Romanticism in Theory

Dedicated to Ernst Behler

ROMANTICISM IN THEORY

Edited by
Lis Møller and Marie-Louise Svane

AARHUS UNIVERSITY PRESS

Copyright: Aarhus University Press 2001

Cover Design: Lotte Bruun Rasmussen

Illustration Philipp Otto Runge's "Cornflowers"

Graphic Design: Jørgen Sparre

Translation: Patrick B. Zöller

Printed by Scanprint, Denmark

ISBN 87 7288 786 9

Published with financial support from

the Danish Council for the Humanities

and Aarhus University Research Foundation

AARHUS UNIVERSITY PRESS

Langelandsgade 177

DK-8200 Aarhus N

Fax (+ 45) 8942 5380

www.unipress.dk

73 Lime Walk

Headington, Oxford OX3 7AD

Fax (+ 44) 1865 750 079

Box 511

Oakville, Conn. 06779

U.S.A.

Fax: (+ 1) 860 945 9468

Preface

In June 1996 the Danish Society for the Study of Romanticism held a conference entitled 'Romanticism in Theory' at Schæffergården, Copenhagen, with the participation of 70 scholars from Scandinavia, Europe, and North America.

This conference was the major and concluding manifestation of a two year network programme 1994-96, sponsored by the Danish Research Council for the Humanities.

The contributions contained in this book are revised versions of a selection of papers from the conference. We believe that the book marks the high and productive level of the current academic debates on Romanticism, showing a cross-section of central issues and delineating some important meeting points between literature, science and theory, as well as between Romanticism and Modernity.

First of all, we would like to thank all the writers for their stimulating contributions to the conference and to this volume. Our gratitude to the Danish-Norwegian Association for kindly allowing us to use Schæffergården for our conference. Thanks also to Aarhus University Press who made it possible for us to have the volume published, and we want to express our special thanks to Mary Waters Lund for her invaluable assistance and great concern throughout the editing process. We are much obliged to the Aarhus University Research Foundation and to the Danish Research Council for the Humanities for their generous sponsoring of the edition. Our special gratitude should also go to the Danish Research Council for the Humanitites, which, in funding the network programme 1994-96, helped us to create the Danish Society for the Study of Romanticism which is still a productive Danish-international forum of debate. Thanks to the Departments of Comparative Literature in the Universities of Aarhus and Copenhagen for their support, and last, but not least, thanks to our colleagues in the Romanticism Society for many inspiring sessions.

Shortly before the conference our invited keynote speaker, Professor Ernst Behler, University of Washington, fell ill. Sadly, he died in 1997. Ernst Behler's scholarly work and its great importance for the modern study of Romantic philosophy and literature, has been felt through decenniums. His writing and editiorial work is, and will be, of lasting influence. We are privileged to be able to publish his conference lecture and to dedicate this volume to his memory.

Aarhus, May 2001
Lis Møller & Marie Louise Svane

Contents

Language and Semiotics

Image, Imagery, Imagination

The Romantic Other

Abbreviations

BAL
Carus, Carl Gustav 1982. Zehn Briefe über Landschaftsmalerei mit zwölf Beilagen und einem Brief von Goethe als Einleitung 1815-1835. *Briefe und Aufsätze über Landschaftsmalerei.*

Blake
Blake, William 1970. *The Poetry and Prose of William Blake.*

CI
Kierkegaard, Søren 1989. *The Concept of Irony.*

D
Nietzsche, Friedrich 1982. *Daybreak.*

DE
Carus, Carl Gustav 1963. *Denkwürdigkeiten aus Europa.*

Foucault
Foucault, Michel 1967. *The Order of Things. An Archaeology of the Human Sciences.*

GE
Nietzsche, Friedrich 1966. *Beyond Good and Evil.*

GS
Humboldt, Wilhelm von 1968. *Gesammelte Schriften.*

GW
Freud, Sigmund 1940-52. *Gesammelte Werke.*

KFSA
Schlegel, Friedrich 1958-95. *Kritische Friedrich Schlegel Ausgabe.*

Kittler
Kittler, Friedrich A 1987. *Aufschreibesysteme 1800/1900.*

KSA
Nietzsche, Friedrich 1980. *Kritische Studienausgabe.*

KSF
Schlegel, Friedrich 1988. *Kritische Schriften und Fragmente.*

KSJG
Grimm, Jacob 1869. *Kleinere Schriften.*

KSWG
Grimm, Wilhelm 1881. *Kleinere Schriften von Wilhelm Grimm.*

L
Coleridge, Samuel Taylor 1981. *Logic.*

LTS
Tieck, Ludwig 1828. *Schriften.*

Mishra
Mishra, Vijay 1994. *The Gothic Sublime.*

NW
Novalis 1978-87. *Werke, Tagebücher und Briefe.*

OL
Humboldt, Wilhelm von 1988. *On Language: The Diversity of Human Language-Structure and its Influence on the Mental Development of Mankind.*

PW
Wordsworth, William 1967-72. *The Poetical Works of William Worsworth, I-IV.*

Ritter
Ritter, Joachim 1974. *Landschaft.*

RL
Gilman, Sander L., Carol Blair, and David J. Parent (Eds.) 1989. *Friedrich Nietzsche on Rhetoric and Language.*

S
Novalis 1975–88. Schriften. *Die Werke Friedrich von Hardenbergs.*

Sprache
Schlegel, Friedrich 1808. *Über die Sprache und Weisheit der Indier.*

SW
Schlegel, August Wilhelm 1967–95. *Sämtliche Werke.*

T
Nietzsche, Friedrich 1968. *Twilight of the Idols.*

Introduction

The essays in this anthology began as lectures and papers presented at the Danish Society for the Study of Romanticism's International Conference 'Romanticism in Theory' in Copenhagen in June 1996. The title of the conference – and of the present publication – lends itself to various interpretations. 'Romanticism in Theory' may be construed as Romantic theory, Romanticism *as* theory, or Romanticism as contemplated from the vantage point of contemporary theory. The fifteen essays selected for publication reflect this ambiguity. The present volume deals with the interconnections between various fields of knowledge and disciplines in the Romantic period, showing how Romantic aesthetics are influenced by scientific ideas and concepts, by linguistics and semiotics, as well as by Romantic theories on the dream and the unconscious. The anthology also includes articles that address the intersections between Romantic literature and philosophy and twentieth-century theory: Essays on Romanticism as reflected and re-read through the prism of modern theoretical paradigms such as speech act theory, psychoanalysis and discourse theory, as well as articles that explore the ways in which Romantic writers anticipate later theoretical developments. Tracing a number of common themes in English, German, French, and Scandinavian Romanticism, the book embraces a wide spectrum of critical approaches thus pointing to the present diversity of Romantic studies as a forum where different humanistic disciplines intersect. Common to all, however, is the attempt to demonstrate the topicality and vitality of Romanticism as a decisive turning point in western literary and intellectual history.

The essays are grouped under three thematic headings: *Language and Semiotics; Image, Imagery, Imagination;* and *The Romantic Other.*

As is stated in a recent study, Romantic theory, 'identified with the critique of language from the start,' contributes 'materially to modern ways of thinking about the condition of language'.[1] The essays in the first section address Romantic theories of language and the various ways in which Romantic philosophy of language and poetics inform each other. In the opening essay, *Ernst Behler* traces the theory of language formulated by the early Romanticists A.W. Schlegel, Fr. Schlegel, and Novalis in connection with their reflection upon the particular nature of poetry.

Michel Foucault, in his seminal study *The Order of Things,* points to the years from 1795 to 1800 – which precisely designate the duration of the early Romantic School at Jena – as decisive for the breakdown of the classical system of knowledge and the development of a new episteme, that is the transition from representation to the concern with the origin and the historicity of language. Foucault's study, however, does not include early German Romanticism. Locating the theory of language developed by the early German Romanticists at the threshold of modernity, Behler's essay thus fills a gap in *The Order of Things.* Furthermore, Behler argues that early German Romanticism, in emphasizing the poetical and metaphorical nature of language, anticipates the philosophy of language in Nietzsche who, according to Foucault, was 'the first to connect the philosophical task with a radical reflection upon language'.

Likewise, Foucault's analysis of the breakdown of the classical episteme provides the point of departure for *Marie-Theres Federhofer's* investigation of the semiotic implications of Fr. Hardenberg's (Novalis) mineralogical studies. Federhofer shows how Hardenberg challenges the scientific discourse of his age by introducing into mineralogy the notion of *Übergang* (transition), derived from the Fichtean concept of *Wechselbestimmung.* The concept of *Übergang* breaks with previous principles of classification in mineralogy as it questions the mineralogical notion of the sign. Focusing on the structural function of the mineralogical sign, the correlation of interior substance and exterior form, Hardenberg unties the sign from the idea of visibility. Semiotically speaking, he replaces representation with structure, thus approximating the mineralogical, non-linguistic sign to the linguistic. In the context of Romantic studies, Hardenberg's preoccupation with mineralogy has been treated as a mere metaphor for his poetological concerns. As Federhofer demonstrates, however, his mineralogical writings are of immediate relevance to the study of the early Romantic philosophy of language.

In the next essay, *Angela Esterhammer* draws connections between nineteenth-century post-Kantian philosophy and twentieth-century analytic philosophy, by proposing that the contemporary theory of speech acts or performative language has an unacknowledged background in the Romantic philosophy of language. Focusing on two representative texts, Humboldt's *Über die Verschiedenheit des menschlichen Sprachbaues und ihren Einfluss auf die geistige Entwicklung des Menschengeschlechts* and Coleridge's *Logic,* Esterhammer shows that the Romantics characterise language as intrinsically performative, in ways that are similar to, and thus anticipate, the arguments of twentieth-century speech-act philosophers such as Austin, Searle, and Benveniste. The striking similarities between Romantic philosophy and contemporary speech-act theory, however, highlight equally striking differences, first of all the emphasis, in Romantic philosophy of language, on mind and subjectivity. Proposing a new synthesis of twentieth-century speech-act theory with the subject-oriented Romantic theories of language as performance, Esterhammer suggests that this extended theory of performative language is particularly relevant to the interpretation of Romantic literature. As an example of such an approach, Esterhammer's essay closes with a reading of Coleridge's poem 'Frost at Midnight'.

In his book *Aufschreibesysteme 1800/1900,* Friedrich A. Kittler has traced the changes that the teaching of reading and writing underwent from the end of the eighteenth century. The child's learning by heart of words and sentences was replaced by the acquisition of written language through phonetic units ('minimal signifiers'), and at the same time the responsibility for the teaching of reading shifted from the father to the mother. This change gave rise to a close connection, hitherto unknown, between the human voice and the printed word. Kittler's study provides the theoretical point of departure for *Otto Fischer's* reading of the Swedish Romantic poet P.D.A. Atterbom whose autobiographical poem 'Minnesrunor' from 1812 thematizes the mother's initiation of her son into the mysteries of reading. Fischer traces the influence of the child's encounter with written language on Atterbom's poetics, the essence of which is the attempt to recreate in poetical writing the presence of the maternal voice.

In the last essay in this section, *Bengt Algot Sørensen* examines the cosmopolitan and nationalistic trends that converge in the concept of literature of German Romanticism. Rooted in the great European poetical tradition of the Renaissance and the Baroque, the idea of universal poetry in the Schlegel brothers and Tieck transgresses national borders. Sørensen demonstrates how the comparative linguistics of A.W. Schlegel inform the early Romantic concept of *Weltliteratur,* and, pointing to Tieck's translations of Shakespeare and Cervantes as catalysts for the new ideas of the prospects of poetry, he emphasises the central role played by the translation. A.W. Schlegel's theory of translation obliterates the boundary between poetry and translation as the poetical translation is conceived as an act of re-creation. Translation is a universal category insofar as 'the human mind cannot but translate, and its entire activity consists in that'. Finally, Sørensen shows how the early Romantic world-panorama in the late phase of German Romanticism narrows down, as the idea of a popular poetry of nature is identified with the myth of the German nation.

The visual aesthetics of Romanticism is primarily concerned with the subject's response to sense impressions and with the pictorial dimension of the creative imagination. The essays in the second section, *Image, Imagery, Imagination,* however, demonstrate the comprehensiveness of the Romantic concept of the image in the contexts of visual art, literature, and philosophy. The Romantic image ranges from vision and prophetic symbol, to the semantic anarchy of the arabesque, and to the hallucinogenic world of hypervisual signs that points towards post-modern aesthetics.

In the first essay, *Alice Kuzniar* addresses the post-Kantian querying of the visual, revealing significant parallels between Romantic and post-modern epistemology and phenomenology. Focusing on Novalis and Tieck, Kuziniar explores the dissolving of the object of perception to prophetic vision and the disruption of the referentiality of the visual signifier. Novalis' futuristic connection of technology of perception and inner visual syntax in *Das Allgemeine Brouillon* is shown to define an ontology of the self. Speed and machine are seen to bear on the nature of the subject, but also on the disparity between perception and its object. Finally, Kuzniar shows the instability of the visual world and its hypnotic impact on the perceiving subject in Tieck's story 'Der Runenberg'.

Tieck and Hoffmann are the central figures in the next essay 'Images and Counter-Images' by *Andreas Böhn*. Böhn suggests a link between Romantic reflection upon genre and post-modern aesthetics and literary theory, arguing that the play with formal and generic schemes in Tieck's 'Der blonde Eckbert' or 'Des Lebens Überfluss' and Hoffmann's *Der goldene Topf* realizes the Romantic programme for a self-conscious literature that blends the genres and reflects its own mode of being. The combination of divergent formal schemes leads to a disorientation of the reader in his or her search for a coherent image of the represented world. Böhn emphasizes, however, that the montages of the fairy-tale and realism, the idyll and the novella should be seen not as an empty game but as a mode of representation pertaining to Tieck's understanding of the world as an intertwining of fantastic and realistic dimensions.

In the next essay, *Klaus Peter Mortensen* explores the motif of mirror-reflection in Turner and Wordsworth in the light of M.H. Abrams' famous dictum on Romantic aesthetics: The mirror turned lamp. Pointing to the blurring of the horizontal line in Turner's late works which dissolves the clear-cut distinction between the reflection and what is reflected, Mortensen argues that these landscapes no longer represent nature as divine creation, but in their totalizing light-effects reflect the divinely creative imagination of the perceiving subject in its dialectical correspondence with nature. Proceeding to Wordsworth's poetry, Mortensen reads the motif of doubling and mirror-reflection in, for instance, 'There was a boy' and 'Elegiac Stanzas Suggested by a Picture of Peele Castle' as reflections upon the relationship between mind and nature, and between the (self)reflecting and the reflected subject.

The relationship between the landscape and the perceiving subject is taken up in *Diana Behler's* essay on the concept of the image in Carl Gustav Carus' *Briefe über Landschaftsmalerei*. Diana Behler argues that the image in Romantic aesthetics is identified as a hermeneutic process, involving the observer as well as the object of perception. Focusing on the landscape, the essay addresses Carus' background in Schelling's philosophy of nature, but points out that Carus' concept of nature as well as his aesthetics of the landscape in important respects diverge from Schelling's philosophy of identity. According to Behler, Carus' concept of symbolic art does not involve a synthesis of mind and landscape, but rather a relationship of complementarity, analogous to the complementarity of art and science.

Finally, *Isak Winkel Holm* explores the literary imagery of Søren Kierkegaard's philosophical works. Taking as his point of departure Kierkegaard's discussion in *The Concept of Irony* of imagination as complementary to philosophical conceptualisation, Winkel Holm reads Kierkegaard in the context of the discussions of the relationship between aesthetics and philosophy in Hegel and Fr. Schlegel. The essay traces the stages in Kierkegaard's attempt to mediate between Schlegel's and Hegel's positions: his acceptance on the one hand of the Romantic idea of the mysterious depths of the imagination, and, on the other hand, his incorporation of the imagination in a dialectics aimed at the totalizing expression of the speculative idea. According to Winkel Holm, Kierkegaard's stance emerges from his own use of literary imagery as the fertile soil of true philosophical thinking.

The essays in the last section, *The Romantic Other*, explore the Romantic preoccupation with the marginalised, the silenced, the repressed – be it the Gothic tradition which shadows Romantic idealism, the hidden recesses of the soul, the fantasmagorical rhetoric of the dream, or the female Other. In the first essay, *Ib Johansen* reads Blake's prophetic poems 'Tiriel' and 'The French Revolution' in the context of the apocalyptic discourse of the French Revolution, exploring the ways in which the poems draw on ideational formations and literary traditions that challenge the neo-classical canon. Focusing on Blake's references to Gothic literature as well as to

Shakespeare's chronicle plays, Johansen demonstrates that Blake's gothic scenarios of patriarchal power gone astray, madness, and destruction culminate in a dysphoric vision in which revolutionary anxiety and the Romantic sublime converge.

The frame of reference of the next three essays is psychoanalytic theory, more specifically Freud and Lacan's theories on the unconscious, the drive, and femininity. The purpose of these essays is twofold: To re-read Romantic literature and aesthetics in the light of psychoanalysis, and to show how Romanticism anticipates psychoanalytic conceptualization. *Cecilia Sjöholm* examines the role and the status of the unconscious in Schelling's philosophy of art and poetry in the light of the psychoanalytic conception of the unconscious as dominated by drives. Reading Schelling's notion of the unconscious as a feminization of matter, Sjöholm argues that the unconscious in Schelling is a concept indicating how poetry surpasses the poet's own limited understanding. The unconscious is nature as the feminine Other who can never be spoken, only shown through the symbolic work of art.

Applying the vocabulary of Lacanian psychoanalysis, *Chenxi Tang* reads the representation of male sexuality in Hoffmann's *Der Elementargeist* as an ironical reversal of the Romantic concept of love as codified in Fr. Schlegel's *Lucinde*. Further, Tang explores the intersections of sexuality and Romantic aesthetics. If Romantic love, conceived as the imbrication of sexuality, marriage, and friendship, correlates with the Romantic conception of progressive universal poetry, the negation of Romantic love in Hoffmann, Tang argues, is bound up with fantastic storytelling.

Suggesting that the American renaissance should be considered as the American counterpart to European Romanticism, *Ide Hejlskov Larsen* examines the representation of the split subject, characteristic of Romanticism, in the poetry of Whitman and Dickinson. Larsen argues that the distinctively American revision of the European Romantic tradition shows itself in the demonization of the unconscious subject, the intertwining of sexuality and power, in Whitman and Dickinson.

With the advent of Romanticism, the dream assumes a new meaning and value. Showing that the Romantic writers associated the dream with imagination, emotion, ecstasy, vision, and inspiration, *Alain Montandon,* in the final essay of this volume, reads the Romantics' conception of the dream as a key to the understanding of Romantic aesthetic and poetological theory. Drawing on a vast number of examples from German, French, and English Romantic writers – including Novalis, Jean Paul, Hugo, Coleridge, Keats, and De Quincey – Montandon shows that the dream is conceived as the paradigm of a poetical language which is synthetic and musical rather than discursive and linear, and he points to the hieroglyph and the arabesque as essential features of the oneiric language of Romantic poetry.

NOTES

1. A.C. Goodson. 'Romantic Theory and the Critique of Language'. In: J. Beer (Ed.), *Questioning Romanticism*. Baltimore 1995, 4.

Language and Semiotics

The Early Romantic Theory of Language and Its Impact upon Nietzsche and Foucault

Ernst Behler

Representation and Historicity

In the last sections of his book *The Order of Things,* Foucault emphatically depicts, in his view, the deep epochal break occurring in the Western world at the turn from the eighteenth to the nineteenth century. This event involved the breakdown of the classical system of rationalism and the Enlightenment, which constituted the last reliable and accomplished system of knowledge in our history. In Foucault's words, at the end of the eighteenth century, our thought 'detached itself from the squares it inhabited before' (Foucault 217).[1] This was 'a radical event that is distributed across the entire visible surface of knowledge' (ibid.). What occurred was a 'fundamental change of those positivities' that had governed the classical age. By positivities Foucault understands basic subject matters of research and world-orientation that mark the interests of humanity during a given period.

Foucault has an undeniable liking for tripartite structures and threefold developments and discusses the epochal break from the Enlightenment to Romanticism in terms of three realms: political economy, natural sciences, and humanities. The basic change brought about by this transition to a new epoch can be noticed first of all in the use of a new vocabulary. During the classical age, political economy presents itself through the notion of *wealth* and through reflections on wealth and trade as firm and objectifiable data; the natural sciences manifest themselves in a tendency to classify their objects and to enlist them on labels, on tableaux, as if they were unchangeable entities; and the humanities show interest in the establishment of a general grammar as an objective basis for the analysis of *discourse*. These subjects now change their names, however. Wealth turns into labour, revealing an interest in how wealth is produced, how wealth comes into being through the human input of labour; the classifying tables of the eighteenth century are replaced by a science of life called *biology,* which reveals an interest in the development and mutation of life and works with concepts such as organism, organic unity, and organicity; and *general grammar* finds its substitute in *philology* and *linguistics,* especially comparative linguistics, investigating the constituent elements of discourse and their historical changes. With regard to language and discourse, Foucault could also have referred to the many treatises at the end of the eighteenth century which define themselves as investigations into the 'origin of language'.

What is obvious in this development of a new episteme, of a new manner of viewing and interpreting the world, is a shift away from representation, from objectifiable entities, and toward history and historicity. The idea of a pre-given being is replaced by that of being in flux, by becoming. Kant and the French Ideologues pay attention to how ideas originate, to what makes ideas possible, to the 'condition of possibility'. With this question about the condition of possibility, an entirely new episteme entered the world, differing sharply from the episteme of the classical age. The central term of the episteme of the Enlightenment seems to have been representation, representation of the objective order of things. Now representation loses its power to define the mode of being common to thought and knowledge, and a different model of thought takes its place, an episteme focusing on development, genesis, and investigations into origin. The point of reference shifts from the outer, objectifiable world to the human subject as the condition of possibility for the new positivities of labour, life, and language. Thought and knowledge withdraw from the space of representation and begin to investigate 'all that is the source and origin of representation': the 'force of labour, the energy of life, the power of speech' (Foucault 243-44). The notion of a 'condition of possibility' obviously relates to Kant, and Foucault indeed states: 'The new positivity of the sciences of life, language, and economics is in correspondence with the founding of transcendental philosophy' (Foucault 244). Labour, life, and language themselves are 'transcendentals', that is, they are 'outside knowledge', but make possible the 'knowledge of living beings, of the law of production, and the forms of language' (ibid.). Foucault states: 'It took a fundamental event – certainly one of the most radical that ever occurred in Western culture – to bring about the dissolution of the positivity of Classical knowledge, and to constitute another positivity from which, even now, we have doubtless not entirely emerged' (Foucault 220). He speaks of an event in which 'the very being of our modernity' is moulded, but is 'largely beyond our comprehension' because 'we are still caught inside it' (Foucault 221).

Foucault, who never had great difficulty in establishing dates, did not overlook this event and believed to be able to situate it 'between easily assignable dates', a period of 50 years from 1775 to 1825, and even to distinguish a nucleus for this event lasting the five years from 1795 to 1800 (Foucault, 221). I will return to these dates later. As far as language is concerned, the main topic of my essay, this subject 'began to fold in upon itself' at this time and started to 'acquire its own particular density, to deploy a history, an objectivity, and laws of its own' (Foucault 296). People usually believe 'that their speech is their servant and do not realize that they are submitting themselves to its demands'. Language gets 'caught up in the trap of philology', and it becomes necessary 'to work one's way back from opinions, philosophies, and perhaps even from sciences, to the words that made them possible' (Foucault 297). All 'techniques of exegesis' are revived because language has resumed the 'enigmatic density it possessed at the time of the Renaissance'. Now, however,

it is not a matter of rediscovering some primary work that has been buried in it, but of disturbing the words we speak, of denouncing the grammatical habits of our thinking, of dissipating the myths that animate our words, of rendering once more noisy and audible the element of silence that all discourse carries with it as it is spoken. (Foucault 298)

This type of exegesis is obvious for Foucault in the first book of *Das Kapital,* which is basically an 'exegesis of "value"'; in Nietzsche, all of whose texts are 'an exegesis of a few Greek words'; in Freud, who undertakes an 'exegesis of all those unspoken phrases that support and at the same time undermine our apparent discourse, our fantasies, our dreams, our bodies'.[2] Foucault says: 'God is perhaps not so much a region beyond knowledge as something prior to the sentences we speak'. If we are inseparable from him, this is perhaps because our language is inseparable from his laws. He quotes Nietzsche, who once stated: 'I fear indeed that we shall never rid ourselves of God, since we still believe in grammar'. Our contemporary mode of interpretation, formed in the nineteenth century,

proceeds from men, from God, from knowledge or fantasies, towards the words that make them possible; and what it reveals is not the sovereignty of a primal discourse, but the fact that we are already, before the very least of our words, governed and paralyzed by language. (Foucault 298)

The 'threshold between Classicism and modernity', Foucault claims, 'had been definitely crossed when words ceased to intersect with representation and to provide a spontaneous grid for the knowledge of things' (Foucault 304). Yet for a long time, philosophical reflection 'held itself aloof from language, and language would not have become a field of thought in its own right until the twentieth century, had not Nietzsche 'been the first to connect the philosophical task with a radical reflection upon language' (Foucault 305). In this 'philosophical-philological space' which Nietzsche opened up for us, 'language wells up in an enigmatic multiplicity that must be mastered' (Foucault 305). Nietzsche no longer asked 'what good and evil were in themselves', but questioned 'who was speaking when one said *Agathos* (good) to designate oneself and *Deilos* (evil) to designate others'. Mallarmé, however, responded to this Nietzschean question of 'who is speaking?', 'by saying that what is speaking is, in its solitude, in its fragile vibration, in its nothingness, the meaning of the word, itself – not the meaning of the word, but its enigmatic and precarious being' (Foucault 305). Whereas Nietzsche was ready 'to irrupt into that questioning himself and to base it upon himself as the speaking and questioning subject', Mallarmé constantly attempted to efface himself 'from his own language' (Foucault 306). And it might very well be that all our questions concerning language 'are presented today in the distance that was never crossed between Nietzsche's question and Mallarmé's reply' (ibid.).

It appears that with these distinctions, Foucault has neatly delineated the scope of my essay 'The Early Romantic Theory of Language and its Impact Upon Nietzsche and Foucault': Early Romanticism toward the end of the eighteenth century; Nietzsche toward the end of the nineteenth, and Foucault toward the end of the twentieth century. The years from 1795 to 1800, identified by Foucault as the nucleus of this event, precisely designate the duration of the Early Romantic School in Jena. To be sure, Foucault did not think of Early German Romanticism when he made this caesura, but related it to the Parisian philosophical school of the Ideologues, such as de Gerando and Destutt de Tracy. These philosophers were also interested in a genealogy of our words and concepts, but operated from a different philosophical basis than the Romantics, that of a sensualist philosophy as established by Locke and Condillac. I will relate the beginning of this event to early German

Romanticism, the Schlegel brothers, Novalis, and Tieck, and attempt, in a Foucault-friendly manner, to fill a gap in his book.

August Wilhelm Schlegel's Language Theory

If one approaches the intellectual and poetic world of the early Romantics, one soon realizes that their preoccupation with language was by no means an incidental activity, but fundamentally involves all that to which romantic reflection extended – poetry and the other arts, rhetoric, philosophy, Bildung, religion, society, and even republicanism. The most immediate subject was of course poetry, in that the Early Romantics proposed to investigate the particular nature of poetry. This was meant as a fundamental reflection upon poetry in the most rigorous sense, that is, a reflection upon the condition of possibility for poetry. And the most fundamental phenomenon that came to light during these investigations was language. Language was prior to all other means previously used for the explanation of poetry, prior to the rules, norms, and genres of the classicist theory; prior to the systematic deduction of poetry within the new systems of aesthetics, prior to situating poetry as a branch in an all-embracing encyclopaedia of human knowledge, and also prior to a comparative analysis of all human faculties such as reason, will and imagination.

The earliest text among the writings of the Romantics that comes closest to this demand is August Wilhelm Schlegel's *Letters on Poetry, Meter, and Language* of 1795. His particular approach in the sense of a fundamental reflection can already be seen in his treatment of meter. He wanted to reach back behind superficial explanations of meter as a mnemonic device and enjoyment of recurrences and deduce meter and tempo from our physiology and base it on phenomena such as heartbeat and breathing. The Dutch philosopher Hemsterhuis, Schlegel's guide in these matters, considered the feeling for time as essential to the human being and said: 'The conception of time is perhaps the first among all our conceptions and precedes even birth, because it seems that we owe it only to the successive pulsations of blood in the neighborhood of the ear'.[3] The human disposition for meter thus leads us, as Schlegel says, into the 'labyrinths of physiology and psychology' (*SW* 7.135).

Schlegel's theory of language takes a similar direction of investigating the anthropological conditions for the possibility of poetry. His *Letters on Poetry, Meter, and Language* originated in Amsterdam, where Schlegel then lived, far removed from Jena, the center of transcendental speculation in Germany. He referred to authors like Moritz, Herder, and Hemsterhuis, that is, to representatives of a more sensualist orientation. Elaborating his language theory, Schlegel went far beyond these sources and related to the entire rich spectrum of language theory of the late eighteenth century: to Rousseau, his *Discourse on Inequality* as well as to the posthumous *Essay on the Origin of Languages;* to Charles de Brosses and his theory of a mechanical formation of language from animal sounds – the most prominent model for a theory of language during the Enlightenment, but especially to Frans Hemsterhuis and his *Letter on Man and his Relationships.*

On the basis of these various materials, Schlegel distinguished three possible theories of language:

1) language has arisen from the imitation of sounds and signs of nature and their constant perfection;
2) language has originated from 'sounds' of feeling and emotion; and
3) language developed from both the imitation of nature and inner sounds, reason and sensuality (*SW* 7.112).

The first theory is that of a mechanical development and constant perfection of our system of signs, originating in the first impressions of the human being and extending to the most perfected computer language. The theory relating to sounds of the soul considers the sounding, sensual element of language most important and establishes an inner relationship between language and poetry, as well as between language and music. The third theory attempts to combine both (*SW* 7.118). The first theory is that of the Enlightenment and originates in the writings of Locke and Condillac. The second refers to Herder, but also to Rousseau, who had characterized human language as a 'cry of nature', who considered passion as the cause of words, and saw the first languages as those of poets. The third theory is a mediation between the two first ones, between rationalism and sensualism, and was maintained by many language theorists of the late eighteenth century, Hemsterhuis the most prominent among them. What distinguishes Schlegel's theory from that of Hemsterhuis, however, is that he does not limit the realm of sensuality and feeling to a first stage in the formation of language, one of 'crude sensuality' and 'untamed passion', one that was lost and overcome during the process of language development. He maintains instead the presence of this sensual, sensitive, poetic element of language up to the most advanced forms of scientificity. This permanent presence of the sensuous-poetic element of our language is evidenced, for instance, in our capability for producing and enjoying poetry (*SW* 7.105).

Schlegel considers language to be the 'most wonderful creation of human poetic power', the 'great, not yet accomplished poem in which human nature represents itself' (*SW* 7.104). Language is a proto-poetry of humanity, an original manifestation of the creativity of the human being, our first spontaneous contact with the world. Language is furthermore a general medium of communication among people. Language is not a product of reason alone, but of a more comprehensive power also embracing the imagination. This original language is the source of the cultivated languages, refined by reason, more perfect in terms of usefulness and precision, but without that original power. The language of science is the farthest removed from this original language and indeed resembles Condillac's conception of language as an 'assemblage of signs established by agreement'. Yet even this language conceals the 'infinite language of nature' (*SW* 7.105).

The question of an origin of language is brushed aside by Schlegel as unanswerable and just as dubious as the question about the origin of poetry (*SW* 7.111). When theoreticians make use of this model, they do so in order to exemplify the order of facts and not to narrate 'real occurrences according to time, place, and circumstances'. The distance between the oldest attainable documents and those original states is so great that one can bridge it only by a death defying leap. Many have attempted such a leap, but they met with a fatal accident. Others have engaged in etymological games disapproved by linguists as well as by philosophers. Others have attempted to deduce all languages from a common root, but only made the philosophical theory that guided them suspicious (ibid.).

According to Schlegel's own theory, we experience daily that the human being uses signs of communication for his sensations and thoughts (*SW* 7.113). These consist in speech and gestures. A bond of communality links all human beings, which is more important for our communication than everything provided by reason. This general capability for communication and understanding is so vast that it includes every child and people of the most distant zones, even of the 'most distant centuries'. This is the 'true, eternal, general language of the human race', the proto-language in all cultivated languages (*SW* 7.114). To explain this relationship, however, both systems of language theory are required, and they become instantly erroneous when they 'proclaim their basic law for the formation of language at the exclusion of the other' (*SW* 7.118). Schlegel elucidates the collaboration of these two formative principles with the 'origin of poetry', which is historically just as unknown to us as the 'origin of language'. If the oldest language was indeed 'the achievement of those communally operative dispositions of human nature', then it was also 'reliably all image and allegory, all emphasis of the passions'. This is certainly meant when according to an old tradition the oldest language is designated as 'poetry and music', although certainly not meant as a technically developed form of poetry and music (*SW* 7.121-22). This relates rather to the originally sounding, rhythmic, and altogether metaphorical character of language as the first organ in our meeting with the world. What matters to Schlegel is that this sphere of language always remains present and that even on the most cultivated level of speech, we still maintain our bonds with it.

I should like to illustrate this always present poetic and metaphorical quality of language with August Wilhelm Schlegel's thoughts on the interrelationship of language and mythology. The first sentence of his Jena lectures *The Philosophical Doctrine of Art* establishes such an interconnection, when Schlegel states: 'Myth is, like language, a universal and necessary product of human poetic power and, as it were, a proto-poesy of the human race'.[4] Mythology is a 'metaphorical language of reason and its kindred power of imagination'. Mythology is a poetry deriving from the proto-poetry of language and forming the basis for poetry in the specific sense. Yet independent of this relationship to poetry in the specific sense, mythology is an essential element of the poetic and metaphorical organization of the human mind. Mythology not only belongs to an early and bygone phase of humanity, but forms, just like language, an essential component of the human being, a structural principle of his mind. Just like language, mythology can lose power and colour during the process of rationalization. Yet even at the most elevated status of reason, the human mind mythologizes. Our kind of world-orientation and world experience always has a spontaneous mythologizing tendency, which manifests itself in a metaphorical transformation of everything we have contact with. This tendency should not be minimized, Schlegel says, as a merely allegorical manner of expression for complicated matters, as the supplement of a fantastic image for a concept. What Schlegel insists upon is a form of mythologizing that belongs to the basic equipment of human beings and without which human experience would not at all be possible. He is of the opinion that the ultimate findings of the natural sciences also have a mythologizing tendency and can be transformed into mythology.[5]

Novalis, Friedrich Schlegel, and Incomprehensibility

One can say that August Wilhelm Schlegel reflects more upon what is possible with language, whereas his fellow Romantics, Novalis and Friedrich Schlegel, reflect more on the limits of language and communication. An especially interesting piece of this type of reflection is a brief text, a fragment, by Novalis, entitled *Monologue*.[6] With a few strokes he emphasizes the roguish character of language that constantly prevents us from achieving what we want to accomplish with its help, namely, a complete and ordered communication of our ideas. People assume, Novalis argues, 'that their talk is about things' and ignore 'what is most distinctive about language, namely, that it is concerned solely with itself' and that 'the capricious nature of language' will cause them to say 'the most ridiculous and mistaken things'.[7] Yet as soon as someone speaks without a specific purpose, 'just in order to speak, he pronounces the most magnificent and original truths'. That is why 'a number of serious people hate language', but they should know 'that it is with language as with mathematical formulas': 'they constitute a world by themselves, they play only among themselves, express nothing but their own marvellous nature, and for that very reason, they are so expressive and mirror the singular interplay of things'. Up to here, the fragment reads like an exercise in language critique, in language scepticism. At this point, however, Novalis reverses the direction of argumentation and focuses on the great capabilities of our language. For it is precisely this non-intentional, involuntary use of language which is the essence of poetry. A true writer is 'but one who is inspired by language'.

Friedrich Schlegel entertained thoughts about language very similar to those of Novalis. We should be careful, however, not to confuse their ideas, which can be characterized as reflections upon the limits of language, with pejorative descriptions of language as a prison. Their attitude is rather a joyful acceptance of the limited character of our language as appropriate to the human condition, but it also reflects the true character of the human being as residing in a constant attempt to transcend these limits through poetry, play, and irony. Friedrich Schlegel and Novalis did not mourn the loss of full communication in an irretrievable past, or project it into a utopian future, but would have instead considered a fully accomplished system of knowledge and understanding as the real prison of the human race. Friedrich Schlegel said in this regard: 'Verily, it would fare badly with you if, as you demand, the whole world were ever to become wholly comprehensible in earnest' (*KFSA* 2.370).[8]

Our essential means for attaining a full comprehension of the world and perfecting our understanding, Friedrich Schlegel argues sarcastically, would be a 'real language' which would permit us to 'stop rummaging about for words and pay attention to the power and source of all activity'. Such a language would appear as the appropriate endowment of an age that proudly congratulates itself on being the 'critical age', and that raises the expectation that everything will soon be criticized 'except the age itself' (*KFSA* 2.364).[9] Christoph Girtanner, a prolific writer of Göttingen, had already put forward this idea of a 'real language', holding out the glorious prospect that 'in the nineteenth century man will be able to make gold'. With Girtanner's prediction and Schlegel's comments, we are at the close of the eighteenth century, when all sorts of expectations were held for the future. He had always admired 'the objectivity of gold', Schlegel assures us, and 'even worshipped it'. In every part of the world, 'where there is even a little enlightenment and education, silver and gold are comprehensible, and through them, everything else'. Once artists possess these materials in sufficient quantity, we can expect them to write their works 'in bas-relief, with gold letters on silver tablets'. 'Who would want to reject such a beautifully printed book with the vulgar remark that it is incomprehensible?', Schlegel asks. The problem is, however, that Girtanner is dead and the nineteenth century has begun, without a fulfilment of the promises of gold and real language (*KFSA* 2.365).

Friedrich Schlegel wonders, however, whether incomprehensibility really is 'something so unmitigatedly contemptible and evil'. One could argue that 'the salvation of families and nations rests upon it', and also that of 'states and systems', as well as the 'most artificial productions of man'. 'Even man's most precious possession, his own inner happiness, ultimately depends on some point of strength that must be left in the dark, but nonetheless supports the whole burden, although it would crumble the moment one subjected it to rational analysis' (*KFSA* 2.370). In an inverse type of reflection, Schlegel maintains that all the 'greatest truths of every sort are completely trivial', and that 'nothing is more important than to express them in ever new ways and whenever possible, ever more paradoxically, so that we will not forget that they still exist and that they can never be expressed in their entirety' (*KFSA* 2.366).

As in the text by Novalis, these playful formulations express a disciplined, unyielding reflection upon language, a scepticism toward language which is not absolute scepticism, but that type of scepticism that is as old as philosophy itself. The form of communication that corresponds to this kind of language is, as with Novalis, indirect communication and indirect writing. The kind of saying and writing in the world of comprehensibility, which is not ours, would be systematic and direct. The kind of saying and writing in the world of incomprehensibility, our world, is the fragment, the aphorism, irony, dialogue, and pluralistic communication. This is a kind of thinking, saying, and writing that does not integrate itself with a superior context because such a context would always be too narrow and stifle us even more than the boundaries of language. This is accompanied by a sense of positive not-understanding, that is, a consciousness of not understanding. This seeming imperfection, however, is the real nucleus of human perfectibility.

Nietzsche and Metaphor

Nietzsche's most important text on language is his essay 'On Truth and Lie in an Extra Moral Sense'. He dictated the text during the summer of 1873 on the basis of his notes on a lecture course on rhetoric, but never published it. In one instance he referred to the text as a 'secretly kept document' (*KSA* 2.370).[10] Among the writings of this time and within the radius of *The Birth of Tragedy,* 'On Truth and Lie' appears as a little sceptical monster, since it denies fundamentally and categorically our ability to make any truth-related statement about the world surrounding us. Nietzsche begins his text with a fabulous framing and writes:

In some remote corner of the universe that is poured out in countless flickering solar systems, there was once a star on which clever animals invented knowledge. That was the most arrogant and the most untruthful moment in 'world history' – yet indeed only a moment. After nature had taken a few breaths, the star froze over and the clever animals had to die. (*RL* 246; *KSA* 1.875)[11]

In a language overloaded with metaphors and exotic images, Nietzsche attempts to show 'how shadowy and fleeting, how purposeless and arbitrary the human intellect appears within nature'. Although this intellect was 'given only as a help to the most unfortunate, most delicate, most perishable creatures, in order to preserve them for a moment in existence', it always accomplishes bringing up 'the most flattering estimation of this faculty of knowledge'. Dissimulation, even 'deception, flattery, lying, and cheating' appear as the true essence of the intellect which makes it hard to comprehend 'how an honest and pure desire for truth could arise among men'. This question is the focus of the text in its further development. With impressive images, Nietzsche describes how the human eye, 'deeply immersed in delusions and phantasmagoria', glides 'around the surface of things' and engages in 'a groping game on the back of things'. Nature conceals almost everything from the human being, 'even about his own body', and locks him within his consciousness – 'unmindful of the windings of his entrails, the swift flow of his bloodstream, and the intricate quiverings of his tissue' – and 'threw away the key'. Woe to the one who would attempt 'peering through a crack out of the room of consciousness' and would suddenly realize 'that man is based on a lack of mercy, insatiable greed, murder, on the indifference that stems from ignorance' – 'as if he were clinging to a tiger's back in dreams' (*RL* 247; *KSA* 1.876-77).

Considering this situation, Nietzsche asks, 'where in the world does the desire for truth originate?' For the conventions of language are hardly products of knowledge, a congruent designation of things, an adequate expression of reality, but rather 'illusions' and 'empty husks'. Only convention, not truth, had been decisive in the genesis of language. Properly speaking, we are not at all entitled to say 'the stone is hard' because 'hard' is only known to us as a 'subjective stimulation'. Just as little are we entitled to 'arrange things by genders' and to designate the tree as masculine and the plant as feminine. If we placed the various languages side by side, we would realize 'that words are never concerned with truth, never with adequate expression; otherwise there would not be so many languages'. The 'thing in itself' is something toward which the 'creator of language' is indifferent, something that for him is 'not worthy of seeking'. He 'designates only the relations of things to men, and to express these relations he uses the boldest metaphors' (*RL* 248; *KSA* 1.878).

In describing this creation of language, Nietzsche uses a transformation theory which states that during the formation of language 'each time there is a complete overleaping of spheres – from one sphere to the center of a totally different, new one.' He writes: 'First man translates a nerve stimulus into an image! That is the first metaphor. Then, the image must be reshaped into a sound! The second metaphor'. At any rate, our language does not relate to things too well. We believe that we know something about the things themselves when we speak of trees, colours, snow and flowers, although 'what we have are just metaphors of things, which do not correspond at all to the original entities'. On the whole, the origin or genesis of language is not a logical process, 'and the whole material in and with which the man of truth, the scientist, the philosopher, works and builds, stems if not from a never-

never land, in any case not from the essence of things' (*RL* 249; *KFSA* 1.879). The inadequate relationship of the human being to objects is further elucidated by Nietzsche's analysis of the transformation from metaphor to concept. This occurs when 'the unique and absolutely individualized experience' which leads to the origin of a word is relinquished in favour of the concept and now has to fit 'countless more or less similar cases, which, strictly speaking, are never identical, and hence absolutely dissimilar'. Nietzsche writes: 'Every concept originates by the equation of the dissimilar'. As if there was something in nature that would correspond to our concepts of 'leaf' or 'honesty!' Only by overlooking what is individual and actual do we arrive at concepts, 'whereas nature knows no forms and concepts, hence also no species' (ibid.). As is obvious in these arguments, Nietzsche's critique of language is a critique of the language of philosophy and the claim to truth traditionally connected with this language. What connects him with the Romantics most directly is his emphasis on the creative, artistic, poetic, and metaphoric character of language, his notion of 'language as art'. 'What is truth?', he asks and responds:

A mobile army of metaphors, metonyms, and anthropomorphisms, in short, a sum of human relations which were poetically and rhetorically heightened, transferred, and adorned, and, after long use seem solid, canonical, and binding. Truths are illusions about which it has been forgotten that they are illusions, worn-out metaphors without sensory impact, coins which have lost their image and now can be used only as metal, and no longer as coins. (*RL* 250; *KSA* 1.880-81)

Nietzsche illustrates this thought with numerous examples. When an investigator operates on the basis of this language, he ultimately discovers 'just the metamorphosis of the world into man'. Just as the astrologer observes 'the stars in the service of men and in connection with their joys and sorrows', so this investigator observes the whole world as the 'infinitely refracted echo of a primeval sound, man; as the reproduction and copy of an archetype, man'. Such an investigator forgets 'that the original intuitive metaphors are indeed metaphors and takes them for the things themselves'. Science originates 'only insofar as man forgets himself as a subject, indeed as an *artistically creating* subject'. If the human being could escape 'from the prior walls of this belief, then his high opinion of himself would be dashed immediately' (*RL* 252; *KSA* 1.883).

Nietzsche's Critique of Metaphysics and the Communicative Value of his Texts

At this point we can break off the discussion of 'On Truth and Lie' because the conception of language Nietzsche outlines in this text has become sufficiently evident. His main argument is that although human language is a superb medium for inter-human communication, it is unfit for philosophy, science, and the communication of objective facts. Now the question arises of course in which way language is capable of communicating thoughts. This is not meant so much as a general question, but more as a question directed to Nietzsche. For after he had realized the unfitness of our language as far as the knowledge and communication of objective facts is concerned, he did not cease talking and writing, but articulated one thought after the other and published one book after the other. On the basis of his theory of language, he was not even entitled to write a text like 'On Truth and Lie'. When he describes in this writing the transformation of a nerve stimulus into a sound, a sound into a word, and a word into a concept, he undoubtedly communicates objective statements, even based on a theory of origin loaded with unproven presuppositions. According to this text, we cannot peer out of the chamber of our consciousness because nature, after having locked us into it, threw away the key. Nietzsche, however, certainly peers out of this chamber and tells us that out there the pitiless, greedy, insatiable, and murderous is dominating, and that we are hanging, in our ignorance, on the back of a tiger. The question, however, that cannot be avoided at this point concerns the organizing principle of Nietzsche's writing, the order of his discourse, the communicative value of his text, and, above all, how we are supposed to interpret him.[12]

In response to this question, I first should like to say that Nietzsche's theory of language as it comes forth in the small text 'On Truth and Lie', cannot be overestimated in its importance for Nietzsche's subsequent thought and our understanding of it. The linguistic analyses of this text had led to the conviction that our language does not permit a knowledge about the true nature of things and that our language encapsulates us into the world of the human being. These critical thoughts are now expanded and transformed into a more general discourse of a critique of metaphysics. One of these transformations takes place in Aphorism 39 of *Human, All too Human* and relates the formation of our language to the genesis of our moral concepts. Nietzsche writes in this instance:

First of all, we call individual actions good or evil without any concern for their motives, but instead on account of their beneficial or harmful consequences. But soon we forget the origin of these designations and imagine that the quality 'good' or 'evil' inheres in the actions in themselves, without regard to their consequences: making the same error as when language describes the stone itself as hard, the tree itself as green – that is, by conceiving what is an effect as the cause. (*H* 1,39; *KSA* 2.62)

In this instance, the choice of examples makes the relationship of Nietzsche's thought to his theory of language still noticeable. Both examples, the hard stone and the green tree, occur in 'On Truth and Lie'. In Aphorism 121 of *The Gay Science*, Nietzsche formulates a similar thought which no longer reveals any link with his earlier theory of language:

We have arranged for ourselves a world in which we can live – by positing bodies, lines, planes, causes and effects, motion and rest, form and content; without these articles of faith nobody now could endure life. (*GS* 124; *KSA* 3.477)

This transformation of his early theory of language also takes shape when Nietzsche transposes it to related realms like consciousness, reason, ability to communicate, and grammar. The theme of grammar is of particular interest in this context. Grammar is of course not to be understood in a technical, linguistic sense, but as that 'unconscious domination and guidance by similar grammatical functions' which governs people of a similar family of languages, of the same 'atavisms', as Nietzsche proposes in Aphorism 20 of *Beyond Good and Evil* (*GE* 20; *KSA* 5.34). In the *Preface* to this text, he had referred to a 'seduction by grammar' as a possible reason for the origin of philosophical systems. In Aphorism 34 of the same text, he equals the 'faith in grammar' with the 'faith in governesses' and asks: 'but hasn't the time come for philosophy to renounce the faith in governesses?' (*GE* 34; *KSA* 5.54).

Many of these thoughts have parallels in Nietzsche's unpublished fragments. In one instance, he relates language to reason and claims that language has provided reason with the 'most naive prejudices'. We read 'problems and disharmonies into things because we think only in the form of language', and we would cease to think 'if we did not do it under the coercion of language'. These reflections lead up to Nietzsche's famous statement: 'Reasonable thinking is an interpretation according to a scheme we cannot throw off' (*KSA* 12.193-94). How Nietzsche thinks about language, grammar, and reason as a unity, is best noticeable in a tour de force of his critique of reason in *Twilight of the Idols,* one of his latest writings. In Aphorism 5 of the section '"Reason" in Philosophy', Nietzsche says that the question about the origin of language would bring us back into an 'age of the most rudimentary form of psychology' and that we would find ourselves 'in the midst of a rude fetishism when we call to mind the basic suppositions of the metaphysics of language — that is to say, of *reason*'. Nietzsche concludes this aphorism with the exclamation: '"Reason" in language: oh, what a deceitful old woman! I fear we are not getting rid of God because we still believe in grammar' (*T* 5; *KSA* 6.78). As these few examples demonstrate, Nietzsche's early theory of language extends far into the finest ramifications of his thought and is perhaps affiliated with the entirety of his text.

This also applies to the expressive character and communicative value of his writings. I believe that Nietzsche remained faithful to his recognition, first formulated in 'On Truth and Lie', according to which we cannot achieve objective knowledge, but only register our impressions, reactions, and interpretations. This is what he has done in his writings. In the most extreme manner, as no other author has ever dared it, he has involved in his text his own person, his sickness and states of euphoria, the places where he produced his writings, his own New Year's wishes, and even his culinary predilections. Every aphorism reflects his own experience. To interpret Nietzsche indeed means, as Derrida has formulated it, to interpret his signatures.[13] Aphorism 119 of *Daybreak* appears to be most revealing in this regard. This aphorism has the title 'Experience and Imagining' and compares our waking with our dreaming state. In both cases, we react to stimuli from the outside and transform them into our human world. This is more obvious in dreams because we can better determine the nervous stimuli for them: 'the motions of the blood and intestines' – 'the pressure of the arm and the bedclothes' – 'the sounds made by church bells, weather-cocks, night-revelers, and other things of the kind'. Our 'imagining reason' imagines causes for those stimuli, this is the same in our waking and dreaming state. Yet in the waking state we do not enjoy that freedom of interpretation as in our dreams. Who knows whether 'our moral judgements and evaluations too are only images and fantasies based on a physiological process unknown to us'. Perhaps, Nietzsche muses, 'all our so-called consciousness is a more or less fantastic commentary on an unknown, perhaps unknowable, but felt text' (*D* 119; *KSA* 3.114). In a more radical manner he asks in the same Aphorism 119 of *Daybreak:*

What then are our experiences? Much *more* than that which we put into them than that which they already contain! Or must we go so far as to say: in themselves they contain nothing? To experience is to imagine? (*D* 119; *KSA* 3.114)

Concluding Remarks

Foucault had maintained that thinking about language in a 'direct and self-related manner' entered the 'field of thought' only toward the end of the twentieth century, after first attempts toward the end of the eighteenth and Nietzsche's radical reflections on language toward the end of the nineteenth century. Indeed, the Romantic occupation with language, although recognized in a few individual studies,[14] was never considered to be a main feature of the Early Romantic theory. Nietzsche's critique of language similarly remained outside the core of his thought in most interpretations of his writings. To be sure, Fritz Mauthner, himself a prominent theorist of language, noticed an immediate link between the critique of language and the critique of knowledge in Nietzsche's theory, in that his critique of morality, for instance, proceeded primarily via a critical analysis of the traditional designations for 'good' and 'evil'. Yet Mauthner eventually characterized Nietzsche's attitude as that of a 'trumpeter of immorality', of a 'moralist' who wanted to set up 'new tablets' and thereby manifested a new belief in language.[15]

Later interpretations, when they turned to Nietzsche's theory of language at all, tended to interpret his conception of language as relating to prior, more originary principles such as grammar, reason, or instinctive moves in the primordial drive for self preservation on the part of the human being, to 'atavisms', and ultimately to physiological conditions. Nietzsche himself seemed to suggest such an interpretative scheme and often expressed it in his texts. In Aphorism 20 of *Beyond Good and Evil* he wrote: 'the spell of certain grammatical questions is ultimately also the spell of *physiological* valuations and racial conditions' (*GE* 20; *KSA* 5.35). Nietzsche's statements on language seemed to require a more basic text for the human being, a text in which instinctual drive, cruelty, and survival techniques are the main features. Aphorism 230 of *Beyond Good and Evil* clearly points into that direction. According to this aphorism, the task is to rediscover beneath all 'flattering colours and make-up' the 'frightful prototext *homo natura*', which means

to translate man back into nature, to become master over the many vain and overly enthusiastic interpretations and connotations that have so far been scrawled and painted over that
eternal basic text of *homo natura*. (*GE* 220; *KSA* 5.169)

As far as the expressive, communicative, rhetorical, and stylistic character of Nietzsche's writings was concerned, especially in regard to their constant contradictions,
one did not use during that time linguistic, but cognitive, epistemological models to
explain this particular character of his text. The most commonly recognized theory
was that of 'perspectivism', that of a continuous switch of 'perspectives' emphasized
by Nietzsche himself in prominent parts of his writings. Karl Jaspers, who studied
Nietzsche's cognitive perspectivism most thoroughly, speaks of an 'infinite reflection', an 'infinite and total dialectic' (unendliche Totaldialektik) that animates Nietzsche's writings, that draws every finite form of rationality into the process of infinite
reflection, and brings all apodictic statements into question through consideration
of new possibilities.

In contrast to this approach to Nietzsche during the first half of our century,
interest in our time has decisively shifted to his theory of language. Investigations
into his language theory and the linguistic aspects of his writings have replaced the
concern with his theory of knowledge and epistemology. His thoughts on language
serve to explain the ambiguity of his statements and to confirm the impossibility of
ascribing a definite meaning to them. This tendency of contemporary Nietzsche
interpretation is obvious in the last part of Foucault's *The Order of Things*. Derrida
focuses his writings on Nietzsche not on 'what' he said but on 'how' he said it, that is,
on his style which Derrida expresses in the plural as 'the styles of Nietzsche'. Of
decisive influence on this trend was the discovery of the importance that rhetoric
had for the formation of Nietzsche's philosophical discourse. It was Philippe Lacoue-
Labarthe who first made this discovery when he focused on Nietzsche's Basel lectures on Greek and Roman rhetoric. Paul de Man continued and broadened this approach by investigating rhetorical tropes and figures of speech in Nietzsche's text.
This preoccupation with language in the case of Nietzsche had an important effect
on the rediscovery of the Early Romantic theory of language. Referring to Nietzsche's question and Mallarmé's answer, Foucault says that 'we know now where these
questions come from':

They were made posssible by the fact that, at the beginning of the nineteenth century, the law of discourse having been detached from representation, the being of language itself became, as it were, fragmented; but they became inevitable when, with Nietzsche and Mallarmé, thought was brought back, and violently so, towards language itself, towards its unique and difficult being. (Foucault 306)

NOTES

1. Michel Foucault 1970. In the text as Foucault with relevant page numbers.

2. See Foucault's earlier text on these three authors: Michel Foucault 1967.

3. August Wilhelm Schlegel, 'Briefe über Poesie, Silbenmass und Sprache'. A.W. Schlegel 1967-95, *Sämtliche Werke* 7.135. In the text as *SW* with volume and page references. Schlegel is referring to Frans Hemsterhuis, *Lettre sur l'homme et ses rapports: SW* 7.119.

4. A.W. Schlegel 1989, 1.49.

5. See the section on mythology in Schlegel's Berlin lectures, 'Über schöne Literatur und Kunst': A.W. Schlegel, 1989, 1.440-61.

6. Novalis: *Monolog.* Novalis 1981, 672-73.

7. The English translation of this text is by Alexander Gelly in: Willson 1982.

8. Friedrich Schlegel. 'Über Unverständlichkeit'. Fr. Schlegel 1958-95, *Kritische Friedrich Schlegel Ausgabe* 2.363-72. In the text as *KFSA* with volume and page references.

9. Translated by Peter Firchow in: 'Friedrich Schlegel' 1971.

10. Nietzsche is quoted from Friedrich Nietzsche 1980, *Kritische Studienausgabe.* In the text as *KSA* with volume and page references.

11. The translation of 'Über Wahrheit und Lüge im aussermoralischen Sinne' is taken from Sander L. Gilman (Ed.) 1989, *Friedrich Nietzsche on Rhetoric and Language.* In the text as *RL* with page references.

12. See my essay, Behler 1996.

13. Jacques Derrida 1984.

14. Eva Fiesel 1927 and Heinrich Nüsse 1962.

15. Fritz Mauthner 1901-2, 1.336-69; Fritz Mauthner 1890, 753-55.

BIBLIOGRAPHY

Behler, Ernst 1996. 'Nietzsches Sprachtheorie und der Aussagecharakter seiner Schriften'. *Nietzsche-Studien*, 25.

de Man, Paul 1974. 'Nietzsche's Theory of Rhetoric'. *Symposium: A Quarterly Journal in Modern Foreign Literatures.*

de Man, Paul 1976. *Allegories of Reading. Figural Language in Rousseau, Nietzsche, Rilke, and Proust.* Yale.

Derrida, Jacques 1979. *Spurs. Nietzsche's Styles.* Chicago.

Derrida, Jacques 1984. *Otobiographies. L'enseignement de Nietzsche et la politique du nom propre.* Paris.

Fiesel, Eva 1927. *Die Sprachphilosophie der deutschen Romantik.* Tübingen.

Foucault, Michel 1967. 'Nietzsche, Freud, Marx'. *Cahiers de Royaumont (Philosophie 6).*

Foucault, Michel 1970. *The Order of Things. An Archaeology of the Human Sciences.* New York. Fr. *Les mots et les choses. Une archeologie des sciences humaines.* Paris, 1966. (Abbreviated as Foucault)

Gilman, Sander L., Carol Blair, and David J. Parent (Eds.) 1989. *Friedrich Nietzsche on Rhetoric and Language.* Oxford. (Abbreviated as *RL*)

Jaspers, Karl 1956. *Reason and Existence.* London.

Jaspers, Karl 1966. *Nietzsche. An Introduction to the Understanding of his Philsosophical Activity.* Chicago.

Jaspers, Karl 1968. 'Zu Nietzsches Bedeutung in der Geschichte der Philosophie'. In: Karl Jaspers. *Aneigungen und Polemik: Gesammelte Reden und Audsätze.* (Ed. Hans Sauer). München.

Lacoue-Labarthe, Philippe, and Jean-Luc Nancy 1971a. 'Le détour (Nietzsche et la rhétorique)'. *Poétique* 5.

Lacoue-Labarthe, Philippe, and Jean-Luc Nancy 1971b. 'Friedrich Nietzsche, Rhétorique et langage'. Textes traduits, présentés et annotés. *Poétique* 5.

Mauthner, Fritz 1890. 'Ola Hansons Schriften'. Deutschland. *Wochenschrift für Kunst, Literatur, Wissenschaft und soziales Leben*, 46.

Mauthner, Fritz 1901-2. *Beiträge zu einer Kritik der Sprache.* Leipzig.

Nietzsche, Friedrich 1966. *Beyond Good and Evil.* (Trans. Walter Kaufmann). New York. (Abbreviated as *GE*)

Nietzsche, Friedrich 1968. *Twilight of the Idols.* (Trans. R.J. Hollingdale). Harmondsworth. (Abbreviated as *T*)

Nietzsche, Friedrich 1980. *Kritische Studienausgabe.* (Eds. Giorgio Colli and Mazzino Montinari). Berlin. (Abbreviated as *KSA*)

Nietzsche, Friedrich 1982. *Daybreak.* (Trans. R.J. Hollingdale). Cambridge. (Abbreviated as *D*)

Nüsse, Heinrich 1962. *Die Sprachtheorie Friedrich Schlegels.* Heidelberg.

Novalis 1981. *Novalis Schriften. Die Werke Friedrich von Hardenbergs.* (Eds. Richard Samuel, Hans-Joachim Mähl, and Gerhard Schulz). Stuttgart.

Schlegel, August Wilhelm 1967-95. *Sämtliche Werke*. Paderborn. (Abbreviated as *SW*)

Schlegel, August Wilhelm 1989. *Kritische Ausgabe der Vorlesungen*. (Ed. by Ernst Behler in collaboration with Frank Jolles). Paderborn.

Schlegel, Friedrich 1958-95. *Kritische Friedrich Schlegel Ausgabe*. (Eds. Ernst Behler, Jean-Jacques Anstett, Hans Eichner. Paderborn). (Abbreviated as *KFSA*)

Schlegel, Friedrich 1971. *Lucinde and the Fragments*. (Trans. Peter Firchow). Minneapolis.

Willson, A. Leslie (Ed.) 1982. *German Romantic Criticism*. New York.

'Transition-Fossiles': Friedrich von Hardenberg's Conception of Transition in His *Werner-Studien*

Marie-Theres Federhofer

Each mineral is a real philological problem.

SCHELLING

Hardenberg at Freiberg

The young Friedrich von Hardenberg (Novalis) having had two years of administrative training in the public service of the Elector of Saxony, was attracted by the 'old idea of independence and by the love of particular sciences'.[1] Therefore, at the beginning of December 1797, having resigned from his position, Hardenberg began to study at the renowned Bergakademie (Mining Academy) at Freiberg, 'but not necessarily with a view to future employment' (*S* 4.287).[2] These studies lasted approximately two and a half years.

This thirst for knowledge *without* a purpose was not, however, compatible with the aims of the Bergakademie. This institution, the oldest technical university in the world, was founded in 1765 with the intention (according to its charter) of offering scientifically based education to serve economic and administrative interests. It was hoped that the students of the Bergakademie could later be employed in the Saxon mining industry or in the salterns and that in addition these newly qualified junior staff members could contribute to the introduction of new technological production methods. In this regard the Saxon government, in an attempt to master the difficulties which followed the Seven Years' War (1756-1763), were in urgent need of acquiring new resources – especially the hiterto unexploited lignite.[3] Also, due to shortage of wood throughout Europe towards the end of the 18th century, the energy situation was so precarious that the economist Werner Sombart spoke of the 'imminent end of capitalism'[4] in his historical–systematic description of modern capitalism.

In the end, the pragmatic objective of the Bergakademie was not without influence on Hardenberg. In his reminiscences of his years of study at Freiberg he remarks:

Many favourable circumstances there have filled me again with courage, with diligence for other purposes, and with devotion to our Saxon constitution. Therefore, this winter I have seriously begun to wish and to hope for employment at the salterns. (*S* 4.287)[5]

This wish was fulfilled as both the Elector and the Saxon Ministry of Finance, which was responsible, among other things, for the employment of personnel in the salterns, were favourably disposed towards employing this young man who was not quite 30 years old.[6] After studying at Freiberg, Hardenberg first worked as an assessor at the salterns at Weißenfels; and, in the search for combustible raw materials he took part in geological investigations in Saxony from the 1st to the 18th of June 1800. On December 6th – shortly before his death – he was appointed 'Supernumerar-Amtshauptmann' (a position resembling senior clerk in the German civil service of the day) in the Thüringischer Kreis (an administrative district in the area of Thuringia).

Referring to Hardenberg's career, Hans Blumenberg points to a fact not always given the deserved attention: 'Looking back, the brief period in his short life following his studies at Freiberg, during which he was engaged in the mining industry, was of greater importance than many other things at the turn of that century'.[7]

Today there is concensus among experts that 'together with Goethe, Hardenberg is the poet most competent in the natural sciences'[8] of the later part of the 1700s.

Mineralogical Conceptions of Transition: A. G. Werner, C. I. Löscher, J. F. Widemann

Literary critics tend to interpret Hardenberg's interest in mineralogy and mining as a metaphor of aesthetic-poetological or psychological conceptions. The latest example of such an approach to the Romantic preferences for mining is Theodore Ziolkowski's monograph to German Romanticism and to its institutions. He says there:

The mine in the German romantic view is not simply a cold dark hole in the ground; it is a vital, pulsing place into which man descends as into his own soul for the encounter with three dimensions of human experience: history, religion, and sexuality.[9]

Of course the interrelationship between professional practice and poetry has often been discussed in different ways,[10] but will not be dealt with here.

Only in a part of his texts does Hardenberg refer to the traditional literary motif of mining as a metaphor, for example in *Heinrich von Ofterdingen* or in *Die Lehrlinge zu Sais*. Thanks to the historico-critical Novalis-edition published in 1960 it has become clear that – and to what extent – respectively, he dealt with geological and mineralogical literature, especially in the so-called *Freiberger naturwissenschaftlichen Studien,*[11] which were carried out while he was a student at Freiberg. They were not intended for publishing, being merely notes taken down from his reading, together with his own connecting thoughts. The *Werner Studien* are one of the most extensive parts of these documents – but even they are not coherent texts. Hardenberg here discusses the first mineralogical work of his Freiberg teacher Abraham Gottlob Werner (1749-1817): *Von den äußerlichen Kennzeichen der Foßilien (On the External Characteristics of the Fossiles* [Leipzig, 1774]).[12] In contrast to modern colloquial usage, 'fossile' in the 18th century stood for 'mineral'. 'Fossile' at that time was defined in the *Ökonomisch-technologische Enzyklopädie* of Johann Georg Krünitz as a 'body dug out of the soil. Such bodies are sometimes called fossiles, sometimes minerals. (…) Every mineral is a fossile'.[13]

In the discussion of the mineralogical literature of his time Hardenberg tries to meet the theoretical and philosophical problems which emerged in the context of mineralogical patterns of explanation. In the Freiberg papers this becomes particularly clear when he tries to specify the – according to his understanding – insufficiently developed idea of mineralogical transitions with Fichte's concept of interdetermination. If this context is reconstructed here, then it is not done in order to classify Romantic philosophy of nature as a prediction of the results of empirical scientific research. Actually, Hardenberg would serve as a good example for such an interpretation since he speculatively anticipates a later insight by insisting on the interrelation between the external attributes and the chemical structure of a mineral which was denied by Werner but later confirmed through the development of methods of chemical analysis.[14]

But the example of Hardenberg also contains aspects of Romantic natural science which, until then, had not been given much recognition. In the historic-scientific context Hardenberg turned out to be a young scholar who critically discussed the contemporary scientific discourse which was influenced by the tradition of the Enlightenment. As Henderson points out, Hardenberg can definitely be considered a representative of modern natural science in this respect since here one is mainly concerned with the 'examination of theories rather than the examination of natural phenomena or the experience itself'.[15] With regard to the discussion of the position of the Enlightenment concerning natural science, it is obvious that Hardenberg accomplishes the change in thinking at the end of the 18th century which was observed as a general trend by Foucault: 'To classify, therefore, will no longer mean to refer the visible back to itself, while allotting one of its elements the task of representing the others; it will mean (…) to relate the visible to the invisible, to its deeper cause (…).'[16]

Of course, Hardenberg never systematically summarized the results of his manifold scientific work. This often leads to a classification of his considerations, which already emerged in his lifetime. In a letter to Schelling (September 1799), Heinrich Steffens notes that he finds 'strict scientific consistency' lacking in Hardenberg's studies, and continues: 'It seems to me that his way of thinking leads to such a fragmentary line of reasoning where one tries to catch nature with witty ideas, ending up in a disordered accumulation of such ideas, in short: the Schlegelianism of natural science' (S 4.637).

Apart from the already mentioned texts by Werner, two rather less epochal works belong to the specialized literature Hardenberg read during his Freiberg years of study: Carl Immanuel Löscher's *Uibergangsordnung bei der Kristallisation der Fossilien, wie sie aus einander entspringen und in einander übergehen (Transition Sequence in the Crystallization of the Fossiles, how they come from one another and turn into one another* [Leipzig 1796])[17] and Johann Friedrich Widemann's *Ueber die Umwandlung einer Erd- und Steinart in die andere (On the Transformation of an Earth- and Rock Type into another* [Berlin 1792]). In contrast to Löscher, Widemann – who is rather difficult to identify – is not mentioned either in the commentary or in the index of the historico-critical Novalis-edition, although Hardenberg specifically refers to the author's name as well as to his work.[18]

Carl Immanuel Löscher (1750-1814) was Chief Miner (Bergmeister) in Bohemia and Freiberg, thus director of a Mining Office in a particular mining district and moreover had the reputation of being a talented mechanic since he invented among other things an easy to handle fire-engine.[19] In his text Löscher terms that process transition, in which 'a crystal is transformed from a certain basic form into another' by 'blunting, sharpening and pointing', that means by a change of the angular sizes, and thereby 'reaches the highest degree of resemblance'.[20] Transition is a process of approximation by means of continuous quantitative change. According to this degree of resemblance Löscher distinguishes different kinds of transition whose description fills the greater part of his work. Demonstrating these transition sequences he makes use of 'proper and thoroughly developed models' since the *Zwischenkristalle* (intermediate crystals) 'remain nevertheless unclear'.[21] 'Since nature does not change the already produced crystals, I would like to show here how they have to be changed if they are to be transformed into other crystals'.[22] Thus transitions are in the first place not a result of observation but of constructions.

Also the Werner-student Johann Friedrich Widemann (1764-1798) understood the transitions as quantitative changes, though he examines the phenomena of transition in the field of minerals from a perspective totally different from that of Löscher. His essay *Ueber die Umwandlung einer Erd- und Steinart in die andere* answers the prize question of the Royal Prussian Academy of Sciences at Berlin in 1791, i.e., 'whether there is sufficient evidence that in nature there are only five simple elements of earth which are transformed into one another, one thus changing into another one, and whether, and how, it was possible to bring about this transformation in an artificial way?'[23] The answer Widemann sends the jury is clear: 'Neither chemistry nor nature are able to transform the five basic substances into one another'.[24] Without doubt minerals can transform themselves into other ones,[25] but these processes do not affect the basic substances. Only the mixing ratios change when a mineral changes its properties. Widemann thus differenciates between chemical elements and external properties – it will turn out that he follows his teacher Werner in this respect – and understands transition as a quantitative and subsequent change of given substances.[26]

Since Werner only payed little attention to the phenomenon of mineralogical transitions in his work about the external characteristics, Hardenberg, who was interested in this problem, probably studied these less popular works of Löscher and Widemann. The term 'transition' is used by Hardenberg in some completely different contexts, though. He notes, for example, shortly after his return from Freiberg: 'Nothing is more poetical than all transitions of heterogeneous mixtures' (S 3.587, No. 221)[27] and thereby establishes a reference between chemical processes and poetic-theoretical considerations.[28] Certainly 'transition' is not just a poetical and linguistic-philosophical concept which was imparted to him through the contemporary chemical literature and – as remains to be shown – last but not least, through Fichte's *Wissenschaftslehre (Science of Knowledge,* 1794) Hardenberg comes across this term also in the cource of his mineralogical studies.

The editors of the historico-critical edition remark in their commentary on Löscher, that Hardenberg possessed his *Uibergangsordnung* and point out that 'in the *Werner-studien* the principle of the *transition sequence* was a thought with which [Hardenberg] wanted to enlarge Werner's principles of classification' (S 3.951-52). It is necessary to trace this in detail. In accordance with Walter Benjamin's call for a commentary on the contents, Werner's position should briefly be reconstructed in this context before Hardenberg's problems are worked out.[29]

The Wernerian Dichotomy

Abraham Gottlob Werner, probably the most famous teacher at the Freiberg Bergakademie at that time, helped the mineralogy of those days to its systematic-scientific basis with his work *Von den äußerlichen Kennzeichen der Foßilien.* His work counts today as the 'first extensive textbook on mineralogy'.[30] It purports to be a diagnostic textbook of mineralogy, i.e., it provides a repertoire of criteria which make it possible to describe and define a mineral. This pragmatically orientated work also had personally valuable consequences for Werner, since he was offered a chair at the Freiberg Bergakademie already one year after its publication in 1775.

In his outline of mineralogical characteristics Werner differentiates four types, the external, the chemical or inner, the physical and the empirical characteristics.[31] Among the external characteristics he counts colour, taste and weight. For pragmatic reasons, he prefers the external characteristics among these four types, since they proved most practical in mining practice. They are 'totally complete, reliably distinctive, best known' and moreover 'the easiest to define and to seek out'.[32] They just need simple instruments to be defined, visual perception. The uncertainty of the physical and chemical methods of analysis of those days was definitely one reason why Werner resisted the use of every technical instrument and plays off the evidence of the senses against scientific instruments. Even the 20th century's geoscience still refers to Werner's terminology, when it counts the external marks among the so-called 'pragmatical characteristics'. The criterion for this classification today – as in those days – is the use of 'simple means'.[33]

Werner's project can be described in a more detailed way if one looks at what is left out. He does not systematize minerals on the basis of species and thus he does not try to reconstruct nature's unity by the help of a natural-historical method of classification. Hardly interested in taking an inventory of single mineralogical objects, he developed instead a systematic manner of mineralogical characteristics. Werner's order of the world of minerals is a nomenclature of mineralogical terms, the use of which is not regulated by an objective given order, but by perception. The 'main topic'[34] ('Hauptgegenstand') of his work is not the single mineralogical object, but its characteristics. Consequently Werner does not use the terms 'Kind' ('Art') and 'Species' ('Gattung') to describe minerals, but to depict their characteristics. 'Generic' ('Generisch') and 'Specific' ('Speciell') are the semiotic, but originally na-tural-historical categories, and he subdivides the 'general generic characteristic' ('das allgemein generische Kennzeichen') colour into the 'specific characteristics' ('speciellen Kennzeichen') white, grey, black etc.

In his translation of Linné's *Natursystem des Mineralreichs (Natural System of the World of Minerals)* the natural scientist Johan Friedrich Gmelin reports that no less than 27 mineralogical systems were developed in Europe between 1647 and 1775. Werner, it seems, as a consequence of this enormously disarranged state of affairs, had come to the conclusion: 'I would rather have a fossile badly ordered and well described than well ordered and badly described'.[35] Consequently, the order of the characteristics does not give information about the order of the minerals.

This connection is dissolved since Werner presumes a fundamental dichotomy, the one between anorganic and organic. The decisive criterion for this division is the specific coherence of matter. Anorganic matter is 'totally simple or composed of pieces of the same kind' whereas 'organic matter is composed of parts which are different'.[36] While components and the whole of an anorganic object differ merely quantitatively, that means concerning their size, the organic objects are as a whole more than the sum of equally structured and independent components. Components and the whole differ qualitatively from each other. These different connecting structures again are responsible for the status of the external characteristics. Whether it is a question of organic – in those days called 'organized' ('organisierte') matter – or of arbitrarily composed matter, respectively, the external characteristics give information about the phenomenon in its entirety – as in botany and zoology – or they do not have any reference to the inner structure – as in mineralogy.[37]

Hardenberg's criticism of his teacher is directed towards these distinctions, towards that of organic and anorganic matter and towards that of external characteristics and inner structures and he tries to dissolve them by the help of the term 'transition' ('Übergang').

Challenging the Wernerian Dichotomy: Hardenberg

'A young scholar has to begin with special criticism' (S 3.380, No. 627).[38] In the *Werner-Studien* Hardenberg tries to fulfil this demand and sums up his criticism of his teacher's paper at the end: 'Werner unconsciously indicates the lack of two mineralogical disciplines and their principles – the science of relationship of the fossiles – and the science of transition characteristics' (S 3.143).[39] With regard to Werner's work he remarkably often criticizes that 'this division is very incomplete' (S 3.135)[40] and thus criticizes Werner's principle of classification with regard to the natural phenomena as well as the characteristics. Hardenberg sees the 'dichotomy' ('Dichotomie'; S 3.138) clearly in Werner's system and uses the term 'transition' in the *Werner-Studien* only at the points where he scientifically and critically refers to 'gaps' ('Lücken') and 'lacks' ('Mängel'; S 3. 140) in mineralogy. Central key-words of the *Werner-Studien* – and as far as I can see only in the *Werner-Studien* – are the terms 'transition characteristic' ('ÜbergangsKennzeichen'; S 3.143), and 'transition nature' ('ÜbergangsNatur'; S 3.140).

Of course it must be mentioned that these terms lack definitional precision. Hardenberg's remarks in this regard are confined to a few sentences. Thereby it is suggested that none of the terms is a component of a conclusive theory. On the contrary, these two terms are to be seen as a sign of a certain intention, and it would be wrong to expect that this intention has been worked out in Hardenberg's notes.

However, the philosophical importance Hardenberg attaches to the problem is to be seen in an elliptic expression in the *Werner-Studien*. Subsequent to the comments on the 'transition nature in essence' ('ÜbergangsNatur im Wesen') he continues: 'the rule of interdetermination in the natural selection and interpretation of the symptoms' (S 3.140).[41] Hardenberg was familiar with the term 'interdetermination' ('Wechselbestimmung')[42] and its synonym, the 'transition' due to the reading of Fichte's *Wissenschaftslehre*. Actually he did not meet the term 'transition' through his special studies in mineralogy, and the use of this term shows how much the view of this philosophically educated coal-, iron- and steel-student had been affected by the Fichtian world of ideas.

In the first discourse of the second part of the *Wissenschaftslehre,* Fichte understands the 'interplay *as* such [...] *as a transition* from one to the other'.[43] As Winfried Menninghaus has shown, the Early Romanticists radicalize Fichte's principle of interdetermination and do not understand an active reflection or an active change, respectively, as a subjective ability in the context of a philosophy of consciousness. Hardenberg does not place the absolute – beyond reflexive interdetermination – within the intellectual intuition as Fichte does. Rather the interdetermination itself is the absolute context.[44] According to Hardenberg, the change is not a subsequent mediation institution between two given quantities, but genuinely synthetical.

As an 'objective structural principle of the order of things and signs'[45] the change is fundamental for the doctrine of the characteristic as for the doctrine of being. Semiotic and ontological reflections thus converge in the model of the transition. On the one hand, the importance of this thought becomes clear when Hardenberg expects the transition characteristic to 'improve the doctrine of the outer characteristics' and thus to make the 'interrelation of the outer characteristics and the inner substances' visible (*S* 3.141).[46] On the other hand, the importance of the thought becomes clear as soon as one brings Hardenberg's idea of a 'transition nature' in relation to the mineralogical conception of transition as it was proposed, for example, by Widemann.

Hardenberg calls such characteristics transition characteristics which 'stand between outer [characteristics] and inner [characteristics] (*S* 3.143).[47] Therefore they are classified between the characteristics perceptible by the senses and those which are to be identified by chemical analysis. Nevertheless, the 'doctrine of the transition characteristics' ('die Lehre von den ÜbergangsKennzeichen') was still a 'weak point' ('Mangel') of mineralogy (*S* 3.143). Further comments on the transition characteristic are not to be found in the *Werner-Studien.* Differing from Werner's external characteristics, Hardenberg's transition characteristics have no representative function. They are not, or not exclusively, the characteristics which are to be seen on the surface of a mineral. Thus Hardenberg separates the characteristics from the principle that hitherto seemed to guarantee its existence: visibility. Hardenberg does not define a mineralogical characteristic with recourse to what it represents. On the contrary, he refers to its relation with other, non-visible characteristics and ascribes to it a structural function, i.e., to relate inner substance and outer form to one another. This correlation is characterized by the transition characteristic. In this sense the demand of the Freiberg students for a 'symptomatology applied to chemistry' ('einer auf Chymie angewandten Symptomatik') is to be understood; he considers this as 'a question of even the highest importance' ('eine Frage, die allerdings von höchster Wichtigkeit ist'; S 3.138).

How far the student's perspective deviates from the teacher's is shown remarkably clearly by the already quoted formulation about 'the rule of interdetermination in the natural selection and interpretation of the symptoms'. In his mineralogical diagnosis Werner chooses the so-called 'natural sequence' ('natürliche Folge') as a semiotic organizing principle: All characteristics 'come one after another in the sequence in which they present themselves to our senses in a fossile'.[48] The optically perceptible characteristics take the first place in this hierarchy 'because they present themselves to us first: We see a fossile before we investigate it by other senses'.[49] This sequence is 'natural' since it is based on sense organs given to man. Werner understands perception by senses as a 'sequence' ('Folge') because, according to him, sense data are not conveyed as a complex general impresssion but are passed on one after another. Intentionally Hardenberg chooses the expression 'natural selection and interpretation' instead of 'natural sequence' and thus raises the question of guidelines for the selection and interpretation of a 'symptom' which Werner does not find interesting. While Werner does not have to, and cannot, decide this question since he assumes the presence of outer characteristics which are taken in by a receptively characterized perceptive faculty and which are passed on to intellectual perception, Hardenberg discusses the state of the characteristics with the term 'rule of interdetermination'.

The idea of a transition characteristic which avoids a representative function and instead of this is assigned a place between inside and outside has, according to Hardenberg, an anti-empirical tendency. He reproaches his teacher for 'dogmatism' insofar as Werner demands 'the complete presence of equational data' ('das völlige Gegebenseyn der Gleichungsdaten'; S 3.139) for mineralogical diagnoses. Unlike Werner, Hardenberg does not assume the presence of outer marks which are to be converted to a descriptive terminology. He rather asks the 'critical' question of the condition of possibility of characterists and prefers that attention be given to which principle should be followed when a mineralogical descriptive model is to be devised (entwerfen). He notes in the *Allgemeine Brouillon:* 'Construction of marks – how do I make a mark – how do characteristics develop' (S 3.413, No. 747).[50] In

Hardenberg's understanding marks or characteristics, respectively, are not given but they are to be 'made' as characteristics.

Furthermore, the accentuation of the transition mark makes it possible for Hardenberg to modify the relation between visible structure and criteria of identity opposite to Werner. While according to Werner the outer marks cannot give information about a mineral's chemical and physical attributes, Hardenberg explains a mineral's existence or its 'essence' ('Wesen') just by the relation between visible and invisible structures. With the term 'transition nature in essence' he pleads against Werner (and against Widemann) for an objective principle of organization in the world of minerals. Thus he refers not just to a comprehensive interdependence-relation between the inner and the outer structures of each single object but also between this object and all other natural objects. In other words, what is specific of an object does not result from an accidental combination of substances, but from a structuring principle. Simultaneously an approach emerges between the anorganic and the organic, a productive interrelation which prevents the possibility of division of nature into two fixed fields.

As described above, Werner refrains from putting the variety of single mineralogical appearances into a natural-historical system and contents himself with the systematization of the description of minerals. Thereby he deviates from a natural-historical, inventory-taking procedure and turns towards a form of presentation of knowledge. This emancipation movement may have fascinated Hardenberg, but it is criticized by him at the same time. Unlike his teacher, the 'arbitrariness' ('Willkühr'; S 3.139) of outer characteristics supposed by Werner is no indication for him that there is nothing more to be found in them than visible attributes. Semiotically speaking, Hardenberg replaces the principle of representation by the principle of structure. Thus a tendency increases in the mining student's theory which was already announced in his teacher's ideas: the separation of the characteristics from their objects. Finally it should be mentioned briefly that his understanding of the mineralogical, and thus non-linguistic characteristic, thereby comes surprisingly close to that of the linguistic sign.

NOTES

*   My paper is dedicated to Fritz Reinitzhuber.

1. 'Die alte Idee von Unabhängigkeit und Liebe zu einigen Wissenschaften'. Script of a letter on Hardenberg's work, sent to Julius Wilhelm von Oppel, presumably by Weißenfels, after mid-June 1799. In: *Novalis* 1965-88, *Schriften. Die Werke Friedrich von Hardenbergs.* Vol. 4.287. In the text as *S* with volume and page numbers.

2. Er 'gieng in der That nicht mit Absicht auf eine künftige practische Anstellung dahin ab.'

3. Cf. Schulz 1963, 280.

4. Sombart 1924,Vol. 2.1137.

5. 'Mancherley günstige Umstände haben mich dort wieder mit Muth, mit Fleis für fremde Zwecke, und mit Anhänglichkeit an unsre sächsische Verfassung erfüllt (…) Dennoch fing ich erst diesen Winter (…) ernstlich an meine Anstellung bei den Salinen zu wünschen und zu hoffen'.

6. Cf. the writings published in *S* vol. 4.

7. Blumenberg 1989, 247. Contrary to all romanticizing ideas about the Romantic sense of nature, Blumenberg shows Hardenberg's understanding of nature as turned towards an intensive control of the world (ibid., 11), which not only lies in the occupational mercantile-technical interest of a mining official, but also is to be seen in his poetic writings which hail the magic of nature as well, as for example in *Die Lehrlinge zu Sais.* Ibid. 247-48.

8. Uerlings 1997, 5.

9. Ziolkowski 1990, 32-33. For similar opinions in literature cf. Dürler 1936, 7, 110; Schulz 1958, 135ff.; Cardinal 1973, 118, 127; Moser 1980, 473-77; Böhme 1988, 77. A concise survey of the different perspectives of the role of mining in *Heinrich von Ofterdingen* is offered in Uerlings 1991, 468-77.

10. Gabriele Rommel, for example, pleads in her informative essay for the close interaction between Hardenberg's philosophy and his professional activity (Rommel 1997, 37). She accuses Hermann Kurzke of a 'pronounced conservative view' (ibid. 36), who insisted: 'Obviously the professional and the poetic took place in different fields which do not form a unity' (Kurzke 1988, 21).

11. Printed in: *S* Vol. 3.34-203. The publication of Hardenberg's scientific studies contributed to a decisive revision of the Hardenberg picture. Cf. Rommel 1997. Rommel explains how the editorial practice conceals the views of the serious natural scientist Hardenberg.

12. In depth studies concerning Hardenberg and Werner are seldom. However, the unpublished dissertation of Schmid from 1951 should be mentioned. Schmid sees the advantage for Hardenberg of the Freiberger mining study not so much in the appropriation of scientific expert knowledge but in the appropriation of a certain method. Werner's course of lectures published in the *Encyclopädie der Bergbauwissenschaften* had inspired Hardenberg to the project of compiling his own

encyclopedia (Schmid 1951, 82ff.). According to Schmid, Hardenberg's study with Werner is a continuation of the study of Fichte's and Kant's philosophical systems. Under the influence of an idealistic philosophy Hardenberg modified Werner's demand for completeness insofar as his encyclopedia-project was not aimed at the complete consideration of empirical knowledge but at the absolute (ibid. 72ff.). Herbert Uerlings stresses in his explanations of the *Werner-Studien* the importance Werner had in the context of Hardenberg's encyclopedia-project (cf. Uerlings 1991, 185-89).

13. Krünitz 1778, 129.

14. Cf. Guntau and Rösler 1967, 68.

15. Henderson 1997, 124.

16. Foucault 1970, 229.

17. Cf. S Vol. 3.387, No. 648.

18. Cf. ibid. 149: 'Widemann vom Übergang einer Steinart in d[ie] Andre'.

19. Cf. Dlabacz 1973, 219.

20. Löscher, 1796, V-VI. Beim Übergang wird 'durch Abstumpfung, Zuschärfung und Zuspitzung', 'ein Kristall von einer gewissen Grundgestalt in eine andere versetzt' und erlangt 'den größten Grad von Ähnlichkeit davon'.

21. Ibid., 13. Er bedient sich 'richtige[r] und sauber gearbeitete[r] Modelle', da die 'Zwischenkristalle', 'doch undeutlich ausfallen'.

22. Ibid.,VI. 'Weil nun aber die Natur an den schon einmal hervorgebrachten Kristallen weiter keine Veränderung unternimmt; so will ich nun hier zeigen, wie an dergleichen Körpern (…) eine Veränderung vorgenommen werden muß, wenn sie in andere Kristalle übergehen sollen'.

23. Widemann 1792, 3. 'Ob hinlängliche Beweise vorhanden, daß nur 5 einfache Elementar-Erden in der Natur vorhanden sind und in einander verwandelt werden, und also die eine in die andere übergehe, und ob, und wie es möglich sey, durch die Kunst diese Umwandlung zu bewirken?'

24. Ibid., 223. Widemann means by 'transformation or change in (…) mineralogy', (Umwandlung oder Verwandlung (…) in der Mineralogie) that a 'fossile due to some kind of power loses its typical characteristics and takes on the properties of another, so that it stops being the former fossile and starts to be another one' (wenn ein Fossil durch irgend eine Kraft seine ihm wesentliche Eigenschaft verliert, und die eines andern Fossils annimmt, so daß es also aufhört, das vorher gewesene Fossil zu seyn und nun ein anderes ist). Ibid. 8-9.

25. 'What I mean by transition is, that a fossile with all these properties which make up its character, approaches the other fossile's properties. (Unter Übergang hingegen verstehe ich, wenn ein Fossil in allen den Eigenschaften, die sein Wesen bestimmen, sich den Eigenschaften dieses, oder jenes andern Fossils (…) nähert). Ibid., 8-9.

26. Widemann's dislike of pure dynamism on the anorganic, as on the organic field, derives from the fear of a transforming universal power leading to chaos, since it removes the stable and specific order of things and exchanges them arbitrarily. However, the aversion to a 'transformation system' ('Umwandlungssystem') does not come exclusively from a scientist's individual uneasiness with magical methods, but is also formed by a historical background, i. e., the embittered debate at the end of the 18th century between *volcanists and neptunists* about the formation of basalt (cf. Blumenberg 1986, especially 476-78). Among his opponents Widemann, in his essay, also numbers Johann Jakob Ferber. Opposed to Ferber's *Untersuchung der Hypothese von der Verwandlung der innerlichen Körper ineinander* (Study of the Hypothesis about the Change of the Inner Bodies into One Another) [Berlin 1788]), Widemann resolutely stands up for his own *Umwandlungssystem* (Widemann 1792, 237). From Italy, Ferber in 1773 described basaltic lava and thus belonged to those scientists who were able to prove the volcanic attributes of basalt (cf. Engelhardt 1982, 31). On the other hand, however, it is known about Widemann that he shared the opinion of his teacher, the neptunist Werner, and in 1787 defended it when answering a prize-question: Was ist Basalt? Ist er vulkanisch oder nicht vulkanisch? ('What is basalt? Is it volcanic or is it non-volcanic?'). (Cf. Guntau 1984, 82). This prize-competition and the basalt controversy are described in detail by Wagenbreth 1955, 183-241. Certainly Widemann was influenced by this conflict when he developed his conception of mineralogical transition. The controversy between *volcanists* and *neptunists* was inflamed by the question of whether basalt was of volcanic origin and thus was a lava, or whether it owed its development to the receding of an ocean and therefore was sedimentary rock. However, behind this conflict something more was hidden than a scientific controversy. The importance the *volcanists* ascribed to the eruptive, volcanic powers was in the eyes of the neptunists seen as a 'decay of trust in the world' (Blumenberg 1984, 477); since thereby the given order of the world was questioned. Widemann may have sensed the danger of another world-outlook coming from the unbridled, permanently modifying, volcanic power. It may have induced him to the opinion of the unchangeability of elementary substances which he energetically held.

27. 'Nichts ist poetischer, als alle Übergänge und heterogène Mischungen'.

28. Cf. Kapitza 1968, 92-93.

29. As a result of the historico-critical Novalis-edition, Uerlings points out that Hardenberg's notes always have to be understood in the specific context – in the context with the basic readings as well as in the context with the contemporary scientific discussion. (Cf. Uerlings 1991, 151-52).

30. Guntau and Rösler 1967, 50.

31. Werner 1774, 32.

32. Ibid., 43. Sie sind 'völlig vollständig, zuverläßig unterscheidend, am bekanntesten' und 'am leichtesten zu bestimmen und am bequemsten aufzusuchen'.

33. Engelhardt and Zimmermann 1982, 129.

34. Werner 1774, 6.

35. 'Ich will lieber ein Fossile schlecht geordnet und gut beschrieben, als gut geordnet und schlecht beschrieben haben'. Without references quoted from Adams 1938, 203. – Although Werner saw the description of minerals as the real aim of his scientific work (cf. Guntau and Rösler 1967, 57) he always strived for a system of minerals during his more than 40 years of teaching at Freiberg. He not only reworked his system several times but increased the number of registered minerals from 183 in the first edition (1789) to 317 in the last one (1816; cf. Guntau 1984, 51).

36. Werner, 1774, 22-23. Anorganische Materie ist 'ganz einfach oder aus einerley Theilen zusammengesetzet (aggregata), organische Materie dagegen besteht 'aus Theilen, so voneinander verschieden sind, (…) (composita)'.

37. Cf. ibid. 26-27.

38. 'Ein junger Gelehrter muß mit specieller Kritik anfangen'.

39. 'Werner indicirt (…) unbewußt den Mangel 2er mineralogischer Disciplinen und ihrer Gesetze – der Verwandtschaftslehre der Fossilien – und der Lehre von den Überganskennzeichen'.

40 'Diese Eintheilung ist sehr mangelhaft'. Cf. also S Vol. 3. 142, 144-45, 155.

41 'Von der Wechselbestimmungsregel in der natürlichen Auswahl und Deutung der Symptome'.

42. Cf. Fichte 1970, 127-50 or Fichte 1979, 52-81 (I, 131-60).

43. Fichte 1970, 150 (I, 161). He understands 'den Wechsel als Wechsel (…) als ein Übergehen von eimem zum andern' (Fichte 1979, 81). (Cf. also Fichte 1970, 155 or Fichte 1979, 87 [I, 167]).

44. Cf. Menninghaus 1987, 92.

45. Ibid., 135.

46. Daß es die 'Zeichenlehre der äußeren Kennzeichen verbessert' und Zusammenhang der äußern Kennzeichen und der inner Stoffe' sichtbar mache.

47. 'Die zwischen äußern [Kennzeichen] und Innern [Kennzeichen] stehn'.

48. Werner, 1794, 84. 'In der Folge, in welcher sie sich an einem Foßile unseren Sinnen darbiethen, nach einander kommen'.

49. Ibid. 'weil sie sich uns zuerst darbiethen: denn wir sehen ein Foßile viel eher, als wir es durch das Gefühl oder andere Sinne untersuchen'.

50. 'Construction von Merkmalen – wie mach' ich Merkmale – wie entstehen Kennzeichen'.

BIBLIOGRAPHY

Adams, Frank Dawson 1938. *The Birth and the Development of the Geological Sciences.* London.

Blumenberg, Hans 1986. *Arbeit am Mythos.* Frankfurt.

Blumenberg, Hans 1989. *Die Lesbarkeit der Welt.* Frankfurt.

Böhme, Hartmut 1988. 'Montan-Bau und Berg-Geheimnis. Zum Verhältnis von Bergbauwissenschaft und hermetischer Naturästhetik bei Novalis'. In: *Idealismus und Aufklärung. Kontinuität und Kritik der Aufklärung in Philosophie und Poesie um 1800.* (Eds. Christoph Jamme and Gerhard Kurz). Stuttgart.

Cardinal, Roger 1973. 'Werner, Novalis and the signature of stones'. In: *Deutung und Bedeutung. Studies in German and Comparative Literature presented to Karl-Werner Maurer.* (Eds. B. Schleudermann et al.). The Hague, Paris.

Dlabacz, Gottfried Johann 1973. *Allgemeines historisches Künstlerlexikon für Böhmen und zum Theil auch für Mähren und Schlesien.* Vol. 2. Prag 1815. Reprint: Hildesheim, New York.

Dürler, Josef 1936. *Die Bedeutung des Bergbaus bei Goethe und in der deutschen Romantik.* Frauenfeld, Leipzig.

v. Engelhardt, Wolf 1982. 'Neptunismus und Plutonismus'. *Fortschritte der Mineralogie* 60.

v. Engelhardt, Wolf and Jörg Zimmermann 1982. *Theorie der Geowissenschaft.* Paderborn, München, Wien, Zürich.

Fichte, Johann Gottlieb 1970. *Science of Knowledge (Wissenschaftslehre)* with the First and Second Introductions. Edited and translated by Peter Heath and John Lachs. New York.

Fichte, Johann Gottlieb 1979. *Grundlage der gesamten Wissenschaftslehre als Handschrift für seine Zuhörer (1794).* Introduction and Index by Wilhelm G. Jacobs. Third edition with an extended Bibliography. Hamburg.

Foucault, Michel 1970. *The Order of Things. An Archaeology of the Human Sciences.* Translated from the French. London. (Fr. *Les mots et les choses. Une archeologie des sciences humaines.* Paris, 1966).

Guntau, Martin 1984. *Abraham Gottlob Werner.* Leipzig.

Guntau, Martin and H.J. Rösler 1967. 'Die Verdienste von Abraham Gottlob Werner auf dem Gebiet der Mineralogie'. In: *Abraham Gottlob Werner. Gedenkschrift aus Anlaß der Wiederkehr seines Todestages nach 150 Jahren am 30. Juni 1967. Freiberger Forschungshefte C* 223. Leipzig.

Henderson, Fergus 1997. 'Romantische Naturphilosophie. Zum Begriff des "Experiments" bei Novalis, Ritter und Schelling'. In: *Novalis und die Wissenschaften.* (Ed. H. Uerlings). Stuttgart.

Kapitza, Peter 1968. *Die frühromantische Theorie der Mischung. Über den Zusammenhang von romantischer Dichtungstheorie und zeitgenössischer Chemie.* München.

Krünitz, Johann Georg 1778. *Oeconomisch-technologische Encyklopädie, oder allgemeines System der Land-, Haus- und Staats-Wirtschaft.* Vol. 14.

Kurzke, Hermann. 1988. *Novalis*. München.

Löscher, Carl Immanuel 1796. *Uibergangsordnung bei der Kristallisation der Fossilien, wie sie aus einander entspringen und in einander übergehen.* Leipzig.

Menninghaus, Winfried 1987. *Unendliche Verdopplung. Die frühromantische Grundlegung der Kunsttheorie im Begriff absoluter Selbstreflexion.* Frankfurt.

Moser, Walter 1980. 'Le soleil souterrain. L'archéologie du sens propre chez Buffon et Novalis'. *Actes du VIIIe congrès international de littérature comparée.* Stuttgart.

Novalis 1975-88. *Schriften. Die Werke Friedrich von Hardenbergs.* Second and third supplemented, extended and improved edition (according to the original manuscript) in four volumes and one supplementary volume. (Eds. von Paul Kluckhohn and Richard Samuel). Stuttgart. (Abbreviated as *S*)

Rommel, Gabriele 1997. 'Novalis' Begriff vom Wissenschaftssystem als editionsgeschichtliches Problem'. In: *Novalis und die Wissenschaften.* (Ed. H. Uerlings). Stuttgart.

Schmid, Heinz Dieter 1951. 'Friedrich von Hardenberg (Novalis) und Abraham Gottlob Werner'. Unveröffentlichte Dissertation. Tübingen.

Schulz, Gerhard 1958. *Die Berufstätigkeit Friedrich von Hardenbergs und ihre Bedeutung für seine Dichtung und seine Gedankenwelt.* Leipzig.

Schulz, Gerhard 1963. 'Die Berufslaufbahn Friedrich von Hardenbergs (Novalis)'. *Jahrbuch der deutschen Schillergesellschaft* 7.

Sombart, Werner 1924. *Der moderne Kapitalismus. Historisch-systematische Darstellung des gesamteuopäischen Wirtschaftslebens von seinen Anfängen bis zur Gegenwart,* Vol. 2. Munich and Leipzig.

Uerlings, Herbert 1991. *Friedrich von Hardenberg, genannt Novalis. Werk und Forschung.* Stuttgart.

Uerlings, Herbert 1997. 'Novalis und die Wissenschaften. Forschungsstand und Perspektiven'. In: *Novalis und die Wissenschaften.* (Ed. H. Uerlings). Stuttgart.

Wagenbreth, Otfried 1955. 'Abraham Gottlob Werner und der Höhepunkt des Neptunistenstreites um 1790'. In: *Freiberger Forschungshefte* D11.

Werner, Abraham Gottlob 1774. *Von den äusserlichen Kennzeichen der Fossilien.* Leipzig.

Wideman, Johann Friedrich 1792. *Ueber die Umwandlung einer Erd- und Steinart in die andere.* Berlin.

Ziolkowski, Theodore 1990. *German Romanticism and Its Institutions.* New Jersey, Oxford.

The Performative in Romantic Theory and Practice: On the Linguistic Philosophy of Coleridge and Humboldt

Angela Esterhammer

The relation between word and thought is not that of belatedly catching up with the thought by means of the word expressing it.
Rather the word is like a flash of lightning that strikes.

H.-G. GADAMER

Ideas of performativity, or the active and dynamic aspect of language and identity, appear with increasing frequency in an increasingly wide range of critical theories. These ideas usually derive in some way from the classic twentieth-century formulation of speech-act theory by the Oxford philosopher J.L. Austin in the 1950s, and by his American student John R. Searle in the 1960s and 70s – and there is a certain irony in the way a major element of contemporary critical theory has developed out of a rather quirky and tangential offshoot of the analytic philosophy of language. Why should the work of Austin and Searle have such wide ramifications in literary and cultural theory? I would suggest that one reason the performative is so compelling is that Austin and Searle only gave explicit and systematic form to a concept that is deeply rooted in post-Kantian philosophy, as well as in Romantic and post-Romantic literature. Neither Austin nor Searle is a tracer of sources, and it is hard to conceive of Searle in particular acknowledging any influences that lie outside the sphere of analytic philosophy. However, some philosophers have recently begun to follow the intellectual roots of speech-act theory back to hitherto unacknowledged sources. One volume of essays on the philosophy of Searle, edited by Armin Burkhardt, locates the origins of speech-act theory in twentieth-century phenomenology, claiming that 'the core of speech act theory undoubtedly originates from the works of the Austro-German phenomenologists within the Brentano-Husserl tradition'.[1] Brigitte Nerlich and other historians of linguistics trace the origins of speech-act theory back another century or more, discovering relevant ideas about the pragmatic and dialogic functions of language in English, German, and French sources from the period around 1800.[2] Meanwhile, the work of comparatists including Andrzej Warminski, Ian Balfour, J. Hillis Miller, and Thomas Pfau has begun to open up the performative dimensions of Romantic-period writers from Wordsworth to Godwin, Kleist, and Hegel.[3] But there is room for a much more comprehensive study of the concept of performativity in the philosophy and literature of the early nineteenth century.[4] Not only would such a study help to fill in an unacknowledged background for twentieth-century notions of performative language, but it might also allow for the development of a re-oriented speech-act theory that is particularly suited to highlight the dynamic aspect of utterance and identity in Romantic literary texts.

Ernst Behler has written that the Early Romantic theory of language, which 'is still virtually unknown', constitutes a 'linguistic revolution' that corresponds to Kant's Copernican revolution in philosophy, and involves 'the recognition of language as the most basic component for our functioning as human beings'.[5] I would add to this that the Romantics' recognition of the fundamental role of language is tied up with their growing awareness of how it functions *performatively,* not only mediating between the human subject and the world but even bringing subject and world into being in the first place. This realization permeates not only philosophy but politics, law, societal institutions, and literature. It emerges in the attempts of the French National Assembly to create a new world-order during the revolutionary age by re-naming citizens, places, dates, weights, measures, and institutions, or in the 1790s debate between Edmund Burke and Thomas Paine over whether the language of a constitution *refers* to already existing rights or whether this language actually *creates* the 'rights of man'. Political philosophy of the Romantic period frequently focuses on socio-political utterances, analyzing their mode of operation as well as their moral status. In his *Enquiry Concerning Political Justice* (1793), William Godwin includes chapters on promises, oaths, libels, and constitutions, and criticizes society's reliance on institutionalized speech acts. Even promises are 'an evil' because 'they call off our attention from the direct tendencies [i.e., the moral foundations] of our conduct, and fix it upon a merely local and precarious consideration', and because they illegitimately exert control over the future, preventing us from applying 'new information' to our future behaviour.[6] His contemporary, the legal philosopher Jeremy Bentham, makes a less critical but more explicit argument about the fictional or constructed nature of the principles on which the social order is founded. Obligations, rights, liberties, powers, prohibitions, privileges, judgements, and many other 'fictitious entities', he writes, owe their 'impossible, yet indispensable, existence' to 'language (…) to language alone'.[7]

As English writers analyzed the role of speech acts in socio-political contexts, German philosophers explored the more phenomenological aspects of performative language – the ways in which language forms subject-object relations as well as relations between speaking subjects. Johann Gottfried Herder discovers a performative moment at the very origin of language. His influential treatise *Über den Ursprung der Sprache* (1772) shows language arising from a hypothetical encounter between a man and a sheep, where the sheep's bleating offers the human subject a distinctive mark or 'word' with which to name it and recognize it again.[8] Herder repeatedly refers to this encounter as an 'act' (Aktus), and the word that is thereby produced must also be seen as an act that connects subject to object and shapes the identity of both. The account of cognition given here, which grounds all of Herder's thinking on philology and epistemology, assumes a living, speaking, acting world (these being one and the same) that marks the human intellect (itself intrinsically active) in a series of dynamic encounters. In this context, too, it is possible to identify the fundamental performativity within German idealism, which reveals itself above all in Fichte's concept of positing or *setzen* as the primary act of the mind, and in his model of experience as a dialogic interaction of *I* and *Not-I*.

The linguistic implications of this essential performativity began to be developed during the nineteenth century in response to Fichte and to Kant, above all by two philosophical-philological thinkers: Samuel Taylor Coleridge and Wilhelm von Humboldt. Both men died in 1834, and each left behind a long unpublished manuscript which he had been revising over the course of several years. These works are Humboldt's *Über die Verschiedenheit des menschlichen Sprachbaues und ihren Einfluß auf die geistige Entwicklung des Menschengeschlechts,* which was published by his brother Alexander von Humboldt within a couple of years of Wilhelm's death; and Coleridge's Logic, which first appeared only in 1981 as part of the ongoing project of publishing the *Collected Works of Samuel Taylor Coleridge.* What follows are some remarks on these texts and on Coleridge and Humboldt as, so to speak, proto-speech-act theorists, along with some indications of their relationship to twentieth-century thinkers such as Searle and Emile Benveniste.

In his letters, Coleridge referred to the work that is now rather misleadingly titled *Logic* as 'my Work on the power and use of *words*'.[9] He conceived of it as a text designed for the use of young men who were preparing themselves for 'the pulpit, the bar, the senate, the professor's chair, or (…) the public press' (*L* 144) – that is, for professions founded on and perpetuated by powerful, public speech acts. To this end, Coleridge analyzes the power of words both constatively and performatively: that is, he *describes* the way basic operations (such as predication) work as mental actions that produce verbal phenomena, and at the same time he *demonstrates* the way his own terminology is formed in and through his own mental acts. In other words, the *Logic* is 'about' performative language on two interrelated levels: Coleridge analyzes words as mental acts of positing at the same time that he performs acts of positing and explicitly reflects on them.

A central principle of the *Logic* is that all things are also acts. 'We cannot conceive even the merest *thing,* a stone for instance, as simply and exclusively *being,* as absolutely passive and *actionless',* Coleridge writes, since even the stone, in reflecting light and holding together many individual particles, manifests an active sense of being. Conversely, lightning (an image that will re-appear in a similar context in Humboldt) is an equally important instance of the conjunction of being and action, for it has existence even though it seems to be purely act: 'as little (…) can we conceive or imagine the purest act, a flash of lightning for instance, as *merely* an act, or without an abiding or continuing somewhat, as the inseparable ground, subject, and substance of the action' (*L* 21). Using examples from geometry, Coleridge later affirms that the geometrical figure that we intuitively take to be the very essence of form or thingness is only the 'image or representation' of an *'energeia theoretike'* or 'perceiving energy' – so that a line might be better called an 'act of length', or a circle an act of circularity (*L* 73).

The coexistence of action and being is encapsulated and made the basis of all language in Coleridge's foundational idea of the 'verb substantive': the 'I am', Latin *sum,* or Greek *eimi* that 'is the act of being' (*L* 16-17). Because all words derive, as Coleridge believes, from the verb substantive, all are hybrids of being and action – 'every substantive a verb, and every verb a substantive' (*L* 19). Situating his concept of the verb substantive in the first of the two introductory chapters to the *Logic,* Coleridge grounds the entire text in a concept of language as performative (i.e., acting) and constative (i.e., being) at once. The starting point of Coleridge's *Logic,* then, foreshadows the conclusion reached by J.L. Austin in his analysis of how everyday utterances relate to the world – namely, the conclusion that 'the dichotomy of performatives and constatives (…) has to be abandoned',[10] for all utterances both state and perform. The difference, for Austin as for Coleridge, becomes purely one of philosophical perspective.

'What is a fact of all human language is of course a fact of all human consciousness', Coleridge writes in his chapter 'On the Logical Acts' (*L* 82), the most important chapter of the *Logic* for establishing the interdependence of mental and linguistic acts. He begins by identifying the primary mental act, the condition of possibility for all consciousness, as the Kantian 'synthetic unity or the unity of apperception' (*L* 76). As in Kant, this refers to the ability of the Understanding to form concepts by recognizing unity in multeity, an act of synthesis that climaxes in the subject's awareness of its own unity as the consciousness that holds all representations of the world together.

But Coleridge, along with Humboldt, regards 'synthetic unity' as the fundamental act of *language*. Both of them identify this mental act with the basic linguistic act of predication. 'Above all', Coleridge writes, 'it is this synthetic unity which first gives meaning and determinate import to the word 'is' in all affirmations' (*L* 76-77): the act of synthetic unity allows us to say 'the house is white' or 'Cerberus is three-headed'. In other words, Coleridge's analysis of the primary mental act explicates *constation* or predication in language (e.g., the statement 'the house is white') as the manifestation of a basic mental *action*.

Not only the verbal proposition, but human identity itself takes the form of performative utterance in Coleridge's *Logic*. Since existence and identity are expressed by the verb substantive, and thus in the form of an utterance or a declarative statement *('I am')*, they already have a profoundly performative dimension in Coleridge's system. But Coleridge goes one step further in establishing the importance of the performative for both knowledge and existence:

The verb *(verbum)*, the word is of all possible terms the most expressive of that which it is meant to express, an act, a going forth, a manifestation, a something which is distinguishable from the mind which goes forth in the word, and yet inseparable therefrom; for the mind goes forth in it, and without the mind the word would cease to be a word, it would be a sound, a noise. If we ask ourselves how we know anything – that rose, for example, or the nightingale hidden in yonder tree – the reply will be that the rose *(rosa subjecta)* manifests itself, that it renders itself objective, or the object of our perceptions, by its colour and its odour, and so in the nightingale by its sound. And what are these but the goings from the subject, its words, its verb? The rose blushes, the nightingale sings. (*L* 82)

The 'word' or the 'verb' of the subject is its fundamental identifying and individuating principle. As in Herder's essay on the origin of language, elements of the natural world impress themselves on human consciousness by uttering a word, and in this act lies the origin of both language and reflection: by announcing themselves as subjects, roses or nightingales render themselves possible objects of our thought.

It may seem a major leap from this Romantic ideal of self-expression to John Searle's standard definition of language: 'speaking a language is engaging in a (highly complex) rule-governed form of behavior'.[11] Yet Searle introduces his idea of constitutive rules for language while confronting a phenomenologically-based question that is not too far from the one Coleridge is trying to answer: namely, the question of how it is possible for someone to perform the act of meaning something, or of expressing a representation of the world, by uttering certain sounds. Searle's philosophy of language is not merely the taxonomy of illocutionary acts such as promising, ordering, and warning to which it is sometimes reduced by both hostile and sympathetic critics. Instead, the real argument of his 1969 book *Speech Acts* is that every aspect of the relationship of words to the world should be seen as an act, and as part of a theory of action. Thus, like Coleridge, Searle analyzes predication as a basic component of all speech acts. According to Searle,

To predicate an expression '*P*' of an object *R* is to raise the question of the truth of the predicate expression of the object referred to. Thus, in utterances of each of the sentences, 'Socrates is wise', 'Is Socrates wise?', 'Socrates, be wise!' the speaker raises the question of the truth of 'wise' to Socrates. (Searle 124)

The effect of this example is to show that the three utterances Searle cites, which perform the different illocutionary acts of asserting, asking, and ordering, all contain the same act of predication: an act of 'the mind's own synthetic power', as Coleridge would put it (*L* 79), that joins the referent 'Socrates' with the predicate expression 'is wise'. Searle's next example illustrates the significance of these predicative acts: 'there is a vast difference between saying of a politician 'Either he is a Fascist or he isn't' and saying of him 'Either he is a Communist or he isn't' (Searle 124), even though neither of these sentences asserts anything but a tautology, and they differ only in the act of predication (or synthesis) that they perform (i.e., joining 'politician' with 'Fascist' on the one hand, 'politician' with 'Communist' on the other).

Like Coleridge, Searle understands language as the communicative intention of a conscious subject; he can only regard a 'noise or mark' as a speech act if he assumes that it 'was produced by a being or beings more or less like myself and produced with certain kinds of intentions' (Searle 16). Of course, Searle would be unlikely to ascribe intentionality to a rose or a nightingale – but this in itself may point to a limitation of his system. Twentieth-century speech-act philosophers tend to *assume* a conscious, intending, and stable human subject. Despite their sophisticated analyses of verbal performativity, including the role of deictics, the interrelation of language and temporality, the pragmatics of the dialogic context, and the dynamics of the speaker's authority, they rarely question the speaker's own status or explore its conditions. This is where Coleridge's work on the active dimension of language can enrich speech-act theory, or at least speech-act readings of Romantic texts: if less analytic, he is nevertheless profoundly concerned with the performative grounding of a subject position in the first place. His concern with a performative subjectivity is especially relevant to Romantic literature with its various explorations of human identity, of the mind's relationship with the world, of the status of the speaking subject as well as the status of reality, and of the effectiveness or ineffectiveness of voice.

The linguistic philosophy of Wilhelm von Humboldt helps mediate between Coleridge's account of logical acts and contemporary speech-act theory, since Humboldt is still more explicit about the performative nature of language and almost prophetic with regard to twentieth-century perspectives on discourse and dialogue. Humboldt anticipates speech-act theorists in his emphatic declaration that *'Language,* in the isolated word and in connected discourse, is an *act,* a truly creative *performance of the mind'*.[12] When Humboldt refers to language as an act, he is first and foremost referring to the moment in which the utterance, by uniting a sound and a concept, objectifies thought and starts a dialogic process of interaction between the mind and the utterance that has just been produced. This speech act is, for Humboldt as for Coleridge, an adaptation of Kant's 'synthetic unity'. Humboldt calls it 'the act of automatic positing through synthesis' (Act des selbstthätigen Setzens durch Zusammenfassung),[13] by which 'the mind creates, but by the same act opposes itself to the created, and allows this, as object, to react back upon it' (*OL* 184).

Once again, Humboldt's concept of utterance as the spontaneous act of an individual speaker may seem to have little in common with Searle's notion of speaking as an activity governed by constitutive rules. Yet unexpected similarities emerge in relation to the examples Humboldt gives of 'synthetic positing'. Humboldt compares the act of automatic positing, as it manifests itself in particular operations of language and parts of speech, to a stroke of lightning. The first example he gives of automatic positing through synthesis is that of joining a root to a suffix that identifies the word as a noun (an example might be 'enjoy-ment'). Through an instantaneous, invisible, and almost magical process, this act of fusing root and suffix evokes the category of substance in the mind as the word is uttered. Humboldt goes on to identify the *verb* in particular as the part of speech to which 'is assigned the act of synthetic positing as a grammatical function' (*OL* 185). The verb makes *synthetic positing* possible on the level of the sentence, joining subject and predicate in such a way as to make the sentence itself an expression of linguistic energy:

Through one and the same synthetic act, [the verb] conjoins, by *being,* the *predicate* with the *subject,* yet in such a way that the being which passes, with an energetic predicate, into an action, becomes attributed to the subject itself, so that what is *thought* as merely capable of conjunction becomes, in *reality,* a state or process. (*OL* 185)

The first example Humboldt provides, once again, is lightning. When we say 'lightning strikes', or when we say 'the mind is immortal', he claims,

We do not just think of the lightning striking: rather, it is the lightning itself that falls. We do not just bring together the mind and the immortal, as capable of conjunction; the mind, rather, is immortal. The thought, if one may put it so concretely, departs, through the verb, from its inner abode, and steps across into reality. (*OL* 185)

That is, the proposition does not merely form a logical or mechanical association between subject ('lightning') and predicate ('strikes'). Rather, the action of the verb somehow manages to make lightning into a thing that strikes; or, better still, in uttering the sentence we *create* lightning *as that which strikes.*

Humboldt's speech act of synthetic positing, then, is fundamentally an application of linguistic rules, yet it is an idea that brings life to grammatical forms, and grammatical forms to life. There is, after all, a certain resemblance to Searle's concept of utterance as action within a rule-governed system. Yet Humboldt's ideas are still more closely related to the work of Emile Benveniste, the structuralist linguist who developed a concept of performative language independently of but at the same time as Austin. Both Humboldt and Benveniste describe the way the speaking subject appropriates the linguistic system and positions people and events in relation to the present moment of discourse. Anticipating Benveniste and H. Paul Grice, Humboldt places one-to-one dialogue at the centre of his model of language: 'All speaking rests on dialogue, in which, even in a group, the speaker always sets himself over against the addressees as a unit' (GS 6.25). The pronouns *I* and *you* provide the only way of bringing the essential condition of reflective thought, the distinction between *I* and *not-I*, into the present instant of discourse: *you*, writes Humboldt, is a *not-I* that has been brought into the sphere of immediate co-operative exchange (GS 6.26). All language is the expression of fundamental dualities, but the immediate and present one that makes speech possible is the duality of *I* and *you:*

The first thing is naturally the personality of the speaker himself, who stands in continuous and direct contact with nature, and cannot possibly fail, even in language, to set over against the latter the expression of his self. But in the I, the Thou is also given automatically, and by a new opposition there arises the third person (…). (OL 95)

One of many parallel statements made by Benveniste comes from the beginning of his 1966 essay 'Le langage et l'expérience humaine':

Each person posits himself in his individuality as an *I* in relation to *you* and *he*. (…). Thus, in every language and at every moment, the one who speaks appropriates the *I*, that *I* which, in the inventory of the forms of the language, is only a lexical given like any other, but which, put into action in discourse, introduces there the presence of the person without whom no language is possible. As soon as the pronoun *I* appears in a speech-act where it evokes – explicitly or not – the pronoun *you* so that together they oppose the *he*, a human experience is established anew and reveals the linguistic instrument that founds it.[14]

Clearly Humboldt and Benveniste share a focus on the opposition of *I* and *you,* along with the equally significant contrast between *I/you* and *he*. The third person, being by definition outside the present instance of discourse, is characterized by both Humboldt and Benveniste as absent and even inanimate, and their concentration on the *I/you* relationship discloses their orientation toward subjectivity and the present moment of active utterance. Yet the above quotations reveal with equal clarity a significant difference between the perspectives of Humboldt and Benveniste on the relative priority of human consciousness and language. For Humboldt, 'the first thing is naturally the personality of the speaker', and this is expressed in – indeed, it creates – the mechanism of pronouns in language. Benveniste, conversely, has the *I* posit itself by appropriating the already-existing mechanisms of language – mechanisms which 'found' and 'establish' human experience itself.

The difference is significant, although not as absolute as it might seem, since both Humboldt and Benveniste make highly ambiguous statements elsewhere about the relative priority of speaker and language.[15] But to the extent that there is a significant distinction between nineteenth- and twentieth-century philosophy of language on this point, it is precisely here that a productive synthesis of the two might be proposed. Humboldt's speech act, like Coleridge's logical act, is a totally dynamic intersection of *I*, word, and world in which each of these terms alters, defines, and (at the same time) expands the others. One might say, in fact, that for these Romantic theorists the utterance somehow establishes the conditions of its own possibility – establishing the speaker's subjectivity in the act of positing a relationship between *I* and *you,* shaping the speaker's thought by positing a new synthesis of grammatical forms. It is this synthetic dynamism that can help adapt the more analytic twentieth-century formulations of speech-act theory in a way that is particularly appropriate to Romantic literary texts, as I hope may be demonstrated here by a brief example from the poetry of Coleridge.

Like many of Coleridge's poems, 'Frost at Midnight' thematizes the mind's need for dialogic interaction with some other person or subject. Idealess and empty at first, the speaker becomes capable of communicative utterance when his mind seizes on the wisp of ash fluttering on a fireplace grate:

Only that film, which fluttered on the grate,
Still flutters there, the sole unquiet thing.
Methinks, its motion in this hush of nature
Gives it dim sympathies with me who live,
Making it a companionable form,
Whose puny flaps and freaks the idling Spirit
By its own moods interprets, every where
Echo or mirror seeking of itself,
And makes a toy of Thought.[16]

Coleridge attributes to the film the same kind of self-expressive act performed by the blushing rose and the singing nightingale in his *Logic:* the fluttering motion is its word, its verb. It cannot achieve the status of a conscious mind because, as Coleridge's philosophy constantly affirms, consciousness depends on the ability of the subject to become an object *to itself.* But by manifesting motion, one of the attributes of a subject, the film makes itself into a possible object of the poet's thought. Becoming both subject and object – becoming, as Coleridge calls it, a *stranger* – the fluttering ash allows the poet to engage in reflection, to find an 'echo or mirror' of his own spirit. And the spirit, once dialogically engaged, finds another companionable echo in the breath of an infant, Coleridge's son asleep in the cradle beside him. Through the stimulus of the infant's breath (or spirit) the poet can, in the second half of the poem, instantiate a dialogue between *I* and *you* for the first time by addressing his son directly.

The speaker's dialogic interaction with the fluttering 'stranger' and the breathing baby leads to a recasting of the entire world in the mode of prophecy and verbal projection. At the end of the poem, the poet creates, in language, a future for his son. He predicts an existence in which the external world itself is experienced as reflection and utterance, transmuted into an eternal, divine language in dialogue with the human subject:

> But thou, my babe! shalt wander like a breeze
> By lakes and sandy shores, beneath the crags
> Of ancient mountain, and beneath the clouds,
> Which image in their bulk both lakes and shores
> And mountain crags: so shalt thou see and hear
> The lovely shapes and sounds intelligible
> Of that eternal language, which thy God
> Utters, who from eternity doth teach
> Himself in all, and all things in himself.

But the poem's ultimate act of reflection occurs when the prophecy of the baby's future turns back into the poet's present situation. The final verse-paragraph creates a possible world through utterance, suspending a vision of nature in the subjunctive mood that hangs on 'whether', 'or', and 'if':

whether the eave-drops fall
Heard only in the trances of the blast,
Or if the secret ministry of frost
Shall hang them up in silent icicles,
Quietly shining to the quiet Moon.

What is crucial here is that these closing lines not only project a vision of the future, but simultaneously transmute Coleridge's immediate physical surroundings into verbal utterance. The final images of the frost's secret ministry and the silent icicles (images strangely reminiscent of frozen lightning) echo the poem's opening line ('The Frost performs its secret ministry') so as to shape the text into a potentially endless spiral. While the beginning of the poem apparently describes the experienced reality of a winter night, its ending rises to a level of meta-discourse in which reality is re-created as a speech act – *and that speech act is only made possible by the act of reflection and dialogue that the poem itself constitutes.* The text, in other words, contains the conditions of its own possibility; the entire poem performs a quiet act of synthetic positing.

In effect, 'Frost at Midnight' is an enactment of Coleridge's linguistically-oriented philosophy of consciousness. Subjectivity emerges here in the act of synthesis by which the mind posits a trace of consciousness in the fluttering film. From an initial encounter with an object in the world, the mind proceeds to a conception of its own unity as the basis for its ability to unify external impressions. It becomes aware that it interprets the external world 'by its own moods' and as an 'echo or mirror' of itself. This is the ground for the poet's ability to say 'I' or 'I am', and to enter into an *I-you* relationship with his son. The 'I am' of the individual mind then leads onward to an affirmation of the eternal 'I am' 'which thy God / Utters, who from eternity doth teach / Himself in all, and all things in himself'. Intriguingly, however, the poet's movement toward an increased objectivity, or an awareness of the divine 'I am' as the ground of external existence, is counterbalanced by the emergence of an explicitly performative language. The constative utterances of the poem's beginning, that fit words to the external world, give way to performative utterances that fit a future, unrealized, potential world to the poem's words. 'Frost at Midnight' thus appears open to a reading grounded in the awareness that Romantic linguistics, adapting the forms of German idealism, affirms the identity of thought and speech, activity and product, utterance and action. Applied to Romantic texts in this way, the marriage of speech-act theory with Romantic philosophy of language might ideally help to liberate the contemporary theory of the performative from the strictures of rules and taxonomies and return it to a more phenomenological focus on the way self, word, and world interconstitute one another.

NOTES

1. Burkhardt 1990, 3.

2. 'It [German pragmatic thinking, and especially the prehistory of speech-act theory] all started in 1795, the year which is generally regarded as marking the beginning of the Early Romantic movement', Nerlich writes, referring to publications by Fichte, G.M. Roth, A.W. Schlegel, and Humboldt in that year (Nerlich 1995, 1-2). The fullest presentation of her argument appears in Nerlich and Clarke 1996, 25-111.

3. For wide-ranging applications of speech-act theory to Romantic texts, see the essays by these critics in the Bibliography.

4. For a longer study of performativity in the work of William Blake, and the beginnings of a 'systematic' approach to speech acts in Romantic texts, see Esterhammer 1994.

5. Behler 1993, 263.

6. Godwin 1976, 218-22.

7. Ogden 1932, 15.

8. Herder 1964, 25.

9. Coleridge 1981, 1. Henceforth *L,* with page references in the text.

10. Austin 1975, 150.

11. Searle 1969, 12. Henceforth Searle, with page numbers in the text.

12. Humboldt 1988, 183. Henceforth *OL,* with page references in the text.

13. Humboldt 1968, 7.213. Henceforth *GS.* Translations from this text, unless otherwise identified, are my own.

14. Benveniste 1966, 3-4.

15. For instance, in 'Subjectivity in Language' Benveniste argues that subjectivity makes language possible and, simultaneously, that language makes subjectivity possible: 'Language is possible only because each speaker sets himself up as a *subject* by referring to himself as *I* in his discourse', yet 'language alone establishes the concept of "ego" in reality' (Benveniste 1971, 224-25). It might even be maintained that this (intentional) ambiguity regarding the reciprocal influence of speakers and language is traceable to Humboldt, whose privileging of the speaking subject is evident from the quotation given in the text ('The first thing is naturally the personality of the speaker ...'), but

who also refers to language repeatedly as an 'external power', an 'independent power', and an independent object (e.g., *GS* 6.121, 180, 181). Moreover, far from being mutually exclusive for Humboldt, the roles of language as *expression of* human consciousness and as *influence* on human consciousness are interdependent: 'Language is an object and independent precisely insofar as it is a subject and dependent' (Die Sprache ist gerade insofern Object und selbstständig, als sie Subject und abhängig ist [*GS* 6.181]).

16. Coleridge 1912, 1.240-41.

BIBLIOGRAPHY

Austin, J.L. 1975. *How to Do Things with Words.* (Eds. J.O. Urmson and Marina Sbisà). 2nd ed. Cambridge, Mass.

Balfour, Ian 1994. 'Promises, Promises: Social and Other Contracts in the English Jacobins (Godwin/Inchbald)'. In: *New Romanticisms: Theory and Critical Practice.* (Eds. David L. Clark and Donald C. Goellnicht). Toronto.

Behler, Ernst 1993. *German Romantic Literary Theory.* Cambridge.

Benveniste, Emile 1966. 'Le langage et l'expérience humaine'. In: *Problèmes de Langage.* Paris.

Benveniste, Emile 1971. *Problems in General Linguistics.* (Trans. Mary Elizabeth Meek). Coral Gables, Florida.

Burkhardt, Armin (Ed.) 1990. *Speech Acts, Meaning and Intentions: Critical Approaches to the Philosophy of John R. Searle.* Berlin.

Coleridge, Samuel Taylor 1912. *The Collected Poetical Works of Samuel Taylor Coleridge.* (Ed. Ernest Hartley Coleridge). 2 vols. Oxford.

Coleridge, Samuel Taylor 1981. *Logic.* Vol. 13 of *The Collected Works of Samuel Taylor Coleridge.* (Ed. J.R. de J. Jackson). Princeton. (Abbreviated as *L)*

Esterhammer, Angela 1994. *Creating States: Studies in the Performative Language of John Milton and William Blake.* Toronto.

Godwin, William 1976. *Enquiry Concerning Political Justice and Its Influence on Morals and Happiness.* Harmondsworth.

Herder, Johann Gottfried 1964. *Abhandlung über den Ursprung der Sprache. Sprachphilosophische Schriften.* (Ed. Erich Heintel). 2nd ed. Hamburg.

Humboldt, Wilhelm von 1968. *Gesammelte Schriften.* (Ed. Albert Leitzmann). 17 vols. Berlin, 1903-36. Rpt. Berlin. (Abbreviated as *GS)*

Humboldt, Wilhelm von 1988. *On Language: The Diversity of Human Language-Structure and Its Influence on the Mental Development of Mankind.* (Trans. Peter Heath). Cambridge. (Abbreviated as *OL)*

Miller, J. Hillis 1992. 'Laying Down the Law in Literature: The Example of Kleist'. In: *Deconstruction and the Possibility of Justice.* (Ed. Cornell, et al). New York.

Nerlich, Brigitte 1995. 'The Notion of "Speech Act" in German Linguistics, Philosophy and Psychology between 1830 and 1970'. In: *Speech Acts and Linguistic Research: Proceedings of the Workshop, July 15 - 17, 1994.* (Ed. Elisabetta Fava). Padova.

Nerlich, Brigitte and David D. Clarke 1996. *Language, Action, and Context: The Early History of Pragmatics in Europe and America, 1780-1930.* Amsterdam.

Ogden, C. K 1932. *Bentham's Theory of Fictions.* London.

Pfau, Thomas 1995. 'Immediacy and Dissolution: Notes on the Languages of Moral Agency and Critical Discourse'. In: *Intersections: Nineteenth-Century Philosophy and Contemporary Theory.* (Eds. Tilottama Rajan and David L. Clark). Albany.

Searle, John R. 1969. *Speech Acts: An Essay in the Philosophy of Language.* Cambridge.

Warminski, Andrzej 1990. 'Facing Language: Wordsworth's First Poetic Spirits'. In: *Romantic Revolutions: Criticism and Theory.* (Eds. Kenneth R. Johnston, Gilbert Chaitin, Karen Hanson, and Herbert Marks). Bloomington.

The Voice of the Mother: On Reading, Writing and Femininity in Romantic Poetics and in the Poetry of P.D.A.Atterbom

Otto Fischer

In the wake of Rousseau the later half of the 18th century saw an increased interest in pedagogical matters, and among the reforms proposed were those that pertained to the initial alphabetization of children.[1] In his thought-provoking and today widely acknowledged *Aufschreibesysteme 1800/1900*, as well as in a number of other texts, the German discourse analyst Friedrich Kittler argues that such reforms in the instruction of literacy had an eminent impact on the relationship between thought, emotion, reading and writing in the period.[2]

Firstly, the significance of the individual letters were now to be apprehended through sounding, which replaced the learning of words, syllables and indeed, at times, entire sentences and texts by heart. Written words and phrases were dissolved into individual phonemes of the human voice, 'minimal signifieds' as Kittler puts it. Literacy was no longer imparted through a corpus of texts but directly through the human voice, and as a result ensued an, in the history of scriptural culture, unprecedented intimacy between sound and letter, between the printed page and the human voice. And what is more: writing and the book became direct links to this voice. Writing hence took on the aspect of a direct outflow of the soul, and in this lies, Kittler proposes, one very important determinant behind the special traits of Romantic subjectivity as reflected in the literary texts of the period. Never before in literal culture had it been possible to establish such an intimacy between written discourse and the human subject.

But this pedagogical reform had another important aspect to it. The responsibility for the child's alphabetization shifted from the father to the mother. The argument was that the mastery of reading and writing was facilitated if the learning took place in the intimacy of the house and was promoted by the child's mother instead of the father or a teacher. This, in turn, went to establish a certain pattern of psychological and generical relations, traces of which are detectable in the texts of the period. The child's primary alphabetization, if I am allowed that expression, was intimately linked to primary genderization and socialization. As a result reading and writing were invested with great psychosexual significance, and the book and the written text as objects became linked to a desire. The literary text can perhaps, although of course not in the strictest sense, even be said to have taken on the aspect of a 'transitory object'. In one of the many anecdotes about initial alphabetization that are remarkably frequent in the biographies of the Romantic writers (at least in Swedish literature), Atterbom tells us how his friend the great epistolary and diary writer Adolf Törneros as a child would not go to sleep unless his mother had put a book under his pillow.[3]

Interestingly enough, we come across the situation of the little (boy)child acquiring literate skills in the poetry of one of the main Swedish Romantic poets, P.D.A. Atterbom. In an early, yet stylistically pre-Romantic,[4] version of his important poem 'Minnes-runor' (roughly translatable into 'Eulogies') Atterbom directs the following verses to the spirit of his deceased father:

> Än vigde Du mig in i första graden
> Af Bokstafskonstens heliga Mysterier:
> Än tolkade Du mig de Gamles Skrifter,
> Och Spartas dygd, och Romas jättestorhet,
> På mina unga Fantasiers Himlar
> Likt vidtkringglänsande Kometer, blänkte [5]

(Now you initiated me into the first degree / Of the sacred mysteries of the art of letters: / Now you interpreted for me the writings of the ancients, / And the virtue of Sparta and the grandeur of Rome, / In the sky of my imagination / Shone like bright comets) .

The education depicted here is of a traditional and scholarly kind. The teaching of reading and writing in the humanistic tradition goes along with the apprentice of classical history. In a later, rather more strictly 'Romantic' version of the poem, the scene recurs but in a quite different setting:

På dessa ställen satt den Oförgätna.

Hon höjer aldrig mer, vid brasans skimmer,

Så mången ljuf, förtrolig vinterafton,

Till andakts sång sin ömma silfverröst!

Ej bokstafkonstens första hemligheter

Vid sländan mer sin älskade hon lär:

Ack nej! ack nej! min engels röst är stum!

I tomma rummen hennes vålnad hviskar.[6]

(Here she sat, the unforgotten / She'll never more on a sweet, intimate winters night, raise her tender silvery voice in a song of devotion / No more will she by the distaff teach her beloved the firsts secrets of the art of letters / Alas! alas! my angels voice is quiet / Her ghost whispers in the empty rooms).

The scene is set in a domestic environment. The boy and his mother are snuggled up by a warm fire, safe from the cold of winter outside, and as the mother teaches her son 'the first secrets of the art of letters' she spins with the help of a distaff. Alphabetization has been clearly separated from the rest of the educational subjects, and indeed it is now, strictly speaking, not a subject of education at all; instead it is associated with leisure, intimacy and playfulness, and the task of learning to read and write is clearly connected with a high amount of pleasure. Whereas the emphasis in the former scene was put on the imagination released by the fathers account of heroic deeds from classical history, the stress is now on the comfort of the mothers voice and another activity associated with her is the singing of hymns. It is also the absence of this voice that appears as most painful to the lyrical subject in the present situation.

For anyone attempting a biographical approach to the poems the existence of two contradictory versions of the same event would naturally pose a problem. The issue here though is of course not to determine whether Atterbom actually acquired literacy from his father or his mother, but I believe that the circumstance of the existence of two different versions indicates that something important is at stake, and should this circumstance complicate a strictly psycho-biographical interpretation of the theme, the presence of the different versions nevertheless suggests that we are dealing with a theme of literary importance.

The classical education is not absent in this version; but the educational tasks have been separated, and whereas the mother now is responsible for the basic skills of reading and writing, the father retains responsibility for teaching the boy history, morals and the secrets of the Christian faith. The scenery here though differs in a significant way from that of the former scene:

> Och när du hemkom sent till lugna kojan,
> Och satte dig i dina lönnars skymning,
> Du talade med mig om Svenska Hjeltar,
> Om Dygden, Äran och Odödligheten.
> Ditt faderslöje följde gossens blickar,
> Som druckna häftade vid talarns läppar
> Och dunkelt brunno af begär till bragder. –
> Nu leder du mig ej på himlens vägar,
> Du tyder ej de Gamles skrifter mer.
> Den gröna höjningen vid kyrkomuren,
> Den grofva stenen som ditt namn förkunnar,
> Är allt, hvad jag har öfrigt nu af Dig.[7]

(And when you returned late to the calm hut / And sat down in the shadow of your maple trees / You talked to me about Swedish heroes / About virtue, glory and immortality. / Your fatherly smile accompanied the gazes of the boy / That drunkenly clung to the speakers lips / And darkly glowed with desire for deeds. – / Now you are no longer leading me on the ways of heaven / You're no longer interpreting the writings of the ancients. / The green mound by the churchyard wall / And the rough stone that proclaims your name / Are all I've got left of you now).

The setting here is outdoors, and the locality, the academic grove, is of course strongly associated with the tradition of classical education. Quite in concordance with this tradition, the instruction offered by the father is also of an altogether oral character. The father/teacher narrates, interprets and guides his pupil. This orality however is not explicitly thematized, and the voice of the father is, very unlike the 'silvery voice' of the mother, nothing but a transparent vehicle simply conveying its contents. Focus is shifted from the signifying medium to the signified contents.

Whereas the relation between teacher and pupil is here of a clearly hierarchic nature, with the boy passively clinging with his eyes to the lips of the talking father, the relation between mother and son is of more interactive nature; in a reworking of the poem for his collected poems in the late 1830s the scene is further elaborated and Atterbom describes how the lyrical subject as a reward for his literate labours is allowed to read aloud from *Heimskringla* to his mother.[8]

The formal parallelism of the two strophes also deserves to be pointed out: a state of lack or of absence is depicted, and the lyrical subject contrasts his remembrance of things past with that which he is left with at the present moment; in the case of the mother this is the whispering of her ghost in the now empty rooms, a whispering which is not actually a proper whispering, but rather a metaphorical representation of silence; in the case of the father it is the grave and the headstone that spells out his name. Reading and writing comes to be contextually associated with the vocal, whereas remembrance of oral instruction is linked to the letters of the fathers rough headstone. This written text though does not call forth a voice of any kind; much in accordance with the associations linked with writing and the letter in western tradition from Plato to Derrida, it rather underlines the absence of a speaking subject. Two contradictory versions of the theme writing are thus to be found parallel in the poem. When writing functions as a trope of absence, as in the description of the fathers headstone, it can do so by functioning as a sign of signification itself and by exploiting the necessary non-coincidence of signifier and signified that is inherent to the notion of sign. And this indeed is the status assigned to writing when it is put in relation to the referential discourse of the father.

In the sphere determined by the 'minimal signifieds' of the mother's voice, writing is perceived in an entirely different manner; it is here an activity associated with the vocal, and hence with presence, immediacy, even intimacy. The power of the medium conveying the significance of the written letters is strong enough to dissemble the signifying nature of the letter, and instead create the illusion of a coincidence between signifier and signified; between the vocal and the materiality of writing. Through a sort of semiotic short-circuit the letters are made transparent to the voice that initially conveyed their meaning, and they disappear as signs, in the proper sense, as their materiality is repressed (Kittler 20).

The written sign then ultimately appears as even more spiritual and less material than the human voice itself, its semiosity is repressed and it takes on the aspect of an immediate outflow of the soul, something quite illustrative in Friedrich Schlegel's account of his sentiments about written texts:

Die Schrift hat für mich ich weiß nicht welchen geheimen Zauber vielleicht durch die Dämmerung von Ewigkeit, welche sie umschwebt. Ja ich gestehe Dir, ich wundre mich,

welche geheime Kraft in diesen toten Zügen verborgen liegt; wie die einfachsten Ausdrücke, die nichts weiter als wahr und genau scheinen, so bedeutend sein können, daß sie
wie aus hellen Augen blicken, oder so sprechend wie kunstlose Akzente aus der tiefsten
Seele. Man glaubt zu hören, was man nur lieset, und doch kann ein Vorleser bei diesen
eigentlich schönen Stellen nichts tun, als sich bestreben, sie nicht zu verderben. Die stillen
Züge scheinen mir eine schicklichere Hülle für diese tiefsten, unmittelbarsten Äußerungen
des Geistes als das Geräusch der Lippen.[9]

One believes to hear what one is in fact only reading, and yet this imaginary audibility of the text is mysteriously superior to the actual audibility of the voice. It
is in some sense purer, less material, and the letter is regarded as a more fitting
medium for the most 'profound' and 'immediate' utterances of the spirit than the
'noise of the lips'. The text has a voice of its own, and upon hearing a text read
aloud Schlegel experiences an abuse being made towards this voice.

This repression of semiosity eventually leads to a challenging of the entire
notion of sign as it is understood in previous rhetoric and semantic tradition, and I
should like to suggest that the two contradictory versions of the theme writing
simultaneously figuring in the poem, does in fact give way to the ongoing transition
between semiotic orders decisive for Romantic and idealist aesthetics.

One could also venture to claim that in this we find a clue as to why the notion
of a bipartite sign appeared so traumatic to Romantic and idealist aesthetics. The
most well known example of this was probably the way in which an ideal of a symbolic work of art, where total coincidence between signifier and signified is demanded, is contrasted to a consciously biased – at least that is how Benjamin will have it[10]
– image of allegory. Perhaps it could even be suggested that the concept of symbol,
as developed in the dominant aesthetic doctrines of the time, can be traced back to a
transposition of the illusion of the identity between sound and letter, experienced in
initial alphabetization, on to the realm of referential signification at large.

Here we also touch upon another important tenet of Romantic or idealist aesthetics: its aversion towards the very materiality of art, which often leads it to assign
poetry a higher status than more immediate material forms of art such as the plastic
arts form; and ultimately to its high estimation of music. This taxonomy of the arts,
based on their relative materiality, is fundamentally, of course, just as illusory as the
coincidence between signifier and signified, letter and voice experienced in writing. Words are not thoughts, and tones are certainly not emotions.

Poetical discourse produced by the subjects of such an education as the one depicted in 'Minnes-runor' would have but one main addressee: woman, in general, and the mother in particular. Romantic writing becomes an attempt to re-establish the presence of the maternal voice that originally called forth written discourse. It aims ultimately at the re-creation of the long lost intimacy of the original pedagogical situation, and becomes as such an extreme illustration of Lacan's dictum: 'Ce que je cherche dans la parole, c'est la réponse de l'autre'.[11] But such texts are already in some respect nothing but mere variants of the original discourse of the mother; she is their origin and the sons/writers can only feed back to her what she has once given them (Kittler 74). It is the son's hand that writes, but once written the text always echoes the voice of the mother. Though I am not aiming at any biographical approach, it is nevertheless interesting how Atterbom in a letter to Schelling writes about his mother: 'wie sie mir denn auch alle die bessern meiner frühesten Gedichte selbst eingegeben und bei deren Vorlesen mitgefühlt als wenn sie ihre eigenen gewesen wären'.[12]

If this is indeed the case, no wonder then, that a contemporary critic could describe Atterbom's poetry as being at heart a 'music signified with words'.[13] What the words of the mothers voice signify is not a semantic content, but the pure presence of this voice itself. And in this lies perhaps one important factor behind the sonority or musicality of Romantic poetry, often at the expense of semantic coherency, that has been so frequently pointed out.[14]

I should like to conclude by showing how the situation depicted above at times also calls forth a text with clearly defined generic positions and in which a female recipient, reader or listener, is inscribed into the text itself. The text in the most extreme case becomes a virtual re-enactment of primary alphabetization. Illustrative of this is Atterbom's 'Erotikon'.[15]

In this, in the usual manner of Atterbom's poetry, a semi-allegorical landscape is depicted in which it is virtually impossible to discern on which ontological level the objects belong; pictures are superimposed on pictures, and metaphorical and literal sense are dissolved into one another. In this landscape a female being of high metaphysical dignity appears; she is simultaneously terrestrial and celestial, at the same time incarnated beauty itself and the imagined object of the lyrical subjects desire. As often in Romantic poetry, platonic eros and erotic desire are seamlessly fused into one. Attracted by the song of the lyrical subject she hurries to meet him and they are united in a kiss, whereby a bolt of lightning 'flies through space'. The union of the lovers is at the same time a sign of the identity between spirit and nature, and the 'Worldspirit' himself rejoices at the sight.

Then something very interesting happens; the female pole of the poem ceases to be a 'She' in the third person and is transformed into a 'You', to which the lyrical subject now turns. But this 'You' is no longer the mythical deity of the first part of the poem; and in the following strophe it becomes apparent that the invoked 'you' is indeed none other than the actual feminine reader of the poem, and Atterbom envisages how his own poem is received by this anonymous female reader. The strophe begins with a 'kanske' (maybe) which marks the hypothetical nature of the following scene, and allows the poetic imagination to revel in a fantasy of the situation. Indeed it becomes a fantasy as powerful as the mythico-allegorical reveries of the first part of the poem, but the setting is now extremely different.

Kanske nu du, vid din gömda båga,
Bakom gröna skydd mot solens låga,
Med tamburn i hand, i tårar ler:
Ty en sång af mig på duken hvilar,
Och din svanhand genom bladen ilar;
Än ett stygn – och än en blick i skriften -
Och en suck du åt Författarn ger.

(Maybe you now by your hidden embroidery-frame / Behind green screens protecting you from the flame of the sun / Smiling in tears, with the tambour in your hand / Because a song written by me rests on the cloth / And your swanlike hand hurries through the leaves / Yet a stitch, and yet a glance at the text / And you give the author a sigh).

Once again a domestic scene is invoked, as in the version of 'Minnes-runor' which we have previously studied, and we even find the female reader embroidering while reading Atterbom's poem, just like the boy's mother was busy with handicraft in the scene from 'Minnes-runor'. It is also worth noticing how the setting is now apparently indoors. The vast perspective of the infinite metaphysical landscape is substituted for the seclusion of the home, where 'green screens' protect the female reader from 'the flame of the sun'. And as it turns out the sojourn in the high heavens of mythico-allegorical poetry constituted indeed nothing more than a shortcut to the intimacy of the living room, where once the primal scene of literacy took place.

But the fantasy intensifies and the lyrical subject imagines how the female reader in her turn fantasises about the poet. Once again a 'Maybe' opens the strophe, and allows the poem to relate the hypothetical thoughts of the female reader.

Kanske ock, 'Hvar vistas han?' du frågar;
'Månne i hans egen lefnad lågar
'Denna dygd, jag i hans dikter fann?
'Skalder sällan äga fromma seder;
'Men om Religion hans Sångmö leder,
'Som den andaktsfulla stämpeln tyder,
'Säkert är han då en ädel man'.

(Maybe you also ask, 'where does he dwell' / 'Perhaps this virtue I've found in his poems also burns in his own life? / Poets seldom have pious customs / But if religion guides his muse / As can be inferred by the devout character / He's sure to be a noble man').

The events of the first portion of the poem repeat themselves; once again the song of the lyrical subject attracts the attention of a female being. But just as the metaphysical setting of the first portion is substituted with a more mundane environment, so is the erotic temperature remarkably lowered. Desire in the text is no longer adult erotic, nor is it a longing for metaphysical infinity, but rather takes the form of an infantile desire for approbation.

NOTES

1. I should point out that the term 'alphabetization' is not used here in its common English sense. This is because I have not been able to find a good English equivalent for the German 'Alphabetisierung', in the sense of a process of making literate, or of being made literate.

2. Kittler 1987, 31ff. In the following as Kittler, with reference to page number in the text. In what follows I will draw quite heavily on Kittler's work, but I would like to point out that this paper is not to be considered a 'kittlerian' reading of Swedish material. In a paper of these dimensions, it has not been possible to do justice to the full scope and far-reaching consequences of Kittler's approach; therefore, while some of the main themes of Kittler's work have been employed, others – by necessity – have been ignored. In this paper I have not so much attempted to carry out an

accomplished study, but rather have tried to outline a possible field of future investigation.

3. Atterbom 1840-42, Vol. 2, p.6.

4. See Edström 1969, 137 f.

5. Manuscript in U.165, Uppsala University Library.

6. Atterbom 1812, 6.

7. Ibid. 7.

8. Atterbom 1863, 303.

9. Über die Philosophie. Fr. Schlegel 1988, 2.171, see Kittler 1987, 70 ff.

10. Benjamin 1990, 139.

11. Lacan 1971, 1.181.

12. Atterbom to Schelling July 3, 1819. (Ed. Berg) 1918, 92.

13. Hammarsköld 1814, col. 793.

14. Cf. Engdahl 1990, 94.

15. Atterbom 1810, 24 ff.

BIBLIOGRAPHY

Atterbom, P.D.A. 1810. 'Erotikon', *Phosphoros.*

Atterbom, P.D.A. 1812. 'Minnes-runor', *Phosporos.*

Atterbom, P.D.A. 1840-42. 'Minnesteckning'. In Adolf Törneros: *Bref och dagboks-anteckningar,* Vol. 2. Uppsala.

Atterbom, P.D.A. 1863. *Lyriska dikter,* Vol. 2 (= *Samlade dikter* Vol. 5). Örebro.

Benjamin, Walter 1990. *Ursprung des deutschen Trauerspiels.* Frankfurt.

Berg, Ruben G. (Ed.) 1918. 'Atterboms bref till Schelling'. *Samlaren.*

Edström, Vivi 1969. 'Atterboms Minnes-runor. Versionsjämförelse och forskningsdebatt'. *Samlaren.*

Engdahl, Horace 1990. 'Atterboms akustik'. In: *Sinnenas rike. Till Per Daniel Amadeus Atterbom.* (Ed. Göran Bergengren). Stockholm.

Hammarsköld, Lorenzo [anon.] 1814. Review of *Phophoros* 1813, *Swensk Literatur-Tidning.*

Kittler, Friedrich A. 1987. *Aufschreibesysteme 1800/1900.* 2nd ed. München. (Abbreviated as Kittler)

Lacan, Jacques 1971. 'Fonction et champ de la parole et du langage en psychanalyse'. *Écrits.* Vol. 1. Paris.

Schlegel, Friedrich 1988. 'Über die Philosophie'. In: *Kritische Schriften und Fragmente. Studienausgabe in sechs Bänden.* Vol. 2. (Eds. Ernst Behler and Hans Eichner). Paderborn, München, Wien, Zürich.

German Romanticism between
World Literature and German Philology

Bengt Algot Sørensen

The first evidence of the term *World Literature* belongs to the cosmopolitan context of the Enlightenment. The term was first found in the work of the Göttinger historian August Ludwig Schlözer[1] and later in 1790 in the private copy of Christoph Martin Wieland's translation of Horace's letters, where he defines the word *urbaneness* as 'this subtile tincture of world knowledge and world literature'.[2] But it was first through the older Goethe that the term became known to the public.[3] At the end of the 1820s the term turns up again and again in his diaries, letters and conversations, and last but not least, also in the review written by himself *Über Kunst und Altertum (About Art and Antiquity)*, the horizon of which is best characterized by the term 'world literature'. The first two numbers of the 6th volume (1827/28) contain, for example, essays about Homer, Euripides and Shakespeare, about Byron's and Manzoni's recent works, about Chinese lyrics and oriental fairy tales, as well as about folk-poetry in several languages. In this review Goethe explicitly declared himself an adherent of the term 'world literature' and therefore in the 6th volume he expressed the expectation 'that with the present, most lively epoch and quite simplified communication, a world literature can soon be hoped for'. Even more convinced and with a polemical point against a national narrowing of the literal and cultural perspective, he had in his conversation with Eckermann on 31st of January 1827 remarked: 'National literature will not say much now; it is the time for the epoch of world literature and everybody has to work to expedite this epoch'. The contrast between the two terms 'national literature' and 'world literature', led Goethe to name an antinomy, the tensions emanating from which would continue into the 19th and 20th century.[4]

The essential difference between the two terms is not so much quantative, but rather what is implied by the terms themselves. World literature, for example, presupposes that each literature can principally be understood and experienced by every nation, whether it be in the translated version or in the original language; hence, the possibility of a net of literary relations crossing political, geographical and linguistic borders. In sharp contrast, during the 19th century and sometimes later it was maintained that the literature of a nation could after all only be experienced and understood by members of the particular national community; not just because of linguistic reasons, but also – and importantly – because language and culture were organically linked with the community and the character of a nation. Accordingly, between the 'own' and the 'foreign' an unbridgeable contrast exists. *World literature* in comparison presupposes an interior, however constituted relationship of all literatures, which refers to an anthropological substance common to all peoples. Through this substance the term *world literature* wins – in spite of all individual and national differences – a dimension through which a mutual supranational understanding and a mutual intercultural communication can be realized with the help of literature.

Such and similar opinions were widely known in the European Enlightenment, although they were formulated differently. But the matter existed, also there where the term *world literature* itself was not used and was still unknown, for example in *Journal étranger,* a French review, which stood for the 'circulation des valeurs parmi tous les peubles cultivés'[5] in the years 1754-1762. With regard to Germany, Johann Gotfried Herder deserves a special position. Although he stood in opposition to the Enlightenment in some respects, he developed further the universality of the Enlightenment in his way and connected it with an organological view of nations and cultures. So supporters of *world literature* as well as supporters of *national literature* could later appeal to Herder. In his treatise *Alte Volkslieder (Old folk-songs),* later (1807) published under the title *Stimmen der Völker in Liedern (Peoples' Voices in Songs)* he not only brought translations and adaptations of almost all the European literatures but also of the Persian, Arabian and Indian literatures, as well as from Greenland, Madagascar, Peru and other countries. One can see, he was not Eurocentrical. For Herder all these peoples were, as he wrote, 'die Brüder unsrer Menschheit' (the brothers of mankind), and the songs a means to get to know and to understand the essence of the cultural character of these peoples.

Unlike the widely held idea that Romanticism and Germanic philology had given up Herder's cosmopolitan tendencies in favour of a narrow-minded national chauvinism, the fact rather was that the Early Romanticists carried on Herder's universality of the Enlightenment and the over-national understanding of literature, changed it, adapted and integrated it in a far-reaching way in poetry, theory and translations. Thus it results here in continuity and contexts, which decisively relativize the otherwise undeniable differences and tensions between the Enlightenment, Storm and Stress *(Sturm und Drang)*, Early Romanticism and the Olympian in Weimar. On the basis of the concept of *world literature* their hopes and interests could converge, although they thought differently to a lesser or greater extent.

In the vocabulary of the German Early Romanticism the European idea was a central concept from the beginning. Well-known is Novalis' (1799) fragment *Die Christenheit oder Europa (Christianity or Europe),* which begins with the sentence: 'These were beautiful bright times when Europe was a Christian country' (Es waren schöne glänzende Zeiten, wo Europa ein christliches Land war), and ends with the more utopic than realistic conclusion: 'The other parts of the world wait for Europe's reconciliation and resurrection in order to join it' (Die andern Weltteile warten auf Europas Versöhnung und Auferstehung, um sich anzuschließen). With regard to the literary contexts, Friedrich Schlegel also played a particularly important role here. Already in his early treatise *Über das Studium der Griechischen Poesie* (1795/96; *About the Study of Greek Poetry)* he had characterized the European literature as 'a coherent whole' (ein zusammenhängendes Ganzes)[6] in which a 'continuous mutual imitation' (eine stete Wechselnachahmung) especially between the Italian, French and English literatures had taken place. This view was repeated and deepened in Fr. Schlegel's lectures in Paris in 1803/04, that is at a time when he was editing the review with the informative title *Europa.* Introductorily it is also established in his Parisian lectures: 'European literature makes up a coherent whole, where all branches are mingled closely, one thing rests on another, explained and completed by it. That can be seen throughout all times and nations until the present day. The new is not understandable without the old' (*KFSA* 11.5; Die europäische Literatur bildet ein zusammenhängendes Ganzes, wo alle Zweige innigst verwebt sind, eines auf das andere sich gründet, durch dieses erklärt und ergänzt wird. Dies geht durch alle Zeiten und Nationen herab bis auf unsere Zeiten. Das Neueste ist ohne das Alte nicht verständlich). That results for Schlegel in the following consequence: 'To concentrate only on the literature of a certain time or nation is impossible because one literature always refers to another and all literatures form a closely coherent and large whole, not only one after another but also side by side' (*KFSA* 11.2; Sich nur auf die Literatur einer gewissen Zeit oder einer Nation einschränken wollen, geht gar nicht an, weil eine

immer auf die andere zurückführt und alle Literaturen nicht allein vor- und nach-
einander, sondern auch nebeneinander innig zusammenhängend ein großes Ganzes
bilden).

This perspective was broadened in Fr. Schlegel's text *Über die Sprache und Weis-
heit der Inder* (1808; *About the Language and Wisdom of the Indians*). By adding a non-
European dimension, Schlegel firstly substantiates the context between Asia and
Europe linguistically by showing a pioneering detection of the relationship of the
Sanskrit with the Latin, Greek, Germanic and Persian languages. At the same time
he transmits this linguistically well-founded insight to the field of literature:

Just as historically the Asians and the Europeans form one large family and one inseparable
whole, one should increasingly make an effort to regard the literature of all educated peoples
as a continuing development and a single, deeply linked building and creation, a large whole,
where some one-sided and limited views would disappear by themselves, where much
would become understandable in the context and all would appear as new in this light. (218;
So wie nun in der Völkergeschichte die Asiaten und die Europäer nur eine große Familie,
Asien und Europa ein unzertrennbares Ganzes bilden, so sollte man sich immer mehr bemü-
hen, auch die Literatur aller gebildeten Völker als eine fortgehende Entwicklung und ein
einziges innig verbundenes Gebäude und Gebilde, als ein großes Ganzes zu betrachten, wo
denn manche einseitige und beschränkte Ansicht von selbst verschwinden, vieles im Zusammenhang erst verständlich, alles aber in diesem Lichte neu, erscheinen würde).[7]

With this small, but in some respect epoch-making treatise, Fr. Schlegel had not
only founded comparative linguistic science, but had also paved the way for future
studies of comparative literature, the direction of which is best interpreted by the
term *world literature*.

Fr. Schlegel's efforts for a comprehensive consideration of *world literature* were
first heavily supported by other Romanticists, but most strongly by his brother
August Wilhelm Schlegel and by Ludwig Tieck who was of the same age. Tieck's
introduction to his edition of the old-German *Minnelieder (Minnesongs;* 1803) is a
characteristic example of the harmony which still existed between the beginning of
Germanic philology – in which Tieck's edition played an important role – and the
Early Romantic idea of a *world literature*. In Tieck's introduction 'all the works of the
most different artists' (alle Werke der verschiedensten Künstler) are regarded as 'parts
of One poetry, One art' (als Teile Einer Poesie, Einer Kunst) since, as follows here:

there is just One poetry, which in itself from the beginning of time into the farthest future with the works we own and with those which are lost which our phantasy will complete as well as with the coming ones which it will foresee make up an unseparable whole (es gibt doch nur Eine Poesie, die in sich selbst von frühesten Zeiten bis in die fernste Zukunft, mit den Werken die wir besitzen, und mit den verlorenen, die unsere Phantasie ergänzen möchte, sowie mit den künftigen, welche sie ahnden will, ein unzertrennliches Ganzes ausmacht).

This feeling of the whole (Gefühl des Ganzen) is depicted by Tieck as a characteristic sign of his own times. He sees it in the industrious activity of translation and in the intensive study of Greek antiquity, of Shakespeare's works as well as the works of Italian poets and Spanish authors, the songs of Provence, the romances of the North and of the Indian imagination (indischen Imagination). After this panorama of world literature Tieck finally comes with remarkable modesty to that which was the actual aim of his task, by writing: 'Under these favourable circumstances perhaps the time is ripe to rediscover the older German poetry' (Unter diesen günstigen Umständen ist es vielleicht an der Zeit, von neuem an die ältere deutsche Poesie zu erinnern). But the European perspective is kept, for Tieck also sees the German medieval Minnelieder in the wider context of European literature, and above all, the literature of Provence; he even thinks that in them 'the lovely ghost of the Orient and Persia and India' (den lieblichen Geist des Orients und Persien und Indien) is to be found.

Closely linked with the Romantic project of *world literature* was the lively activity of translation from many different languages. The German Early Romanticism presented translations of Shakespeare, Cervantes, Calderon, Ariost, Petrarca and a lot of other Spanish, Italian, and Portuguese works, as well as antique works, which generally remained unmatched until the present day. In the years 1797 till 1810 A.W. Schlegel produced his justifiably famous translation of 17 Shakespearean dramas, a task which was continued and finished by Tieck. In an independent volume of almost 700 pages A.W. Schlegel's *Poetische Übersetzungen und Nachbildungen (Poetic Translations and Imitations)* were later edited as a collection; there were translations from the Indian, Greek and Latin languages, but the Italian, Spanish and Portugese transcriptions of poems preponderate by far. The importance the German Early Romanticists ascribed to these literary translations is shown as well by the fact that the most extensive poetic text in the review *Athenäum,* the core of German Early Romanticism and edited by the Schlegel brothers, is formed by the translation of the eleventh song from Ariosto's *Orlando Furioso*. Subsequent to these 30 pages of translation there was a supplement by the translator Johann Diederich Gries, who was in close contact with the Romanticists and who addressed Tieck here in order to thank him for his translation of *Don Quijote*. Gries then added the confession: 'I think one is on the way to invent the real poetic art of translation; this fame was reserved for the Germans' (Ich glaube man ist auf dem Wege, die wahre poetische Übersetzungskunst zu erfinden; dieser Ruhm war den Deutschen vorbehalten).[8]

Beside the art of translation the German Early Romanticism developed a theory of translation in which the activity of translation gained a matchless theoretical status. It was linked here with the postulate of a universal translatability of everything into everything. The remark by Novalis to A.W. Schlegel in his letter dated 30th November 1797: 'Finally all poetry is translation' (Am Ende ist alle Poesie Übersetzung) was taken up and developed further by Schlegel in his Berlinian lectures 1802/03. Schlegel abolishes the border between translation and writing of poetry here by characterizing the poetical activity of translation as 'a true writing of poetry, a new creation' (ein wahres Dichten, eine neue Schöpfung) since, as it says here: 'the human mind cannot do anything else but translate, all its activity consists in that' (der menschliche Geist könne eigentlich nichts als übersetzen, all seine Tätigkeit bestehe darin). That this theory of translation was closely associated with the idea of *world literature,* can be seen in Schlegel's Berlinian lectures as well, in which it says:

The aim is nothing less than to unify the advantages of many nationalities, to go into all of them and to get into their spirit and thereby to establish a cosmopolitan centre for the human mind. Universality and cosmopolitanism are the real German characteristics. (Es ist auf nichts Geringeres angelegt, als die Vorzüge der verschiedenen Nationalitäten zu vereinigen, sich in alle hineinzudenken und hineinzufühlen, und so einen kosmopolitischen Mittelpunkt für den menschlichen Geist zu stiften. Universalität, Kosmopolitismus ist die wahre deutsche Eigentümlichkeit).[9]

In spite of this programmatically announced universality it must not be overlooked that the German Romanticists with predilection translated only those foreign works into German which they already considered to be 'Romantic' (Romantisch). Here of course the question turns up as to which non-German works the German Romanticists called 'Romantic'? Firstly we can establish that for the German Early Romanticists the Modern and the Romantic were not at all identical, which follows from Fr. Schlegel's (1800) *Brief über den Roman (Letter about the Novel)*. After Fr. Schlegel had emphatically refused identification of the Romantic with the Modern, he continued:

So I search and find the Romantic in the older Modern ones, in Shakespeare, Cervantes, in the Italian poetry, in that age of knights, of love and fairy tales from which the idea and the word come. (Ath. III, 122; Da suche und finde ich das Romantische bei den älteren Modernen, bei Shakespeare, Cervantes, in der italienischen Poesie, in jenem Zeitalter der Ritter, der Liebe und der Märchen, aus welchem die Sache und das Wort kommt).

A few years later (1803-04) he laconically established in his lectures *Geschichte der europäischen Literatur (History of European Literature):* 'In the older Spanish poetry everything one calls Romantic is unified' (*KFSA* 11, 156; In der älteren spanischen Poesie ist gleichsam alles, was man romantisch nennt, vereinigt).

In his lectures (1802/03) *Geschichte der romantischen Literatur (History of Romantic Literature),* A.W. Schlegel for his part called Dante and Calderon 'the cornerstones at the beginning and the end of Romantic poetry' (*KFSA* 4.7; die Eckpfeiler am Anfang und Ende der romantischen Dichtung). At the same time Tieck completed his great play about *Kaiser Octavianus,* a major work of German Romanticism. Looking back he later wrote about the development of this work:

Being filled with enthusiasm about the allegorical poetry of Calderon, I tried also in this wondrous fairy tale to encapture allegorically, lyrically and dramatically what in my opinion is romantic poetry (Vom Calderon für die allegorische Poesie begeistert, versuchte ich es in diesem wundersamen Märchen zugleich meine Ansicht der romantischen Poesie allegorisch, lyrisch und dramatisch niederzulegen).[10]

Tieck's romanticization of the old German folk-book about Kaiser Octavian, which led him thematically to the very popular Carolingian cycle of legends – so loved by Italians and Spaniards – concurred with the statement he made under the spell of the admired Calderon.

Despite all terminological deviations and inaccuracies concerning the use of the word 'Romantisch', it was – beside Shakespeare – mostly the poets of the Italian and Spanish Renaissance, and of the Baroque, who embodied the spirit and the style of what the Schlegel brothers as well as Tieck and other contemporaries called

'Romantisch'. The fact that there were at the same time terminological open margins towards the German and European literature of the Middle Ages, and that the Orient's literature was praised as the 'highest Romantic' (höchste Romantische), for example in Fr. Schlegel's *Rede über die Mythologie (Speech about Mythology)*, does not change anything in this regard.

However, the German Early Romanticists were not content with translating and commenting on the works of their favourite authors which they characterized as Romanticists. On the basis of their works they rather formed – to a degree not fully appreciated – their own poetological imaginations as well as the style and the structure of their own poetry. In a communiqué to the public in the *Intelligenz-Blatt der Allgemeinen Litteratur-Zeitung* from 17th January 1798 *(Intelligence-paper of the General Literary View)* Schlegel stressed Tieck's soon to be published translation of *Don Quijote* with the following words:

Don Quijote is one of the works, (…) which we must try to copy more and more perfectly, that means faithfully, as long as our language is still in a developing process (*Don Quichote* ist eins von den Werken, (…) die wir, so lange unsre Sprache noch im Fortschreiten ist, suchen müssen immer vollkommner, d. h. treuer nachzubilden).[11]

Schlegel's reasons are remarkable insofar as the importance of the *Don Quijote*-translation is seen in the German language's ever increasing possibilities of expression, which – according to Schlegel – was still at this time (1798) in a process of development (Fortschreitens). He expressed himself more clearly on the occasion of his Calderon- and Shakespeare-translations. With well-founded pride he stressed here:

That by the help of these works new sources would be opened in the German language, and that much was now possible which was almost impossible a few years before. (Daß durch all diese Arbeiten neue Quellen in der Sprache geöffnet wurden, und daß sich schon jetzt vieles bewerkstelligen läßt, was vor wenigen Jahren noch geradezu unmöglich war).

As can also be seen in an advertisement in the *Intelligenz Blatt* from the year 1800, in which Tieck and A.W. Schlegel drew attention to Tieck's recently edited *Don Quijote*-translation, it was the poetic works of German Romanticism which should first and foremost benefit from these 'new sources' opened by the translations. Here the two Romanticists declare:

With the direction German poetry is taking, it is essential to gain an extensive knowledge of such a unique and profound artist as Cervantes (daß bey der Wendung, welche die deutsche Poesie zu nehmen anfängt, eine so viel möglich vollständige Bekanntschaft mit einem so einzigen und tiefen Künstler, wie Cervantes war, zu den wesentlichen Bedürfnissen gehört).[12]

In other words, to encourage this initial change in German poetry, i.e., the promotion of Early German Romanticism, a translation of Cervantes' works should be undertaken as completely as possible. Fr. Schlegel had expressed it even more directly in *Athenäum* in 1799 when he pointed out the importance of the Spanish prose of Cervantes for the aspiring German Romantic novel, and finally exclaimed:

Let us forget the popular writing of the French and the English and strive after these models (i.e. the Spanish ones). (*Ath.* II, 327; Laßt uns die populäre Schreiberei der Franzosen und Engländer vergessen, und diesen Vorbildern [d. h. den spanischen] nachstreben).

With the example of the novel *Don Quijote* the importance of the Romanic literature for the development of an Early Romantic theory and poetry in Germany can be illustrated. Fr. Schlegel's theory of the arabesque would not have been possible without *Don Quijote* translated by Tieck. In Cervante's novel Schlegel found 'that great wit of the Romantic poetry which is not to be seen in single ideas but in the construction of the whole' (jenen großen Witz der romantischen Poesie, der nicht in einzelnen Einfällen, sondern in der Construktion des Ganzen sich zeigt) as it is said in *Gespräch über die Poesie (Talk about Poetry)*. Moreover Schlegel stresses features in the context of this novel which entered, more or less unchanged, his own poetological theories – as for example the 'artifically (i.e., artistically) arranged confusion' (künstlich [d. h. kunstvoll] geordnete Verwirrung) or: the 'charming symmetry of contradictions' (reizende Symmetrie von Widersprüchen), or: the 'change of enthusiasm and irony' (Wechsel von Enthusiasmus und Ironie). Finally Schlegel establishes here that the organization of the novel *Don Quijote* was identical with the arabesque, 'the oldest and original form of human fantasy' (*Ath.* 3.102; der ältesten und ursprünglichen Form der menschlichen Fantasie). Also in *Gespräch über die Poesie* Schlegel subsequently fantasizes about a theory of the novel which was a novel of its own and in which Dante and Petrarca's Laura would walk in front of us and 'Shakespeare would have an intimate conversation with Cervantes; and there Sancho

Pansa would once more make merry with Don Quixote. – That would be a real arabesque' (Shakespeare mit Cervantes trauliche Gespräche wechseln; und da würde Sancho Pansa von neuem mit dem Don Quijote scherzen. – Das wären wahre Arabesken) it finally says. Involuntarily one thinks of the sketch with the title 'Zu den Arabesken' (To the Arabesques), which was found among the papers Schlegel left behind. Obviously it is about the plan of a novel-arabesque after the model of *Don Quijote* which Schlegel never realized and to which this sketch refers again and again.

After the *Athenäum*-years Schlegel once more was diligently occupied with the novel by Cervantes in his Parisian lectures *Geschichte der europäischen Literatur (History of European Literature)*. In the chapter about the Greek comedy he defines what he calls 'the poetry of the wit' (die Poesie des Witzes). As an example of such poetry he first refers to Tieck's *Prinz Zerbino oder die Reise nach dem guten Geschmack* (1799; *Prince Zerbino or the Journey to Good Taste)*, a comedy which simply bubbles over with wit, fantasy, irony, satire and parody. Here Dante, Ariost, Petrarca, Tasso and Cervantes walk in the garden of poetry. But Schlegel did not find the poetry of the wit only in Tieck's *Prinz Zerbino* but above all in the Italian and Spanish poetry, last but not least in Cervantes' *Don Quijote,* 'one of the most profound products of wit and parody' (eines der allergründlichsten, tiefsten Produkte des Witzes und der Parodie), which , as it says here, 'can count as one of the most perfect masterpieces of higher Romantic art in every respect' (*KFSA* 11.161; zu den vollendetsten Meisterwerken der höheren romantischen Kunst in jeder Hinsicht zählen kann). Above all it was here that Fr. Schlegel discovered the wit which was adopted as a central category in his aesthetic theories. The following excerpt can illustrate the status of the wit:

What the *Divina Commedia* is for seriousness, *Don Quijote* is for mockery and wit, which, due to its implication, comes close to profound seriousness when it is intensified to a certain degree. (*KFSA* 11.161; Was die *Divina Commedia* des Dante für den Ernst, das ist *Don Quijote* für den Spott und den Witz, der freilich, wenn er bis auf einen gewissen Grad gesteigert wird, durch seine Bedeutung nahe an den tiefsinnigen Ernst grenzt).

As for Schlegel's theory of the arabesque, it would seem that *Don Quijote* was of decisive importance for his theory of the wit as well. And this is an important part of the literary-historical context in which Schlegel's aesthetic theories were embedded.

Since Schlegel exemplarily illustrates the affinity of parody and wit to 'profound seriousness' (tiefsinnigsten Ernst) as well as the symbiosis of wit, parody and poetry, using Cervantes' novel, it looks perhaps less surprising that the translator of *Don Quijote,* Schlegel's friend Ludwig Tieck, conceived similar ideas at approximately the same time – also with reference to Cervantes' novel. In the introduction to his edition of the *Minnelieder* from the year 1803, Tieck speaks, for example, about the spirit which is effective in *Don Quijote:*

in which parody constantly is real poetry, and in which it is impossible to decide whether the poetry of this work were not to be taken completely as as parody, since there shines, one would like to say, such a bright wit through the whole work that one cannot establish with certainty whether one clearly sees or whether one is just blinded (p. 22 f.; dem Parodie beständig ächte Poesie ist, so wie man nicht bestimmen kann, ob die Poesie dieses Werkes nicht ganz als Parodie zu nehmen sei, denn es scheint, möchte man sagen, ein so heller Witz durch das ganze Werk, daß man fast nirgend mit Sicherheit angeben kann, ob man deutlich sieht, oder nur geblendet ist).

The intimate solidarity of witty parody and poetry, the possibility of their mutual identification belongs to the characteristic findings of the German Early Romanticism. At the same time it principally distinguishes the romantic interpretation of *Don Quijote* from the enlightened reading of this work. For the people of the Enlightenment *Don Quijote* was just a pure satire after all, a parody of the romances of chivalry and of enthusiasm. Everything that would not fit into the frame of this simplifying tendency of interpretation, as for example the poems, narrations and short stories just loosely linked to the plot, was critized by the people of the Enlightenment and possibly removed from their translations of *Don Quijote.* The Romanticists on the contrary saw in the loose composition of this novel, and in his mixture of several forms and styles, a typical Romantic feature they admired and which corresponded to the work's ironic-poetical double character. In a letter to A.W. Schlegel, Tieck himself characterized these deep reception- and translation- problems by writing about the *Don Quijote*-translation by Bertuch, a man of the Enlightenment from Weimar, which was published 1775-77:

therefore the Bertuch is not a *Don Quijote* at all. It is entirely another book in which almost the same occurrences are to be found. He had no sense for the real Romantic of the novel, for the magnificent verses, for the sweet depictions of love. He thought he was giving a big present to his readers by leaving most of it out. How poorly the magnificence of this work is actually recognized: One thinks of it as a book of amusing farces only (darum ist der Bertuch gar kein Don Quijote, er ist ein ganz anderes Buch, in dem bloß dieselben Begebenheiten ohngefähr sind, für das eigentliche Romantische der Novelle, für die herrlichen Verse, für die süßen Schilderungen der Liebe hat er keinen Sinn gehabt, er hat gemeint, seinen Lesern ein großes Geschenk zu machen, wenn er das meiste davon ausläßt. Wie wenig ist überhaupt die wahre Herrlichkeit dieses Romans erkannt: Man hält es doch immer nur für ein Buch mit angenehmen Possen).[13]

Between the reception of *Don Quijote* by the Enlightenment and the reception of Tieck's early work, exists a remarkable agreement which does not seem to be quite accidental as seen against the outlined background. As known, the young Tieck turned away from a moralizing petty bourgoisie and a narrow-minded utilitarian Enlightenment with comedy-like fairy tales such as *Der gestiefelte Kater, Prinz Zerbino, Ritter Blaubart (Puss in Boots, Prince Zerbino, Bluebeard the Knight)* as well as with the narrative *Die sieben Weiber des Blaubart (The seven wives of Bluebeard)*. These early works mainly dominated by farces, parody and satire do not lack a poetical element but this was mostly overlooked or misunderstood. In the traditional literary history these works were above all regarded and depreciated as documents of a polemic-aggressive process of liberation of the young Tieck who wanted to free himself from the publishers Nicolai and the rationalistic Enlightenment represented by them. In this way these works were downgraded in a similar fashion as the rationalistic Enlightenment had done with *Don Quijote*. But Tieck's works were intended to be more than just satire and parody. Here the free play of an autonomous fantasy is developed alongside parody and satire at the same time, which is expressed by a colourful mixture of forms and styles as well as by a vast variety of world literary allusions. Obviously Tieck wanted to combine poetry and wit in the form of literary arabesques, a term he explicitly chose for some of these works,[14] in order to create a German-language equivalent to the works of Cervantes, Ariost and others. If it is so, one should not estimate Tieck's early works as a marginal note of Romanticism but rather as an attempt to realize the intentions of Early Romanticism in the context of the European patterns admired by the German Romanticists.

In the Berlin lectures *Geschichte der romantischen Literatur (History of Romantic Literature)*, A.W. Schlegel pointed out in 1803 that the Germans had come to know the influence of foreign countries in various ways without having a retroactive effect. This statement led him to the following considerations:

If, thus, the Germans play such an insignificant role in a general history of Romantic poetry, almost disappearing from it, (…) then it may comfort us, that in contrast to general prosaic dying, the feeling for real poetry has been resurrected among us; that we have living artists who not just follow the old masters in a successful way but (…) have begun to rise to a yet unreached level, to form a new style of Romantic art which was brought about by the changes subsequently adapted by the human spirit (Wenn demnach in einer allgemeinen Geschichte der romantischen Poesie die Deutschen eine so unansehnliche Rolle spielen, ja fast daraus verschwinden (…) so können wir uns damit trösten, daß unter der allgemeinen prosaischen Erstorbenheit bei uns das Gefühl für echte Poesie wieder erwacht ist; daß wir mitlebende Künstler besitzen, die nicht nur den alten Meistern mit Glück nachfolgen, sondern (…) eine noch nicht erreichte Stufe ersteigen, einen neuen Stil der romantischen Kunst zu bilden angefangen haben, wie ihn die Wendungen fordern, welche der Menschliche Geist seitdem genommen).[14]

A.W. Schlegel's reaction is characteristic of German Early Romanticism before the national changes caused by the wars of liberation against Napoleon. The painful lack of a literary past of their own according to the values of Romanticism was first compensated by reference to the present. Their promising literature, criticism, philosophy and natural science, should secure an outstanding position for the Germans in a higher epoch of world literature, which the Early Romanticists of the first years of the new century were still convinced was to come.

Nevertheless, interest in German literature of their own past, above all of the Middle Ages, increased constantly. The centre of interest was the medieval lyric of the *Minnelieder* as well as the *Nibelungenlied*. Beside the actual Early Romanticism a growing interest developed at the same time in the old Norse language and literature, not uncommonly based upon a questionable equalization of the old German with the old Norse culture.

Above all Tieck and A.W. Schlegel gave important impulses to the rising Germanic philology of those days. Tieck's already mentioned edition of the medieval *Minnelieder* in 1803 was, according to his own statement, a crucial experience for Jacob Grimm. Although Tieck in no way aimed at a historic-philological edition but rather avoided all findings with scholarly or scientific inclinations, modernized the language and romanticized the style, his edition found adherents and led in the following years to numerous popular editions of old German texts. Besides the edition of the *Minnelieder* Tieck was also engaged with the *Nibelungenlied* for some years, even referring to the medieval manuscripts in his studies. Nevertheless it was also a revision and not a scientific edition in this case. When the Germanist Friedrich H. von der Hagen in 1807 stole the march on him with his own revision of the *Nibelungenlied*, Tieck had to abandon his intention. His *Nibelungenlied* remained unfinished and was published first after his death by von der Hagen.

As we have seen with the example of Tieck's edition of the *Minnelieder*, Tieck saw the old German literature with which he was very occupied in the years 1802 till 1807 in the context of world literature. The tension between cosmopolitanism and nationalism which unceasingly grew at the beginning of the century, due to the political events – above all the dissolution of the Deutsches Reich, the French occupation and the wars of liberation against Napoleon – and which characterized the beginning of Germanic philology, apparently did not change Tieck's literary concept. It was different in A.W. Schlegel's case.

Schlegel's importance for the Germanic philology lies above all in his contribution to a better historical and aesthetical understanding of the *Nibelungenlied*. Schlegel first presented his opinions in the Berlin lectures *Geschichte der romantischen Literatur (History of Romantic Literature)* in 1803. Among the audience was the above mentioned Friedrich Heinrich von der Hagen who, under the influence of Schlegel, found his way to the old German literature, and who as professor introduced the study of Old German at the University of Berlin in 1810.

A.W. Schlegel's Berlin lectures give an equivocal impression if one looks at them with reference to the rising tension between cosmopolitanism and nationalism, world literature and national literature. On the one hand the Romanticist Schlegel still takes the view of world literature by characterizing Romantic poetry in the word's sense of those days as a 'not just nationally and temporarily interesting but universal and everlasting poetry' (*KSB* 14; nicht bloß national und temporär interessante sondern universelle und unvergängliche Poesie); the same is true when he, with reference to the German national literature, establishes: 'We thus certainly ought to know what in German national literature is excellent, but not because it is German but much more because it is excellent' (*KSB* 28; Kennen sollen wir also allerdings das deutsche Vortreffliche (…), aber nicht bloß weil es deutsch ist, sondern weit mehr weil es vortrefflich ist). On the other hand, the already mentioned patriotical pride of the Early Romanticists in the intellectual and literary achievements of those years is enhanced by him to a really hybrid cultural nationalism. So here Schlegel calls Germany 'Europe's Motherland' (*KSB* 37; Mutterland Europas); he explains – without wavering – the Germans' interest in the literature of the Romance peoples by the latters' 'German blood' (deutsches Blut) 'which is mixed though with Roman blood and has become warmer and more abundant by the effect of a southern sky, but which still boils in the veins of these nations' (*KSB* 36; welches wiewohl mit römischem vermischt, und durch die Einwirkung eines südländischen Himmels wärmer und üppiger geworden, immer noch in den Adern jener Nationen wallt). His opinion of the *Nibelungenlied* makes a similar equivocal impression: On the one hand, it is praised as an embodiment of the German national character (Nationalcharakter) and thus as a miracle of nature (ein Wunderwerk der Natur), on the other hand, it is estimated as a 'sublime work of art' (*KSB* 109; ein erhabenes Werk der Kunst) and analysed as such.

Eight years later A.W. Schlegel devoted himself to the Nibelungenlied once more, in the review *Deutsches Museum (German Museum)* edited in Vienna in 1812 by Fr. Schlegel. In the meantime he had gone through the national changes and had accordingly altered his literary yardsticks. Literature should contribute to national education now, the *Nibelungenlied* should – alongside the *Bible* – become a 'major work in the context of educating German youth' (ein Hauptwerk bei der Erziehung der deutschen Jugend), if – as it says further – 'the Germans do not completely lose the feeling of being an independent, from very ancient times unmixed, glorious and inseparable people' (die Deutschen das Gefühl eines selbständigen, von uralter Zeit unvermischten, glorreichen und unzertrennlichen Volkes nicht ganz einbüßen).[15] Neither did A.W. Schlegel stand alone in those days with the racistic conception of a people 'from very ancient times unmixed' (von uralter Zeit unvermischten), nor with the idea of a national servitude of literature. For example the above mentioned Friedrich Heinrich von der Hagen held the view of a plan of national education as well which obviously made the way to the Berlin professorial chair easier for him.

When the national intoxication gradually fizzled out after 1815 the bell rang for the historic-philological, text-critical Germanic philology, for example in the shape of Karl Lachmann, who published the first text-critical edition of the *Nibelungenlied* in 1826. With sheer brutal frankness Lachmann in a letter to Schlegel dated 7th June 1826, characterized the latter as an overrated aesthete and dilettante, overestimated by public opinion, making an impression by 'a blinding illusion and a fashionable pomp of words' (blendenden Schein und vornehmen Wortprunk).[16] Meanwhile Schlegel was offered a chair at the recently founded University of Bonn in 1818 where he opened his academic profession with lectures about the history of the German language and poetry but apart from that devoted himself to the studies of the Indian philology and since then stayed away from the fields of Germanic philology.

Two of the most important representatives of the Germanic philology in those years of foundation were without a doubt the brothers Wilhelm and Jacob Grimm who should only be regarded here insofar as their relation to national literature and world literature is concerned. From the outset the interest of the Grimm brothers was directed towards national literary types such as folksongs, fairy tales of folk origin and myths; the scientific investigation of this kind of literature required a comprehensive international orientation, since the epic and mythic motifs and subjects of such a folkloristic poetry could not be reduced to *one* national literature. The Grimm brothers quickly acquired the necessary international orientation in this field; this is also to be seen in their first publications, for example in Wilhelm Grimm's translation of the old Danish epic songs in 1811 and of the old Scottish songs in 1813, as well as in Jacob Grimm's edition of Spanish romances, *Silvia de romances viejos,* in 1815. But their primary aim was and remained the old German poetry. Since they approached this aim by the help of a sharp separation of poetry of nature and poetry of art, whereby the poetry of nature was glorified at the expense of the poetry of art, it soon became a rejection of what one could call the Early Romantic conception of world literature. The close solidarity of the national literatures in the medieval Europe could not arouse their enthusiasm:

One normally says: in those days poetry spread throughout the whole world; but this can only refer to those who got to know it in foreign countries, not from the nation; each nation has taken pleasure in its own characteristic, native poetry (Man sagt gewöhnlich schön: damals klang eine Poesie durch die ganze Welt, welches aber nur auf diejenigen bezogen werden darf, welche sich im Ausland damit bekannt gemacht hatten, von der Nation nicht, eine jede hat sich ihrer eigentümlichen, bei ihr einheimischen erfreut).[17]

They even criticised the courtly epic poetry and lyric of the German medieval period, not just because of the art-character of this literature but above all due to the so-called 'foreign influences' (*KSWG* 108; fremde Einflüße) which allegedly distorted the German character of these two kinds of literature. However, in comparison the Nibelungenlied is effusively praised because it had its origins in an older, allegedly true – and still not estranged – German literature of which, moreover, is said: 'this absence of foreign influences is to its advantage' (*KSWG* 108; Jenes Entferntsein von fremden Einflüßen gereichte ihr zum Vorteil).

The terminology of the young Wilhelm Grimm is remarkable : He characterizes the middle-high German poetry of art with the word 'Romantic' (Romantisch), and that means as he explanatorily adds: 'those which are translated from the Romance languages' (*KSWG* 62; die aus dem Romanzo übersetzten). Actually the young Wilhelm Grimm, 1809, regarded the translations carried out on Parzival, Tristan, Iwain and many more, as 'translations of foreign myths' (*KSWG* 63; Übersetzungen fremder Sagen) which had lost the innocence of the poetry of nature and which were 'completely distorted' (*KSWG* 62; völlig entstellt) due to the highly artistic treatment. This so-called Romantic poetry of art had not participated in the 'essence of real German poetry' (*KSWG* 112; Wesen echt deutscher Poesie). According to Wilhelm Grimm, that forms a contrast between a European focussed Romantic (Romantischen) poetry of art of the Middle Ages, on the one hand, and a real German poetry of nature or national poetry on the other. One realizes that in this vocabulary 'national poetry' (Nationalpoesie) is equivalent to 'poetry of nature' (Naturpoesie); according to which Germanity and nature are identical terms, whereas a highly artistic form was something 'un-German' already in itself.

In an essay about the *Nibelungenlied* from the year 1807, Jacob Grimm had already anticipated these opinions of his brother. In this essay the *Nibelungenlied* is characterized as a national epic which is 'matchless in the whole Modern literature and for which one would like to give away the whole circle of the German novels of the Round Table' (das in der ganzen modernen Literatur ohne Beispiel ist, und für welches man, wenn es sein müßte, den ganzen kreis der deutschen tafelrundromane (…) hingeben möchte).[18] According to Jacob Grimm, the *Nibelungenlied* belonged also to the time 'before the French poems of chivalry became popular and were imitated, when poetry bloomed independently and free of foreign categories, in characteristic beauty' (*KSJG.* 4.1; ehe noch die französischen rittergedichte bekannt und nachgeahmt wurden, die poesie selbständig und frei von fremden bestimmungen, in eigentümlicher schönheit geblüht). Later Jacob Grimm revised his opinion about the middle-high German poetry of art, whereas he kept a rejecting,

almost hostile attitude towards foreign, and particularly towards the Romance literatures; in a review of Gervinus' *Geschichte der poetischen Nationalliteratur der Deutschen*
(History of the Poetic National Literature of the Germans) in 1835, Grimm stated his
blunt judgements publicly. Here it says for example:

Something with which I do not agree with the author in general is his admiration of 'the
great Italians', with whose yardsticks he very often judges our older poets. Lessing and A.W.
Schlegel, among others, have freed us from the French classics, and there is no fear of their
getting a firm footing in Germany again (*KSJG* 5.178; Etwas worin ich allgemein betrach-
tet nicht des verfassers ansicht theile, ist seine verehrung 'der großen Italiäner', mit deren
maßstab er sehr häufig unsere älteren dichter beurtheilt. Von den französischen classikern
haben uns Lessing bis auf A.W. Schlegel freigemacht, und daß sie jemals wieder festen fuß in
Deutschland gewinnen, steht nicht zu befürchten).

In the following he speaks about the, as it says, 'smooth, coloured Ariosto destituted
of all epic truth' (glatten, geschminkten, aller epischen wahrheit baaren Ariosto); the
middle-high German Titurel is set above Dante's work and about Petrarca's sonnets
it is said: 'they cannot compete with our best minnesongs, neither with regard to the
innocence of perception nor with regard to expression' (ibid.; sie können sich mit
unsern besten minneliedern weder in unschuld der empfindung noch des ausdrucks
messen). In a letter to Karl Lachmann two years earlier, dated 7th October 1833,
Jacob Grimm had already expressed himself in a similar manner. After he also here
had depreciated the Italian poetry and had upgraded the old German literature he
explanatorily added:

But I do not mind that one loves and studies them (the Italian poets) in Italy; one should let
us love and study our old ones (poets) as well (Aber ich habe nichts dawider, daß man in
Italien sie [die italienischen Dichter] liebe und studiere; man soll uns auch unsere alten
[Dichter] lieben und studieren lassen).

This explanation by Jacob Grimm shows how he imagined the European literary
map: every nation should love and study its national literature; the foreign literatures
are dispensable and recede into the background; like the nations the literatures best
remained neatly parted. One can hardly imagine a greater distance from the literary
system of values of the German Early Romanticism.

This attitude had weighty consequences for the German philology and for the studies of German literature, of course. The Grimm brothers expressed themselves unmistakably about the sense of these studies in their 'speech to the students upon their ovation for the Grimm brothers on 24th February 1843' (Rede an die Studenten bei deren Ovation für die Brüder Grimm am 24. Februar 1843). For Jacob Grimm the aim was, as it says here, 'to investigate the German character' (die erforschung des deutschen wesens); Wilhelm Grimm added:

these studies cover our native country; they have got their own fascination which the native always has for everybody, and which cannot be substituted by something foreign (*KSJG* 8.465; diese studien umfassen das vaterland; sie haben den eigenen reiz, den das heimische für jeden immer besitzt, den nichts fremdes ersetzen kann).

Thereby the world of literature was divided into the native – which was adored, and the foreign – which was met with distrust and hostility. Thus the danger of an ideological abuse of the German Germanic philology had reached a critical stage.

It can hardly surprise that the idea of world literature in this mental climate was not just brought into discredit but was fought passionately. Ernst Moritz Arndt can serve as a symptomatic example. In Rudolf von Raumer's *Geschichte der Germanischen Philologie (History of Germanic Philology)* from the year 1870 we read:

'Arndt's importance for Germanic philology does not lie in his performances in the linguistic field but in his enthusiastic awakening of the German mind' (317; Arndt's Bedeutung für die germanische Philologie besteht nicht in seinen Leistungen auf dem Gebiet der Sprachforschung, sondern in seiner begeisterten Erweckung des deutschen Sinnes).

This awakening of the German mind was expressed in the course of the French occupation by Arndt's ardent, patriotic songs and led to essays after the end of the Napoleonic Wars in which Arndt continued to call for hatred against the French. In his fight against the French language he went so far as to claim that, 'the German, who let his daughters be instructed in the Roman language would, so to speak, educate them as whores of the foreign' (daß der Deutsche, welcher seine Töchter in welscher Sprache unterweisen lasse, sie gleichsam zu Huren des Fremden bilde). This hatred of the foreign made Arndt attack Goethe's statements concerning world literature, which he tried to depreciate as a symptom of Goethe's supposed decrepitude:

not each word of a great man is gospel (…). Among much careless and light talk, hints and remarks, the word 'world literature' is spoken (nicht jedes Wort eines großen Mannes ist Evangelium (…). Da ist denn unter manchen sehr leichten und dünnen Gesprächen Winken und Hinwürfen das Wort Weltliteratur ausgesprochen).[19]

Immediately before that, Arndt had questioned whether 'Goethe would not have developed his talents much more magnificently and truly German in his high nature' if he had stayed in Frankfurt the whole of his life (Arndt 307; viel herrlicher und deutscher in seiner hohen Natur (…) entfaltet haben würde). The widely travelled Arndt referred in this context to the old German proverb: 'Stay at home and live sparsely' (Bleibe zu Hause und nähre dich redlich), which in his opinion absolutely had to be 'valid in the field of art' (Arndt 309; von der Kunst durchaus gelten muß). It disturbed him immensely that the catchword 'world literature' had been taken up by the younger literary generation with enthusiasm. About these young people Arndt writes:

They did not know that for centuries the Germans were ravaged and polluted by foreigners: Spaniards, French and others; that a lot of the very best and most original German still lies overwhelmed and covered with foreign filth and dirt, and that the fresh and bold youth is called (…) to retrieve much of the buried German treasure in its original form and bring it into the light of the sun (Arndt 312 ; Sie wußten nicht, daß die Deutschen Jahrhunderte lang von fremden Verwüstern und Verunreinigern, von Spaniern und Franzosen und anderen überfahren worden , daß Vieles des allerbesten und allereigensten Deutschen noch mit fremdem Unrath und Unflath überschüttet und zugedeckt liegt und daß die frische muthige Jugend berufen ist (…) so manchen vergrabenen deutschen Schatz wieder in seiner Gestalt an das Licht der Sonne zu bringen).

Arndt's metaphorical language about the treasures covered by 'foreign filth and dirt' (fremden Unrath und Unflath) was fatal, of course, and cannot be taken seriously from a present day point of view. But this choice of words and this way of thinking lived on in the national tradition and reached its climax in the propagandistic texts of National Socialism.

Finally we establish that the bold project of the Early Romanticists to form a universal poetry of world literature on the basis of the German language only realised its beginning. This was in spite of the industrious activity of translation, in spite of the literary theories developed primarily by the Schlegel brothers, and in spite of certain poetical works of the young Tieck. These promising beginnings had hardly seen the light of day before they were suffocated in the political and cultural confusion of the time. It was not the epoch of world literature that had begun as the older Goethe had thought, but the epoch of nationalism. In the Germanic philology of those days, which saw itself as a national resurrection, world literary contexts served mainly – as long as they were actually considered – to create a better understanding of the possessive 'own'. The *idea* of world literature was perceived less and less by German philologists in the 19th and in the first half of the 20th century. But it never disappeared completely from the minds of the authors and the literary public. For example the overwhelming success of the Danish critic Georg Brandes in his European-supranational texts of the 1870s and 1880s[20] points much more to a latent requirement to study literature – even German literature – in supranational contexts. But the opposition in the Wilhelminic Germany was great and increased in intensity up until World War I.

Today the situation has changed completely. The subject 'world literature' in the broadest sense of the term has become a crucial point in the comparative and Germanic science of literature. With regard to this field of research, the science of literature seems to converge with the deep changes of the European and global reality. Thereby it might benefit from a reference to German Early Romanticism.

NOTES

1. Manfred Schmeling 1995, 1.

2. Hans-J. Weitz 1987, *Arcadia 22*, 206–8.

3. Fritz Strich, *Goethe und die Weltliteratur*, Bern 1946; Hans Joachim Schrimpf, *Goethes Begriff der Weltliteratur*, Stuttgart 1987; Hendrik Birus, 'Goethes Idee der Weltliteratur', in Manfred Schmeling 1995, 5–28.

4. Victor Lange 1972, 15–30.

5. Marek Zybura 1994, 19.

6. Fr. Schlegel, *Kritische Ausgabe* 1.225. In the text as *KFSA*, with reference to volume and page number.

7. *Über die Sprache und Weisheit der Indier*, 218. In the text as *Sprache*, with reference to page number.

8. *Athenäum* 2.281. In the text as *Ath.* with reference to volume and page number.

9. A. W. Schlegel, *Kritische Schriften und Briefe* 4.36. In the text as *KSB*, with reference to volume and page number.

10. Ludwig Tieck, *Schriften* 1.xxxviii. In the text as *LTS*, with reference to volume and page number.

11. Tieck 1971, 261.

12. Zybora 1994, 45.

13. Tieck 1971, 260.

14. The title page, Vol. 9, *Schriften*, 1828.

15. *Deutsches Museum*. Vol. 1, Wien 1812, 20.

16. *Briefe aus der Frühzeit der deutschen Philologie an Georg Friedrich Benecke*, Wiesbaden 1966, 68.

17. *Kleinere Schriften von Wilhelm Grimm* 1.113. In the text as *KSWG*, with reference to volume and page number.

18. Jacob Grimm, *Kleinere Schriften* 4.1. In the text as *KSJG*, with reference to volume and page number.

19. E. M. Arndt 1845, Part 3, 311. In the text as *Arndt*, with reference to volume and page number.

20. Bengt Algot Sørensen 1980, 127–45.

BIBLIOGRAPHY

Arndt, E.M. 1845. *Schriften für und an seine lieben Deutschen.* Leipzig.

Athenäum 1960. Ausgabe der Wissenschaftlichen Buchgesellschaft, Darmstadt.

Birus, Hendrik 1995. 'Goethes Idee der Weltliteratur'. In: *Weltliteratur heute. Konzepte und Perspektiven.*
(Ed.) Manfred Schmeling. Würzburg.

Grimm, Jacob 1869. *Kleinere Schriften.* Berlin. (Abbreviated as *KSJG*)

Grimm, Wilhelm 1881. *Kleinere Schriften von Wilhelm Grimm.* Berlin. (Abbreviated as *KSWG*)

Lange, Victor 1972. 'Nationalliteratur und Weltliteratur'. In: *Goethe-Jahrbuch* 1972, Weimar.

Schlegel, A.W. 1965. *Kritische Schriften und Briefe.* (Ed. Edgar Lohner). Stuttgart.

Schlegel, Friedrich 1808. *Über die Sprache und Weisheit der Indier. Ein Beitrag zur Begründung der Altertum-
skunde.* Heidelberg. (Abbreviated as Sprache)

Schlegel, Friedrich 1958-95. *Kritische Friedrich Schlegel Ausgabe.* (Eds. Ernst Behler, J.-J. Anstett, Hans
Eichner). München. (Abbreviated as *KFSA*)

Schmeling, Manfred (Ed.) 1995. *Weltliteratur heute. Konzepte und Perspektiven,* Würzburg.

Sørensen, Bengt Algot 1980. 'Georg Brandes als "deutscher" Schriftsteller'. In: *The Activist Critic.* (Eds.
Hans Hertel and Sven Møller Kristensen). Copenhagen.

Tieck, Ludwig 1828. *Schriften.* Berlin. (Abbreviated as *LTS*)

Tieck, Ludwig 1971. *Dichter über ihre Dichtungen,* Vol. 9,2. München.

Weitz, Hans-J 1987. '"Weltliteratur", zuerst bei Wieland'. In: *Arcadia* 22.

Zybura, Marek 1994. *Ludwig Tieck als Übersetzer und Herausgeber. Zur frühromantischen Idee einer 'deutschen
Weltliteratur'.* Heidelberg.

Image, Imagery, Imagination

Hypervisuality in German Romanticism, or 'The Crystal Revenge'

Alice Kuzniar

It is far easier to see how modes of representation, perception, and communication have radically changed in our postindustrialist, high technological consumer age than it is to recognize continuity with former epistemes or ways of knowing. The result is that, despite the numerous debates a few years ago on the ties between modernity and postmodernity (a debate which has now almost totally exhausted itself), postmodernism as a era, movement, or concept appears unprecedented; its uniqueness is fetishized. Consequently, Fredric Jameson, for one, has repeatedly pointed to the need to historicize understanding of our own times. To be sure, many critics have noticed the citation of previous design in postmodernist architecture or the nostalgia for the past, even for the recent sixties, in films of the nineties, but historical contextualization of postmodernism need not and should not content itself with a discussion of rétro style.

Postmodernism's relation to the past is not solely an issue of parody and pastiche. Instead, one needs to investigate in terms of epistemological and phenomenological paradigms what the conditions for the possibility of postmodernism are. In what ways is it profitable to link the present day to previous periods with respect to how time, even novelty itself, is conceptualized, how objectivity is defined, or how representation functions? Without falling into the paradoxically opposite danger of dehistoricizing either period, is it possible to fold postmodernism back into Romanticism? What new insights are uncovered when one searches for an inflection of simulated, automatized reality 200 years earlier? In other words, how may current modes of seeing and knowing help one rethink Romanticism? And can a residue or sediment of Romanticism be found today? A focus on vision and visuality may help answer these questions. The aim will be to reassess commonplaces about the Romantic seer or prophet as well as nuance, with reference to the Jena circle, the dialectic between the perceiving subject and perceived object that defined transcendental philosophy in the wake of Kant. Specifically, the dream spaces and fabricated visual scenes in German Romanticism prove to resemble the virtual, simulated reality of advanced computer graphics technology, where too there is 'no reference to an observer in a real world'.[1] Genealogically speaking, postmodernism may be linked to the stations of the baroque, romantic, and surrealist with regards to the status of the image and its observer. Romanticism thereby promises to signal a pivotal chapter in an understanding of the complexities of the optical register.

Several well known scholars have noted the hypervisuality of postmodernism. In his introduction to *Signatures of the Visible,* Fredric Jameson writes: 'Were an ontology of this artificial (…) universe still possible, it would have to be an ontology of the visual, of being as the visible first and foremost, with the other senses draining off it; all the fights about power and desire have to take place here, between the mastery of the gaze and the illimitable richness of the visual object.[2] Meaghen Morris describes the present world of 'hypervisibility: the terror of the all-too-visible, the voracity, the total promiscuity, the pure concupiscence of the gaze'.[3] Jacqueline Rose similarly observes that 'the postmodern world, its hallucinogenic hyperreality, an undifferentiated vision of the world in the present (…) deprives the subject of the ability to locate her or himself either in time or space'.[4] And the most vociferous writer on hyperreality and postmodernism, Jean Baudrillard, notes: 'sur les écrans en général, et à la faveur de toutes les techniques médiatiques et télématiques, c'est l'objet qui se livre *en puissance'*.[5] Later in *La transparence du Mal* he develops this notion of the tyranny of the object with respect to the photographic image: 'On sent qu'une chose veut être photographiée, veut devenir image, et ce n'est pas pour durer, c'est au contraire pour mieux disparaître (…) Par l'image, le monde impose sa discontinuité, son morcellement, son grossissement, son instantanéité artificielle' (159). Yet if the image is discontinuous, instantaneous, and fleeting, the subject is as well: 'Il faut qu'une image ait cette qualité-là, celle d'un univers dont le subjet s'est retiré' (159). 'Le subjet n'est que l'agent de l'apparition ironique des choses' (158). Baudrillard would respond to Jameson that, in the struggle for the mastery of its gaze, the subject loses out, reduced to a passive, compliant spectator that does not so much mediate between empirical reality and the image but cedes dominance to the latter. Thus the alluring, manipulating visual medium robs the viewer of the freedom and mastery traditionally granted the eye, which is no longer discerning and disinterested but seduced.

Initially it would seem that the gaze in Romanticism is vastly different. As M. H. Abrams classically stated, the inspired Romantic poet is the source – metaphorically speaking the lamp as opposed to the mirror – of illumination. He not only casts philistine reality in an unfamiliar, magical light but is the vaunted origin of the hitherto unimagined, of the fantastic. The Romantic gaze is said to be turned inward to expose the dark recesses of the soul or the unconscious. Moreover, insofar as Romanticism subscribes to the belief that artistic powers may change the world, it reinforces the division of modernity from postmodernity, where, by contrast, individual agency is seen to disintegrate before multinational corporate interest and media uniformity and control.

One major aspect of Romanticism, however, is the role of hallucination and dream in the interior vision. It is a tenet of enlightenment and subsequently modernist faith that visuality may be reconciled with rationality and lucidity. But the Romantics break with the belief in vision as knowledge and clarity and instead see it as enchantment, subverting realism through spectacle and illusion. They no longer glorify observation and the disembodied gaze as a way of knowing the world but envision reality through the prism of desire and fantasy. Scientific investigations bolstered such perspectivism. As Goethe concluded on the basis of his experiments on afterimages and the interference of the body in perception, seeing is temporal and incarnate. Anticipating Goethe, Novalis studied the physiology of the eye and noted how perception of light and colour were modified by distance from the self and proximity to other objects.[6] Other contemporaries – as disparate as Kleist, Jean Paul, and Hoffmann – do not so much glorify interiority as they register unease at the implications of an individualized, even private vision that is susceptible to distortion, anamorphosis, and hallucination. It is not merely a matter of the perceived object being transformed under the fanciful poetic eye. More importantly, the bizarreness and peculiarity that cling to the object seem to detach it inexorably from its source in the Romantic subject. With the promise of overabundant meaning, Romantic vision may be excitable; yet it can reverse into depression and melancholy when the visual signifier appears isolated and its referentiality unmoored or, in terms of Novalis's *Monolog,* when language points enigmatically to itself. In writing about recent French thought, Martin Jay observes: 'When the visual is cast out of the rational psyche, it can return in the form of hallucinatory simulacra that mock the link between sense (as meaning) and the sense of sight'.[7] He could as well be writing about Romanticism. Using such various contemporary intertexts on hyper-visuality and hyperreality, I want to examine in works by Novalis and Tieck (who prepare the way for the irony in E.T.A. Hoffmann) a kind of revenge of the object on the subject's claim to posit the world around it and hence ways in which specta-cle, illusion, and chimera overwhelm and disempower the gaze.

Recently, a number of fascinating studies have cogently periodized modes of seeing, in particular, Jonathan Crary's extraordinary examination of the major para-digm shift that vision underwent in the nineteenth century. Crary sees in the first few decades of the 1800s the surfacing of an 'autonomous vision, of an optical ex-perience that was produced by and within the subject' as well as 'the introduction of temporality as an inescapable component of observation'.[8] The derangement and dislocation of vision in German Romanticism begs to be recognized as a key philo-sophical moment that prepared the ground for the scientific experimentation that Crary details later in the century. The excellence of his book *Techniques of the Observer* lies in the careful precision with which he demarcates historical change. Other critics on the geneology of vision have been less circumspect in establishing diachronic comparisons, but their work is no less stimulating. In classifying the three scopic regimes that he sees dominating Western discourse since the Renaissance, Martin Jay adds to the regime of Cartesian perspectivalism and the Baconian realm of dispassionate observation and description, that of the baroque visuality in which the subject is dazzled and confused by odd shapes, dizzying perspectives, and an ecstatic surplus of images. This is the model Jay finds returning in postmodernism: 'if one had to single out the scopic regime that has finally come into its own in our time, it would be the 'madness of vision' Buci-Glucksmann identifies with the baroque'.[9] In her books, *La raison baroque: De Baudelaire à Benjamin* (1984), *La folie du voir: De l'esthétique baroque* (1986), and *Tragique de l'ombre: Shakespeare et le maniér-isme* (1990), Christine Buci-Glucksmann discusses how baroque images blind their observer with their opacity, indecipherability, and excess. According to her, the baroque eye is captivated by allegorical enigma and the fetishized fragment; it advo-cates a hermeneutics of surprise and bewilderment. Yet despite its fascination before the scintillating spectacle, 'l'oeil baroque de la merveille, du pluriel jouisseur, de la différence est aussi celui de la déillusion (*desengaño*), un spectacle fatal, un théâtre d'affliction et de deuil. Comme si l'immersion totale dans l'image détruisait tout voir'.[10] It is this oscillation between enthusiasm and melancholic depression, one may argue, that characterizes Romanticism as well with its ecstatic, labile production of strangely abstract, ghostly images that seem haunted by visual transience. Paradoxically, the more the romantic, postmodern, or baroque eye delights in the rapid array of images, the more it is reminded of what it cannot see and hence its dwindling agency before the dazzling object. This blinding is nowhere more evident than in the writings of the Romantic visionary par excellence, Friedrich von Hardenberg.

In *Das Allgemeine Brouillon* Novalis compares the respective mutability of object and subject: '[Alles Objekt] ist ein *Geronnenes* – und das Subj[ect] ein Flüssiges, eine Atmosphäre. Es ist eine beständige Größe – das Subj[ect] eine Veränderliche – Beyde in *Einer Funktion*' (*NW* 2.682). This fragment is perplexing insofar as Novalis first aligns the pair in their fluidity, only then to suggest the subject is variable, while the object remains constant. How can it be that the object is both 'beständig' and yet 'ein Geronnenes'? And would one not presume the subject to be the bearer of continuity, if only in Kantian terms as the enduring sum of its successive representations, as the unity of apperception? The idea of a subject in flux is not an anomaly that only this fragment presents. Friedrich Schlegel defined the self as 'ein durchaus bewegliches, flüchtiges, flüssiges Wesen'.[11] Indeed, shortly after the fragment just cited, Novalis similarly speaks of 'ein *transitorisches* – Punctähnliches Ich' (*NW* 2.683). The ideal of a transformative, variable self links Novalis and Schlegel to Fichte's philosophy of ever renewed voluntaristic striving. Yet these fragments suggest the subject is not so much flexible and self-determining in its drive to self-development as, in anticipation of Ernst Mach's theories, transitory to the point of atomistic dispersion. By contrast, the object gains in constancy, even though perception of it is instantaneous and fleeting, making it too appear as 'ein Geronnenes'.

Although the poststructuralist interrogation of the nonunitary subject in Romanticism has been exhaustively debated, the question does pertain to the status of the perceived object and hence the issue of vision. It bears stressing, that subject and object form a relational 'function', as Novalis states, in other words that the object is filtered through the mind as representation. The objects that pass before the inner eye are continuous with it. The term 'object' in this Idealist discourse refers not to some empirically verifiable externality but to something mediated or created via 'Vorstellung' and 'Darstellung'. As Kant wrote in the preface to the second edition of the *Kritik der reinen Vernunft*: 'unsere Vorstellung der Dinge, wie sie uns gegeben werden, richte sich nicht nach diesen, als Dingen an sich selbst, sondern diese Ge-

genstände vielmehr, als Erscheinungen, richten sich nach unsererVorstellungsart'.[12]
Transcendental philosophy consists, by Novalis's similar definition, in this 'Zurük-
weisung ans Subjekt' (*NW* 2.670). But contact with the world does not narcissist-
ically reinforce the boundaries of the subject for Novalis; nor does the subject sub-
sume what is unfamiliar to it. On the contrary, Novalis is committed to a procedure
of consistent self-estrangement: 'Wir verstehen natürlich alles Fremde nur durch
Selbst*fremdmachung* – *Selbstveränderung*' (*NW* 2.670; on 'Alienation' see 2.11, 341 and
on 'Selbstheterogenëisirung' see 2.383). Paradoxically, it is only insofar as the subject
can render itself alien to itself – a process Novalis ironically emphasizes is natural –
that the uniqueness of the object too can be appreciated. Transformative power thus
lies in making self and other strange, 'Selbstfremdung' meaning both making the self
strange and making (the other) strange to oneself.[13] The hermeneutic process of
'verstehen', though, threatens to collapse under the escalating irony of the alienation
process. The subject alienates itself from itself to such an extent that neither objective knowledge nor subjective self-assurance are possible. It loses its grasp over agency. At this point, the object – the initial vehicle of alterity and difference – threatens
to overwhelm and disorient the subject. Novalis writes vividly of such absorpti
on and dissolution: 'Das Phaenomenon scheint uns einzuziehen – Die Welt ist
verschwunden' (*NW* 2.672). To what extent then does the object, once the subject
implodes, have the potential of taking on a phantom, hyperreal life of its own, of
becoming hypostatized?

Yet another passage from *Das allgemeine Brouillon* discusses the mutable, hetero-
nomous subject in terms of its perception of foreignness, in this case via the instantaneous phenomenal trace imprinted on the subject. Novalis turns to the indisput-
ably modern (as well as postmodern) metaphor of perception altered through rapid
motion to illustrate the transience of the subject and the world around it: 'Die
Veränderungen – sowohl zeitliche, als räumliche – der Dinge und selbst unsers
eignen Phaenomenons gleichen den Fortbewegungen der Bäume an der Straße, die
man schnell durchfährt' (*NW* 2.655). Technologization of appearances comes to define Novalis's ontology of the self. Thus he continues: 'Ich und d[ie] andern Men-
schen etc. sind im veränderlichen Zustande'. The example is an early one of how
speed and machine are brought to bear not only on the nature of the subject but
also on the disparity between perception and its object. Just as optical instruments
alter vision, so too can the eye modify the empirical world. Moreover, not only is
the eye a technological device, but the entire body itself becomes cyborgized:

'Zunge und Lippen etc. sind Theile eines Telegrafs (…) Die Augen sind Fernröhre' (*NW* 2.639). This technology, though, does not so much lend precision to sight as it anamorphotically transforms it. If in Novalis's accelerated vision, there is no fixed vantage point, how can one be certain of what one sees?

If external reality can appear modified through movement in time and space,[14] are internal perceptions, say in the dream world or the fictive creation of the fairy tale, constitutively different? Does Novalis here enter a timeless realm? Or in what ways can the technologization of perception equally apply to the production of dreams or poetry; what science does the latter obey? Novalis compares the fairy tale to the dream in its chaotic, unpredictable logic of association: 'Ein Mährchen ist eigentlich wie ein Traumbild – ohne Zusammenhang' (*NW* 2.696); '[Der Traum] ist oft bedeutend und prophétisch, weil er (…) auf Associationsordnung beruht – Er ist, wie die Poësie bedeutend – aber auch darum unregelmäßig bedeutend – *durchaus frey*' (*NW* 2.693).[15] A few fragments earlier in *Das Allgemeine Brouillon* Novalis similarly wrote that poetry was based on the intentional, idealist production of chance (*NW* 2.692). To read the dreams and fairy tales in Novalis's writing is to find numerous examples of this radically discontinuous, random syntax of images, where vision is accidental rather than substantial. In this poetic realm Novalis realized the science of a 'Darstellung der allaugenblicklichsten Thatsache' (*NW* 2.137).

The clearest example, Klingsohr's fairy tale, begins by narrating an increasingly movemented play of figures choreographed to the accompaniment of constantly variegated light:

[Die Figuren] bewegten sich lebhafter, je stärker das röthliche Licht ward, das die Gassen zu erleuchten begann. Auch sah man allmählich die gewaltigen Säulen und Mauern selbst sich erhellen; Endlich standen sie im reinsten, milchblauen Schimmer, und spielten mit den sanftesten Farben. Die ganze Gegend ward nun sichtbar, und der Wiederschein der Figuren (…) (*NW* 1.338-39).

Vision here is multiple and chaotic. Its richness is enhanced by the entire scene being mirrored in a sea: 'alles dies spiegelte sich in dem starren Meere (…) und (…) ward bis in die Mitte mit einem milden Abglanz überzogen' (*NW* 1.339). Yet despite the numerous references to light and the verb 'sehen' and 'sichtbar', the description is too fleeting and sketchy to impart anything but passing impressions. Metonymies of armour – 'das Getümmel der Spieße, der Schwerdter, der Schilder,

und der Helme' (ibid.) – for instance, substitute for personal reference to their wear-
ers. Novalis himself then comments: 'man konnte nichts deutlich unterscheiden'
(ibid.). Instead of precise detail, we are told only of the 'Mannichfaltigkeit und Zier-
lichkeit der Gestalten' (ibid.) and how they circulate. 'Widerschein', 'Abglanz',
'Gestalten', and 'Figuren': this highly mobile, transient universe could not be
rendered more abstract. Yet it is also self-consciously illusional and spectacular.[16] In
fact, were one to project Novalis's tale onto a screen, it would resemble more the
digitally rapid flow of flashing images in a video game, with its lack of visual resolution, than it would the precision of 32 mm or even that of early Disney animation.
To extend the cross-period associations further, one could say that the melancholi-
cally tinged abstraction of Novalis's imaginings presage the faceless dreamscapes of a
Dali, Tanguy, or De Chirico and later the cipher-like, hypostatized signs in pop art
and postmodernist consumer culture.

The link of poetic representation to oneiric indecipherability and syntax evokes
in addition the way in which the dream image is digitally yet imperfectly reconstructed in the futuristic film *Until the End of the World*. Here Wim Wenders ascribes
to technology the capacity to replay dreams on video. The simulated dreams, however, remain private and indecipherable, though they totally engross their viewer to
the exclusion of all else. If Baudrillard has described the video terminal as visual
simulacrum of the mind, a trope that Wenders actualizes, then the page of Novalis's
text likewise copies the alacrity, liquidity, and opacity of mental images, if you will,
of their data flux. Not surprisingly, Novalis conceptualizes signifiers in terms of
mathematical formulae; they are pure signs set up in contingent constellation to
each other. 'Sie machen eine Welt für sich aus: sie spieln nur mit sich selbst', he
writes in the *Monolog* (*NW* 2.438). Poesis thus coincides with mathematics in 'einer
poëtischen mathem[atischen] und abstracten Welt' (*NW* 2.682). The visual representation of this universe with its instantaneous permutations is likewise registered, as
Novalis's example of accelerated vision illustrates, by the automatized eye.

Novalis's flickering, kinetic signifiers – self-referentially designated as such with
the words 'Zeichen', 'Figuren', 'Bilder', 'Sternbilder' – function furthermore to de-
narrativize Klingsohr's fairy tale. Novalis writes in sequences comprised of discontinuous, unexpected forms and immediate, singular perceptions. Again connecting
poetry and speed, he speaks of 'Zahlen und Wort *Gestalten*lehre, z. B. Reihen etc.
Zahlen und W[ort] Mechanik – Geschwindigkeitslehre' (*NW* 2.687). The epipha-
nic, autonomous, and fragmentary 'Augen-blicke' of his story-telling delay intro-

duction to the main actors in the Klingsohr tale, but even their entry does little to mitigate the sensory overload and vertigo that his style induces. In fact, the constantly shifting scenarios in this tale seem to presage a Benjaminian aesthetics of visual shock, inoculatively administered in eventually dulling, rapid succession. For the visionary characters of Novalis's stories, however, this visual exposure is intoxicating: 'In große bunte Bilder drängten sich die Wahrnehmungen seiner Sinne' (*NW* 1.202), the narrator writes of the teacher in *Die Lehrlinge zu Sais.*

The *Lehrlinge* opens with an enchanting passage on the cipher-like writing of nature that can be discerned in wings, egg shells, clouds, snow, crystals, frozen water, and stars. There are moments, Novalis writes, when one senses the significance of these forms but 'nach kurzen Zeiten schwimmt alles wieder, wie vorher, vor [den] Blicken [des Menschen]' (*NW* 1.201). Notably, these natural hieroglyphs are not just present in nature but are observed by the attentive examiner of her book. The reader, however, cannot make sense of their scintillating, absorbing lines. Here contemplation fails to recenter the subject in consciousness either of itself or the objects in nature. This illegibility illustrates well the fundamental Lacanian distinction (to which I shall return) between the eye and the gaze. Far from the subject being able to decipher nature through an intelligent vantage point and perspective, as would be the case were the 'eye' efficacious, here surface design captivates and entices. In Lacanian terms, it were as if nature itself had a pre-existent gaze with which it solicited its viewer, only to remind him of his blindness. If in *Heinrich von Ofterdingen* the blue eyes of a girl glisten like crystal, then here the crystals in nature are the ones who see, for their observer cannot. Accordingly, nature possesses radiant eyes: 'Die Ströme sind die Augen einer Landschaft' (*NW* 1.331). In this passage from *Heinrich von Ofterdingen* eyes glisten like water in their reflection of light; but they do not initiate vision or direct their activity outward. In the *Hymnen an die Nacht* it is night personified that opens 'die unendlichen Augen' inside us (*NW* 1. 151). In *Heinrich von Ofterdingen* it is the power of song that pours light into our eyes (*NW* 1. 239), and Mathilde is described as having a 'mildes, empfängliches Auge' (*NW* 1. 327). Then in the Teplitzer Fragments Novalis calls eyes a 'Lichtklavier' for their physiognomic reflection (*NW* 2. 400). Eyes are thus passive, albeit luminous mirrors or receptacles rather than the source or agent of vision.[17] Furthermore, sight in Novalis is repeatedly clouded by tears, a milky blue light, mists, or twilight.

Rather than reason stepping in to correct this blurred vision, or the mind redirecting awe toward itself when challenged by the sublime vista, the subject indulges in the engulfing fantasy. One final and necessary example to mention of this labile viewing is the famous dream sequence in the third hymn to the night, usually taken to epitomize quintessential Romantic vision. In it the speaker experiences on the grave of the beloved her resurrection and the birth of a new world dedicated to worship of the night and its source of illumination, the beloved herself. For a dream about immersion into the unfathomable depths of the soul, it is intriguingly short and elliptic. On the one hand, this brevity could signify the ineffability of the sublime encounter; yet on the other hand, the mystic event is also the origin of poesis, the proliferation of words. Indeed, for the Romantics, poetry commands precisely this paradoxical ability to represent the unrepresentable (see *NW* 2.840; Schlegel *KFSA* 16.241, #115). Thus the noumenal appears before the sensual imagination: 'alles Sichtbare haftet am Unsichtbaren' (*NW* 2.423). But what visual form does this representation take?

In the hymn, the parataxis of each sentence enhances the quick tempo. The vision of eternity (literally: 'In Ihren Augen ruhte die Ewigkeit' *NW* 1.155) is belied by verbs of transience and dissolving ('zerrann', 'floh', 'floß', 'Jahrtausende zogen abwärts in die Ferne'). As in the Klingsohr tale, Novalis seems here more indebted to an aesthetics of visual distraction, where the phantasmagoric in its scintillating imagery reigns, rather than to inner, silent contemplation. What is fascinating is the minimal extent to which Novalis tries to interpret the oneiric unconscious. The pure visuality of the experience takes precedence over its meaning, almost as if it were the cause not the result of the ecstatic surrender of the viewer. It could also be argued that none other than the experience of Sophie's untimely death made Novalis depict transience in the form of his ever fluctuating imagery. But rather than, à la baroque, darkly painting the parade of worldly possessions subject to decay and demise, Novalis chose a brush that rendered ephemeral objects diaphanous, unreal, and paradoxically timeless in their very instantaneousness. The ultimate symbol of the phantasmal is, after all, the blue flower – the imaginary, apparitional object (like the simulacra without empirical grounding) that represents an alternative center to the self and dictates its unconscious desires.

While Novalis excitingly ushers into their own being the creations of his imagination, for Tieck these emanations from the self are frightening and uncanny, in the Freudian sense as something intimately known. For Tieck, the object embodies the fearsome possibility of representing to the subject more about itself than the subject ever thought imaginable. As evidenced in his story 'Der Runenberg',[18] the exterior eye sees profoundly more than the visually impaired subject sees of itself. Although there are other famous examples of blindness in Romanticism from Jean Paul to Hoffmann, this tale alone illustrates vividly the ascendancy of the visually enticing and powerful object, which in its very materiality scotomizes and denigrates the subject.

I earlier mentioned that according to Lacan, the gaze comes from the object and not, as we usually assume, from the subject. He writes, 'I see only from one point, but in my existence I am looked at from all sides'.[19] Lacan reminds me that I never look from a safe, objective distance, for another gaze will always catch me unawares. The story of 'Der Runenberg' begins with its young protagonist wandering through unfamiliar mountainous terrain. Out of nowhere the Lacanian gaze appears first in the guise of a stranger whose presence startles Christian and then in the form of a mysterious castle the stranger points to in the distance, exclaiming 'wie schön und anlockend das alte Gestein zu uns herblickt' (189).[20] Arriving at the castle walls, Christian peers in a window to see a beautiful naked woman. Yet despite his overt voyeurism, he cannot be said to be the bearer of a manipulating male gaze. Instead the woman glances back at him, reducing him to an object, in fact, an inanimate one. He eucharistically devours the tablet of gems that she gives him, beginning a series of events that lead to his heart turning to stone, while the stones themselves start to have eyes. Like the blond Eckbert, a character in another of Tieck's stories, Christian comes to paranoically believe that, in Lacan's words he is 'looked at from all sides'. The gold an old man leaves in his safe keeping comes to haunt its new owner: when Christian awakens in the night to count the gold entrusted to him, these 'gelbe Augen' (200) gaze at him in return.

Beginning with the unobtrusive remark of the stranger, the mortifying stony gaze resurfaces repeatedly in the tale. Progressively Christian becomes captivated by objects in nature, imagining that they are looking back at him. Even a stream has shining orbs that eye him (197). Christian confesses his g(u)ilt-ridden attraction: 'wie es mich jetzt wieder anblickt, daß mir der rote Glanz tief in mein Herz hinein geht' (200). In onanistically fingering the gold, it becomes even redder: the body imparts its warmth to the inorganic and, in response, the heart pulsates not with its own blood but with the glow of a mineral substance. In a kind of reverse personification the veins of the stone have become Christian's own, while their medusa-like look has turned him into granite. As if wanting to come back to life, Christian then wakes like a vampire at night, drinking with his eyes the blood in the gold. Anemic, he thirsts for the 'Erz' that will sustain his 'Herz'. His father refers to 'der fürchterliche Hunger' (201) that consumes his son, an appetite he later more precisely diagnoses as 'den verwüstenden Hunger nach dem Metall' that has been 'gepflanzt' in him (202). Ironizing the Idealist nondifferentiation between subject and object, 'Der Runenberg' presents the interior and exterior, organic and inorganic as interchangeable.

As the object of the gaze, Christian fundamentally does not see: not only is he blind to his condition, but his eyesight literally fails him. What frightens his wife Elisabeth most are his unfocused, wandering eyes: 'sein Blick [sei] irre und fremd' (201). Christian recounts that when the sun shines all he can see are the yellow eyes of the gold that draw his attention to them, targetting, soliciting, and seducing him 'wie es mir zublinzelt' (200). The protagonist, in fact, suffers from scotoma, as others pass in and out of his field of vision, reminding him of the periodicity of his sight. For instance, he can't see enough of the naked woman in the castle yet later cannot determine if she reappears in the guise of an old man or hag. The confusion about not only the identity but gender of this apparition in the forest fascinates and immobilizes Christian's eye. On both occasions, what captures and displaces his attention is the compensatory fetish, the magic, glistening tablet. The polymorphosis of the mysterious Other gives him/her a certain omnipotence that evades all efforts of the studious eye. It also grants omnipresence, for Christian always fears the gaze upon him in one form or another. The glistening of the Other's belongings, be they the bejewelled slate or the gold, also attest to the Other's power, crystallizing it into the hypnotic object that freezes the look.

Runes are, of course, a hieroglyphic, exclusively visual language whose meaning is irretrievable; they are ruins of a former script. Just as the stranger seems oddly familiar to Christian, so too do runes evoke memory loss and signify vision as the uncanny resurfacing of something previously known. In addition to Christian, the reader too is visually deceived, forced to look twice, as Tieck surreptitiously inscribes the word 'rune' into the intentionally misspelled 'Alrunenwurzel'. The mandrake root in its ability to emit a human cry (186), like the stones that have eyes buried within them (207), represents a repressed past, a forgotten memory that involuntarily resurges. The stony, anamorphotic gaze of these (un)natural objects allegorically alludes to death: the sphinx-like eyes of Tieck's stones recall Olimpia's soulless eyes in Hoffmann's 'Der Sandmann', the enucleation in Kleist's reading of Caspar David Friedrich's seascape, or the heavy eyelid in Jean Paul's 'Rede des todten Christus' that opens only to reveal the absence of an eye or the empty, bottomless eyesocket. Traditionally, the eye represents the window to the soul, deriving its luminosity from the latter. In Tieck, though, the glitter from the stones reveals no internal light but solely a mask displaying all surface and no depth, behind which lies only the hardness and impenetrability of the object. Romanticism thus does not always extol the visionary all-perceptive imagination. In fact, Christian's moments of blindness – the 'Augenblicke' when the eye shuts – call into question the very agency of the eye, including the unifying vision of Idealist 'Anschauung'. In the end, a petrified Christian vanishes from sight, and the last lines reads: 'Der Unglückliche ward aber seitdem nicht wieder gesehen' (208). Lacan notes, 'from the moment that this gaze appears, the subject tries to adapt himself to it, he becomes that punctiform object, that point of vanishing being, with which the subject confuses his own failure' (83).

Traditionally, Romanticism has been privileged in the history of hermeneutics. The Romantics have been seen both to acknowledge that subject and object are disparate and to endeavor to surmount this difference. As Géza von Molnár writes à propos of Novalis, 'his awareness of self and its powers to bridge the gap between subject and object is his consistent point of departure and return'.[21] The reading of Tieck and Novalis I have proposed, though, expresses hesitancy with regard to the agency of the self. As the examples of these two authors suggest (but one could add the names of many others), the Idealist reciprocity between subject and object, including the correspondence between mind and nature, can be upset and not necessarily in favor of the autonomous, intuitive, or even ironic subject. The Romantic artist proves not to be a self-present beholder conscious of his own activity but dispossessed of self insofar as he is under the sway of the object his imagination creates. Via its terror or tyranny, the crystal takes revenge, as Baudrillard observes in reference to our digitalized, consumerist era.[22]

On final account, then, the Romantic visionary is cut off from what he sees, unable to master what passes before his eye. However, if the subject no longer guarantees, as it does in Fichte, the ground of the world, it does not follow that instead the object, as in Spinoza, lends substantiality to the world. Clearly, this analysis is far from rehabilitating the metaphor of an organic nature in Romanticism. As the fabrication of either the inspired or the hallucinatory individual, the object becomes unmoored from a spatial referent. It has no external correlate or grounding. This referential gulf is what links Romanticism to postmodernism and separates together these periods from the enlightenment tradition which would have discounted and marginalized such fabricated vision as the fanciful flight of a sick imagination. What is postmodern as well in Romanticism is the vibrancy of the hypervisual realm before which empirical reality pales. Although it was not their intent or aim, the critics initially cited – Jameson, Morris, Rose, and Baudrillard – do portray the postmodern addiction to hypervisuality as novel and unprecedented. One conclusion would be to suggest that, before we fall prey to the tyranny of optical, simulated illusion in our present culture and the impression it gives of ahistorical immediacy, we recognize the ancestry of such visual captivation.

NOTES

1.   Jonathan Crary 1990, 2.

2.   Fredric Jameson 1992, 1.

3.   Meaghen Morris 1984, 97.

4.   Jacqueline Rose 1988, 116.

5.   Jean Baudrillard 1990, 63. All future references appear parenthetically.

6.   Novalis 1978-87, 2. 618-19. *NW* in the text with volume and page numbers.

7.   Martin Jay 1993, 589.

8.   Jonathan Crary 1990, 98.

9.   Martin Jay 1988, 19.

10.   Christine Buci-Glucksmann 1986, 31.

11.   Friedrich Schlegel 1958-95, 12. 408. *KFSA* in the text with volume and page numbers.

12.   Immanuel Kant 1975, 5.27.

13.   On the history of 'the aesthetics of making strange' from Romanticism through recent photography, see Simon Watney, 1982, 154-76. On the tradition to which Novalis responds, see Hans-Joachim Mähl, 1992, 161-82.

14.   On temporality in Novalis see Kuzniar, 1987, 80-93.

15.   On the concept of chaos, see Joyce Walker, 1993, 43-59.

16.   Novalis acknowledged the inevitability of representational illusion and recognized that the tenacious belief in a perfect correspondence between image and original is in error: 'Auf Verwechselung des *Symbols* mit dem Symbolisirten – auf ihre Identisirung – auf den Glauben an wahrhafte, vollst[ändige] Repraesentation – und Relation des Bildes und des Originals ... kurz auf Verwech-

selungen von Sub[ject] und Obj[ect] beruht der ganze Aberglaube und Irrthum aller Zeiten, und Völker und Individuen' (*NW* 2.637).

17. An exception is the description of Heinrich's father as demonstrating the desire to be 'ein wahres Auge, ein schaffendes Werkzeug' (*NW* 1.374). But see also *NW* 2.650: 'Das Fernrohr oder Auge ein receptives Lichtwesen'.

18. For a lengthier discussion of this story see my article: Kuzniar 1995, 50-64.

19. Jacques Lacan 1981, 72.

20. All references to Ludwig Tieck's works are to Volume 6 of his *Schriften* (Ed. Manfred Frank), 1985. All page numbers mentioned in the text refer to this volume.

21. Géza von Molnár 1987, xxxiii.

22. Jean Baudrillard, 1990.

BIBLIOGRAPHY

Baudrillard, Jean 1990. *Fatal Strategies: Crystal Revenge.* (Trans. Philip Beitchman and W.G.J. Nieslu- choswki). New York.

Baudrillard, Jean 1990. *La Transparence du Mal: Essai sur les phénomènes extrêmes.* Paris.

Buci-Glucksmann, Christine 1986. *La folie du voir: De l'esthétique baroque.* Paris.

Crary, Jonathan 1990. *Techniques of the Observer: On Vision and Modernity in the Nineteenth Century.* Cambridge, MA.

Jameson, Frederic 1992. *Signatures of the Visible.* New York.

Jay, Martin 1988. 'Scopic Regimes of Modernity'. In: *Vision and Visuality.* (Ed. Hal Foster). Seattle.

Jay, Martin 1993, *Downcast Eyes. The Denigration of Vision in Twentieth Century Thought.* Berkeley.

Kant, Immanuel 1975. *Werke in sechs Bänden.* (Ed. Wilhelm Weischedel). Darmstadt.

Kuzniar, Alice 1987. *Delayed Endings: Nonclosure in Novalis and Hölderlin.* Athens, GA.

Kuzniar, Alice 1995. 'Stones that Stare, or, The Gorgon's Gaze in Ludwig Tieck's *Der Runenberg'.* In: *Mimetic Desire: Theories of Narcissism and German Literature/Culture.* (Eds. Jeffrey T. Adams and Eric Williams). Columbia, SC.

Lacan, Jacques 1981. *The Four Fundamental Concepts of Psycho-Analysis.* (Trans. Alan Sheridan). New York.

Mähl, Hans-Joachim 1992. 'Verfremdung und Transparenz: Zur theoretischen Begründung der "Tropen- und Rätselsprache" bei Novalis'. In: *Jahrbuch der Freien Deutschen Hochstift.*

Molnár, Géza von 1987. *Romantic Vision, Ethical Context: Novalis and Artistic Autonomy.* Minneapolis.

Morris, Meaghen 1984. 'Room 101 or A Few Worst Things in the World'. In: *Seduced and Abandoned: The Baudrillard Scene.* (Ed. André Frankovits). Glebe, Australia.

Novalis (Friedrich von Hardenberg) 1978-87. *Werke, Tagebücher und Briefe.* (Eds. Hans-Joachim Mähl and Richard Samuel), 3 vols. Munich. (Abbreviated as *NW*)

Rose, Jacqueline 1988. 'Sexuality and Vision: Some Questions'. In: *Vision and Visuality.* (Ed. Hal Foster). Seattle.

Schlegel, Friedrich 1958-95. *Kritische Friedrich Schlehel Ausgabe.* (Eds. Ernst Behler, J.-J. Anstett, and Hans Eichner). München. (Abbreviated as *KFSA*)

Tieck, Ludwig 1985. *Schriften.* (Ed. Manfred Frank). Frankfurt.

Walker, Joyce 1993. 'Romantic Chaos: The Dynamic Paradigm in Novalis's *Heinrich von Ofterdingen* and Contemporary Science'. In: *German Quarterly 66.*

Watney, Simon 1982. 'Making Strange: The Shattered Mirror'. In: *Thinking Photography.* London.

Images and Counter-Images:
Quotations of Forms and Genres in Tieck
and E.T.A. Hoffmann

Andreas Böhn

Tieck and Hoffmann were, neither of them, major theorists, but in their literary production they reflect crucial points of the Romantic program, in a way which makes them, in our view, very 'modern' and shows parallels even to postmodern issues and discussions. Their use of literary forms and genres is a very sophisticated one, which tends to combine divergent formal schemes. The result is a disorientation of the reader in his or her search for a coherent image of the represented world in the text. In narrative texts like Tieck's 'Der blonde Eckbert', 'Die Elfen', 'Des Lebens Überfluß' or Hoffmann's *Der goldene Topf* or 'Prinzessin Brambilla' we are confronted with highly impressive and visualized, even synaesthetic sub-worlds, which are related to specific literary forms or genres as modes of representation, e.g., the fairy tale or the idyll. These pictorial sceneries are counterplayed by contrasting elements and structures of other formal traditions, like the novella.

The interrelation of the different formal elements often resembles that between text and quotation. Embedded in the frame of a main or basic structure, we find a different structure, which is syntactically and semantically not an integrated part of the main structure. As in the case of quotation, the implications of what is quoted are, in a way, suspended. It does not work in the usual way, but as an index of its previous use. The quoted forms or genres are therefore exposed as certain modes of representation, which are related to a historic period or a subjective state of mind.[1] The constant change between these different modes in Tieck's and Hoffmann's texts leads to a perturbation in the experience of the protagonist(s) and of the willing and following reader, too.

The play with divergent artistic forms, text-worlds and aesthetic experiences can be related, on one hand, to the aesthetic theory and particularly to the reflections on genre of the early German Romantics, Schlegel, Novalis and Schelling, and on the other hand to 20th century discussions of mimesis, intertextuality and the modes of representation. It explains the attraction of Romantic literature, not only Romantic theory, for modern and postmodern literary theory.

At first sight, literary forms and genres do not seem to have much to do with imagery and figural language. They are situated on a much higher level of abstraction than the figures and tropes of poetic language that should supply the senses of the reader with evidence. But, poetic images, metaphors etc. are themselves abstract schemes that allow the reader to relate a concrete and unique case to a more general pattern. If I use a pair of scales as an image for justice, I take the abstract concept of comparison and equation from my knowledge about the working of balances, and relate it to legal procedures. Images can provide orientation, because they are able to connect something new and unfamiliar to schemes and concepts that are related to familiar experiences and habitual modes of behaviour.

In the case of literary texts, we have a need for orientation, because of the lack of pragmatic contexts and defined social functions. This need gives forms and genres their prevalent role in literature and other art forms. They orientate the reader in his or her aesthetic experience of the text. They provide him through the perception of basic characteristics with a first overall *image* of the text and therefore set a frame of expectations about what and how the text will be. This image defines fulfillment and denial of these expectations and the relation of redundancy and surprise in the reading of the text.

This schematic image, created by the use of traditional forms and genres, is *usually* the redundant part of the text, which in the process of reading functions as an unreflected background. The concrete realisation of this scheme and possible modifications are the focus of attention and the source of astonishment and aesthetic pleasure. This relation of background and foreground is subverted in the case of the combination of forms and genres, particularly in the case of the quotational use of forms and genres. First I would like to give examples of the renewal and modification of an old genre under new and counterplaying circumstances, and after that an example of the combination of divergent, even contradictory genres in one text.

Tieck's 'Der blonde Eckbert' (1797) plays an important role in the renewal of the fairy tale in German literature. The interest in this genre is closely related to central and programmatic aims of Early Romanticism. It served as a model for an autonomous poetic world, including the fabulous and the supernatural. A prerequisite for this view was the rehabilitation of popular forms of art by Herder and others. From over-looked and de-valorized anachronisms they were transformed into eminently poetic ressources, because they were intimately connected to a naive, but powerful 'Volksgeist'. Once their supposed organic and unconscious production was seen no more as an artistic deficit, but as a necessary condition of their value and their formal characteristics, a resurrection of this genre by a modern, reflective artist could not take place through simple continuation. The resumption of the production of fairy tales by an author would have been in itself an important modification, compared to the production through an anonymous popular tradition.

Tieck solves this problem by introducing the fairy tale in the form of a framed narrative, making it the object of reflection and thus in a way the object of represen-tation, ultimately subverting the established hierarchy of formal levels in the text.[2] The tale begins with a realistic presentation of the protagonists and the situation. Eckbert causes his wife Bertha to tell the story of her youth to their friend Walther. This story has all the characteristics of a fairy tale, but the *telling* of the story is quite different from the absolute, seemingly unmediated narration that we know from fairy tales. Bertha relates something temporally remote, which is connected with her childhood, and she describes the emotional effects, which the fairy-tale-like elements and events had on her. She psychologizes these elements, and thus in nar-rating she produces an interpretation, too, that relates the objective, represented world of her story to a subjective development.

Topics that are characteristic of fairy tales merge with the stimulating effects which reading has on the imagination and with the tribulations caused by the experience of erotic desire in puberty. The genre 'fairy tale' is set in relation to its historical embedding. It belongs to the 'fabulous stories' Bertha reads in 'written' – not printed – books. Therefore on the one hand it is experienced as something archaic, on the other – or maybe because of that – as something mediated, which lives no longer in an oral tradition, but is read as written text. As an element of the phylogenetic past it is associated with the ontogenetic past, that is childhood, and the relation between both of them is represented and reflected from a distance, from a point of view in present time. The *outside* world of the fairy tale is accompanied by Bertha's *inside* state of mind as its counterpart, which reveals a reception and an interpretation of this world and of the form that mediates it.

Looking at the text up to the point when Bertha finishes her story we could speak of a quotation of the formal elements associated with fairy tales in a context characterized by modern reflective subjectivity. This quotation of form is well motivated and integrated, by the combination of framework story and framed story, adulthood and childhood, present and past. But in Bertha's story we already find a mixture of forms, and in the unfolding of the text the hierarchy of the textual levels and the related forms is totally subverted. Walther is revealed as belonging to the fairy-tale world and thus there is a mixture of text-worlds, which inside the text drives the protagonists into madness and death. What is told here, is not a fairy tale, but the story of modern people, who unexpectedly find themselves in the world of a fairy tale, without having turned over to the consciousness of a fairy-tale hero.

Therefore the text as a whole constitutes a new genre, which is the reconstitution of an old genre under different circumstances. The artistic fairy tale reflects, in a individual consciousness, the collective images and schemes that are inherent to the form of the fairy tale, and makes the resulting ambivalence of the text-world its mere object. The quotation of form is dissolved in the construction of the new genre of the artistic fairy tale. Once established, Tieck continues this pattern in texts like 'Der Runenberg' (1804) and 'Die Elfen' (1812), without having any more need to legitimize the fact that he is using the elements of the fairy tale. The split of text-worlds and the states of mind related to them continues to be a central characteristic.

The new genre is taken up by other authors, too. In E. T. A. Hoffmann's *Der goldene Topf* (1814) its main structure is already mentioned in the subtitle: 'Ein Märchen aus der neuen Zeit'.[3] The twofold world of modern Dresden, on the one hand depicted in precise detail, while a timeless, fabulous sphere on the other hand is reflected in the consciousness of the student Anselmus. He is guided from the first into the second world mediated by the confusing whispers of the golden snakes and the old scriptures that he has to copy. The transition between the opposed worlds is narrated in a way that keeps the reader in the same state of undecidability as the protagonist. The protagonist is in doubt about what he perceives, whether it is reality or imagination and how to relate it to known patterns and form a coherent image out of it. The only information the reader gains is this mental process of the protagonist, not objective representations of the external world.[4]

At the end of 'Prinzessin Brambilla' (1821) however the fairy-tale world is revealed as the effect of theatrical machinations. It appears therefore like a counter-piece to 'Der blonde Eckbert', where the fairy tale was introduced as a framed story, then intermingled with the framework story, driving the protagonists into madness and death; here the tribulations and confusions are revealed to be a well-ordered play, which contributes to the good fortune of everyone in the story. The aim behind all this is the public acceptance of another mixing up of genres, the combination of tragedy and commedia dell'arte. That is the theatre reform of Celionati, who pulls the strings in the story. This reform is intended to put an end to the modern evil of 'chronical dualism', the gap between reality and imagination, which Celionati wants to overcome and which was so well expressed in the modern artistic fairy tale Tieck had created.

Tieck's late text 'Des Lebens Überfluß' (1839) uses elements of the fairy tale, too, and the dualism of fantasy and reality is also one of its topics. But at the structural centre of this text we have the counterplay of two other genres, the novella and the idyll. It is characterized as novella not only by its subtitle and the context of its publication, but, even more important, also by the fulfillment of some central and unquestionable prerequisites of the somehow dubious and vaguely defined genre. It has a structural centre, an unprecedented event, involving a violation of confinements, a transgression of social norms, which is the cause of the conflict. This centre of the story is condensed in a symbolic object, and intensified up to a peak. But on the other hand we find in the text the contradictory elements of the idyll: unchanged ongoing of life instead of dramatic events, isolation and contemplation instead of conflict, conversational reflection instead of physical action. The use of this divergent pattern has to be seen in the light of genre traditions and reader expectations formed by those traditions.

The idyll depicts a confined space, in which basic forms of human life are realized. The confinement is the necessary condition of the autonomy and self-sufficiency of the represented world. It is of great importance whether this relation is made visible in the text and the interdependency of the idyll and its constraints is made clear, or not. In the first case the idyll is presented as a certain mode of representation, as an image of the world seen from a certain viewpoint; in the second case it appears as the totality of an idyllic world.

In 'Des Lebens Überfluß' we have a social conflict, which is the reason for the protagonists, the young couple Heinrich and Clara, to hide themselves in a flat in the middle of a town. They remodel their isolation to an idyll.[5] When they look out of the window, they see odd walls all around them; but they compare them to the landscape of the alps, with the sun-glow on the mountains (or the bricks of the walls). In doing so, they likewise invert the development of the genre 'idyll', which had converted outdoor into indoor spaces in the late 18th century. More than such imaginative interpretations, they use literary references and quotations to expand their little world, or rather to integrate the big world into their small one.[6] They have to use their memory for this, because the only book left to them is Heinrich's diary. Reading one's own diary and talking about it is self-reflective anyway. In reading it from the end to the beginning, as he does, he performs the figure of a circle, which indicates as well the constraint of their situation as the circular completeness of the idyllic world.

It is a crucial point for my argumentation, that we have a polarity of idyll and novella in this text, which is very different from the combinations of those genres to be found in Biedermeier literature elsewhere and not at all a continuous transformation of one into the other. Goethe's *Unterhaltungen deutscher Ausgewanderten* (1795), to which our text alludes with the word 'Schonung' (respect), is a main text of reference for the novella in German 19th century literature. It had presented a concept of sociability and respect as remedy and antidote against revolutionary confusion. That was the meaning of the conversational framework story in the *Unterhaltungen*. In 'Des Lebens Überfluß' the frame of public conversation is but a hint, and the revolution is only an object of grotesque misunderstandings. But in the light of the tradition this is of significance, too. Political discussion and social utopias have withdrawn from the framework to the interior of the story, into the isolation of the couple and their conversations.[7]

The novella is no longer a product, but a prerequisite of sociability. The novellistic core of the action, the conflict-inducing transgression of a norm by the protagonists, leads to their social isolation. By artistic imagination and charging with literary patterns it is heightened to an idyll, which makes a functioning society (in its minimal form) possible. The novellistic action and the framed form of the idyll are interdependent. One is the condition of the other; but they are a threat for each other, too. The burning of the wooden staircase is intended to keep up the idyll and the isolation, because of the lack of any other material to heat the place. But it brings forth the inevitable intrusion of the real society of the town into the retreat of the couple.[8]

The staircase is the central element of the textual structure. It is also the focus of the dichotomy of idyll and novella. When the staircase has been burned completely, their contradiction is intensified up to a point, where the catastrophe seems unavoidable. It can be avoided only through the fairy-tale-like intervention of a new 'staircase'. This metaphor is applied in the text to a book, an early edition of the

Canterbury Tales, which Heinrich had sold for need of money and which by its uniqueness can work as a sign for his friend Vandelmeer to find his way to Heinrich and Clara. He brings back Heinrich's money, which he had given to Vandelmeer as an investment and which has increased quite a lot. This way of solving the economic problems of the couple is therefore not at all anachronistic like a fairy tale, but very modern and up-to-date.

The fairy-tale element of the friend, who comes surprisingly to solve all problems, guided by the old book which serves as a helping object, is combined with modern capitalist principles to solve the problem of the textual structure, the dichotomy of idyll and novella. Both are deficient in themselves and interdependent of each other, and in order to overcome them the fairy-tale plot needs a complementary element, too. What makes these genres and formal elements deficient are the contemporary social conditions, including a money-based economy. They are constantly mentioned in the text and form the background of the structures and dichotomies described. The wood of the staircase is a synonym for money, and the lack of heating material is a metonymy for economic need, that threatens the idyllic life of the couple. The burning of the staircase helps to keep up the idyll, but involves a social conflict and leads to the novellistic plot of the text, when it is discovered.

The simplicity of the idyll can be reached only through conflict-bearing actions; the sociability of the novella can be produced only in the artificial world of a self-constructed idyll; and the phantasmatic rescue in the manner of a fairy tale can only be acceptable in combination with economic realism. The genres and their formal elements do not appear as separate worlds, impenetrable for each other, nor do they simply shade one into the other. They are opposites that build a functional interdependency. Therefore they do not work any more in a self-evident way as patterns of representation, orientating the reader, giving him a general image of the created text-world. On the contrary, they are presented as possibilities of representation and orientation that are constrained in their value and related to each other.

That means, they are not used in the usual way as instruments of literary technique; they are *mentioned* – in the sense of the logical distinction between 'to mention' and 'to use' an expression. They shift from the background of reader perception to the foreground, are no longer frames of reference, providing implicit knowledge about the text-world which helps the reader to understand what is going on in the text, but are the focus of attention now themselves. It is appropriate to speak of quotations of these genres and forms, because as in the quotation of utterances they are not used as they were used in the quoted case. Instead, this former use is mentioned, the genre traditions are referred to. The described structural and functional interdependencies are the frames, which orientate the reader in dealing with the different forms. The fairy tale, the idyll or the novella were forms that referred to a certain species of text-world, now it is this mode of representation and its former use that is referred to in the text.

That does not necessarily harm the figural quality of the text. The formal sub-worlds may be nevertheless highly impressive, visualized, even synaesthetic, as is actually the case in Bertha's memories of her youth in 'Der blonde Eckbert', the adventures of the protagonists in 'Der Runenberg', *Der goldene Topf* or 'Prinzessin Brambilla'. Particularly in 'Des Lebens Überfluß' the play with forms itself reaches a new figurality. The device of quotation balances the different forms in an ironical equilibrium. The oscillation between those forms is the 'figura' that can be seen in the text and that the mental activity of the reader can follow. And this is a means of orientation, too, though a second-order-orientation, an orientation that shows how to find your way through first-order-orientations – forms and genres.

Relating different forms has some parallels to relating different media and different arts, which also play an important role in the Romantic movement. It can be seen in the light of the genre theory of Early Romanticism, which in its call for transgression of genre boundaries had set the emphasis on the effects of a dialectics between opposites. It was regarded as mere ornamental play, as arabesque combination, but taking into account the important role formal elements and genre traditions have it is obvious that there is more at stake. The formal quotations in Romantic texts are an early step on a way that leads to forms of collage or montage, where hierarchies between formal elements hardly exist any more and texts reach a new level of 'openness'.

NOTES

1. For a brief theoretical sketch of the concept 'quotation of literary genres and forms' cf. Böhn 1994. The following considerations are part of a project dealing with this concept. Menninghaus (1995) uses the expression 'quotation' with reference to forms and genres without dealing explicitly with the methodological implications of this terminology. His analysis of Tieck's *Blaubart* shows many affinities to my reading of Tieck's and Hoffmann's texts, but his scope is a specific 'poetics of nonsense' in Early Romanticism. Therefore it should be made clear that quotations of genres and forms do not necessarily lead to an effect of 'nonsense', as I will demonstrate in the discussion of my examples.

2. Cf. Klussmann 1976, 362-72 and Schlaffer 1976; Kreuzer 1983, 157-87 tries to show that 'Der blonde Eckbert' is an artistic fairy tale, but does not adequately take into account the mixture of genre elements in the text.

3. Cf. Willenberg 1976.

4. Cf. Just 1964 and Holländer 1984; for the mediating function of the scriptures and the copying, see Nygaard 1983.

5. Cf. Klussmann 1986 and Diekkämper 1990, 258-97.

6. For intertextual references in the text, see Gould 1990 and Pöschel 1994, 92-108.

7. Cf. Oesterle 1983, 249-51.

8. Cf. Ottmann 1990, 62-70.

BIBLIOGRAPHY

Böhn, Andreas 1994. 'Das Formzitat als kultureller Austauschprozeß'. In: *Bausteine zu einem transatlantischen Literaturverständnis. Views on Literature in a transatlantic Context.* (Eds. Hans W. Panthel & Peter Rau). Jubileum presentation celebrating 20 years of parnership between the University of Waterloo, Canada and the University of Mannheim, Germany. Frankfurt.

Diekkämper, Birgit 1990. *Formtraditionen und Motive der Idylle in der deutschen Literatur des neunzehnten Jahrhunderts. Bemerkungen zu Erzähltexten von Joseph Freiherr von Eichendorff, Heinrich Heine, Friedrich de la Motte Fouqué, Ludwig Tieck und Adalbert Stifter.* Frankfurt.

Gould, Robert 1990. 'Tieck's "Des Lebens Überfluß" as a self-conscious text'. In: *Seminar* 26/3.

Holländer, Barbara 1984. 'Augenblicke der Verwandlung in E.T.A. Hoffmann's Märchen *Der goldene Topf*'. In: *Augenblick und Zeitpunkt. Studien zur Zeitstruktur und Zeitmetaphorik in Kunst und Wissenschaften.* (Eds. Christian W. Thomsen & Hans Holländer). Darmstadt.

Just, Klaus Günther 1964. 'Die Blickführung in den Märchennovellen E.T.A. Hoffmanns'. In: *Wirkendes Wort* 14.

Klussmann, Paul Gerhard 1976. 'Die Zweideutigkeit des Wirklichen in Ludwig Tiecks Märchennovellen'. In: *Ludwig Tieck*. (Ed. Wulf Segebrecht). Darmstadt.

Klussmann, Paul Gerhard 1986. 'Idylle als Glücksmärchen in Romantik und Biedermeierzeit. Bemerkungen zu Erzählungen und Taschenbuchnovellen Ludwig Tiecks'. In: *Idylle und Modernisierung in der europäischen Literatur des 19. Jahrhunderts*. (Eds. Hans Ulrich Seeber & Paul Gerhard Klussmann). Bonn.

Kreuzer, Ingrid 1983. *Märchenform und individuelle Geschichte: Zu Text- und Handlungsstrukturen in Werken Ludwig Tiecks zwischen 1790 und 1811*. Göttingen.

Menninghaus, Winfried 1995. *Lob des Unsinns. Über Kant, Tieck und Blaubart*. Frankfurt.

Nygaard, L.C. 1983. 'Anselmus as Amanuensis: The Motif of Copying in Hoffmann's *Der goldene Topf*'. In: *Seminar* 19/1.

Oesterle, Ingrid 1983. 'Ludwig Tieck: "Des Lebens Überfluß" (1838)'. In: *Romane und Erzählungen zwischen Romantik und Realismus. Neue Interpretationen*. (Ed. Paul Michael Lützeler). Stuttgart.

Ottmann, Dagmar 1990. *Angrenzende Rede. Ambivalenzbildung und Metonymisierung in Ludwig Tiecks späten Novellen*. Tübingen.

Pöschel, Burkhard 1994. 'Im Mittelpunkt der wunderbarsten Ereignisse'. In: *Versuche über die literarische Auseinandersetzung mit der gesellschaftlichen Moderne im erzählerischen Spätwerk Ludwig Tiecks*. Bielefeld.

Schlaffer, Heinz 1976. 'Roman und Märchen. Ein formtheoretischer Versuch über Tiecks "Blonden Eckbert"'. In: *Ludwig Tieck*. (Ed. Wulf Segebrecht). Darmstadt.

Willenberg, Knud 1976. 'Die Kollision verschiedener Realitätsebenen als Gattungsproblem in E.T.A. Hoffmanns *Der goldne Topf*'. In: *Zeitschrift für deutsche Philologie 95*. (E.T.A. Hoffmann Sonderheft).

The Metaphysical Implosion:
Reflections upon Reflections of Landscape
in Turner and Wordsworth

Klaus Peter Mortensen

The Mirror of Nature Inverted

The fundamental Christian concept of the book or mirror of nature plays an important part in 17th- and 18th-century thinking about nature. According to this idea, which can be traced all the way back to St. Paul (The Epistle to the Romans Ch.1,20), man has two sources of knowledge of God: the Holy Scripture and the Book of Nature. The Christian God is not in nature and thus cannot be observed, but as God's creation nature bears witness to his power and grace. From the existence of God's works and their inherent wisdom man can deduce his being. In physical nature you can find his footprints as one popular 17th-century metaphor goes, he is the great painter and nature his painting, another claims. Let me offer just three examples as an illustration of this richly varied notion and thereby close in on my subject.

In his *Night-Thoughts* from 1742-44, Edward Young states:

> *Nature* is the glass reflecting God,
> As, by the *sea,* reflected is the *Sun.*

In the Halle 1734-edition of the widely read *Vier Bücher vom wahren Christenthum* by the influential 17th-century theologian Johann Arndt, one can find a perfect illustration for Youngs statement in which the reflecting sea is replaced by an emblematic mirror.

Mit aufgedecktem Angesicht.

The words 'Mit aufgedeckten Angesicht' allude to St. Paul's Second Epistle to the Corinthians Ch. 3,18, according to which the followers of Christ – contrary to the children of Israel but like Moses (an allusion to Exodus Ch. 34) – are able to see the glory of God with faces unveiled – *as* in a mirror. This again alludes to Exodus Ch. 34,33-35 where Moses protects the Israelites from the light of God emanating from his face by veiling it. Johann Arndt puts this notion of indirect vision like this in *Liber naturae; eller Natvrspeyel,* (i.e. mirror of nature) 1618: 'What is the beauty of heaven and the whole of creation other/ (…) than a mirror/ in which shines the supreme Creator's masterpiece?' 'For GOD has built into all creatures a sign or foot-mark/ by which he can trace the Creator.' It is only possible to trace or to sense God in His work indirectly, as the extremely elaborate frontispiece to O. Traber's *Nervus Opticus,* 1675 suggests.[1]

The light of God, himself unseen, is reflected by the sun, the sun in turn is reflected by way of a heavenly, spiritual mirror (contrasting the speculum to the right reflecting physical light) reflecting and revealing the name of Christ which is in turn illuminating or heading a blank mirror (signifying the mirror function of Nature as parallel to the revelating aspects of the Holy Scripture) and thus finally reaching man, the reader of both the book of nature and the word of God.[2] The zig-zag course of this communication is at the same time an interpretation of the words of St. Paul in his First Epistle to the Corinthians Ch. 13,12: 'For now we see through a glass, darkly; but then face to face' – in the illustration alluded to by the words: 'Nunc Per Speculum'.

Now, it is my intent to argue:

1) That this concept of the Book or Mirror of Nature is secularised in the 18th-century.
2) That one important feature of this process is the aesthetic discussion of the Sublime.
3) That the process has far reaching consequences and thus plays a decisive role in shaping the movement we know as Romanticism, especially its concern with nature and the human mind.
4) That this transformation can be observed in Turner and Wordsworth.

In his famous *System des Transcendentalen Idealismus,* 1800, Schelling claims that:

Die Natur ist dem Künstler nicht mehr als sie dem Philosophen ist, nämlich nur die unter beständigen Abschränkungen erscheinende idealische Welt, oder nur der unvollkommene Wiederschein einer Welt, die nicht ausser ihm, sondern in ihm existiert.[3]

The key-word here is 'Wiederschein'. But the fundamental idea of something being reflected or reflecting itself in something else has been turned upside down or inside out if we compare with Young and Arndt. One might call it a metaphysical inversion or implosion in which the mind of earthly man is placed in the very position formerly occupied by the invisible and immeasurable divine power. The inversive or implosive movement from Young to Schelling consequently seems to be a perfect equivalent to M.H. Abrams' famous, fascinating *and* problematic dictum: the mirror turned lamp. As I will attempt to show, it is not quite as simple as that.

Turner's Turn

You can observe this inversion in Turner's art. Not as a clear break, but as a gradual movement showing how the new way of seeing or thinking about the world evolves from the Christian tradition in a complicated artistic process. This I can only outline roughly by way of some – hopefully – illuminating examples. The first one marks Turner's familiarity with and indebtedness to the old metaphysical tradition in his famous boasting match with Claude Lorrain's *Seaport with the Embarkation of the Queen of Sheba,* 1648. *In Dido building Carthage; or the Rise of the Carthaginian Empire,* 1815, Turner just like Claude obviously subscribes to the old notion of the liber naturae, according to which the divine sun reflects itself in earthly nature very much like the Arndt-illustration shows. In the light of this sun all human enterprises take place. People and societies, even the mightiest, perish. The sun endures.

Now, what happens in the development of Turner's work is, that the world as consisting of distinctive phenomena is dissolved into light (and – if you will – shade) within the realm of colour – that is: within the interaction between the eye with all its inherent powers *and* cosmic light reflected in physical nature. Put succinctly: the two suns become one. This can be seen in the *Regulus,* 1828, completed in 1837. Here Turner tells the story (from Horace) about Regulus's blinding by the Carthagians who cut off his eyelids exposing his eyes to the blazing sunlight. This all-pervading, sublime – simultaneously life-giving and destructive light – is the true object of Turner's ambition. From his contemporaries we know that the light emanating from the canvas seemed so shockingly strong that they could not bear to look at it.

This amazing painting heralds Turner's later works in the 1840s (especially from Venice and Lake Geneva) in which the horisontal line separating heaven from its spiritual reflection in earth or water is dissolved or at least blurred. By doubling light in reflection and simultaneously erasing the separating horisontal line Turner creates an image of total light or colour. *Sun Setting over a Lake,* ca. 1840, can serve as an example of this breathtaking destruction of the old mirror of nature.

This revolution in Turner's painting could be summed up by comparing two versions of the same motive, *Norham Castle,* from respectively 1798 and ca. 1840-45. In the older one the sun is reflected in physical, created nature: water and cliffs, in the younger the earthly world itself is penetrated by light, the light or the sun being an omnipresent part of matter.

The two suns thus becoming one does not, however, result in the total dis-appearance of the horisontal line as a means of composition and the abandoning of the mirror function – the cow in the Norham Castle painting from 1840-45 is actually mirrored. But the appearance and significance of these elements of struc-ture change radically. In this respect one could truly speak of one sun and a new kind of sun. From being a reflection of a reflection – i.e. an indirect mediation of the true, invisible eternal light – the *lux intelligiblis,* God, who cannot be perceived through the human senses – the mirror-reflection now takes on a new impact. In-stead of upholding a clear distinction and a one-way vertical line of communication between the divine and the human, the function of mirroring now consists in creating a horisontal correspondence between the sensing subject and the sensed object. The eyes of the perceiving subject are no longer situated within a vertical pattern of seeing, but are directed inwards at the depths created by the blurred hor-isontal line and the single and obscure source of light.

Thus with the dissolution of the horisontal line heaven and earth are no longer separate pictorial entities. But this change is not exclusively technical. Its implica-tions are ideological insofar as there is no longer need for a reflecting/mirroring ob-ject or function mediating between the eye that sees and the sun seen as in the en-graving from Traber's *Nervus Opticus* or Arndt's *Liber naturae.* In this fundamental transformation of the direction of the eyes a new kind of metaphysics and a corre-sponding phenomenology arise.

Turner's true *sujet* then is not the sun casting its rays on and being reflected in the landscape as in *Llanberis* ca. 1799. To the old Turner nature (as landscape) is no longer the object of his exploration of artistic possibilities, but material light presenting itself in colour and its eternal dialogue with darkness. So Turner proceeds from landscapes bathed *in* light to landscapes *of* light. In this daring move – and the resulting suspension of the sharp contours of phenomena including the horisontal line – the difference between the divine and the human power of seeing is erased.

This however should not be mistaken for solipsism on Turner's part. What the painter depicts is not his own projected notions, but the natural laws inherent in both colour and the active human eye. The eye is both object and subject. By insistingly attempting to catch the interrelation of eye and light in colour, the old Turner took his own obstinate and boundary-crossing consequences of the metaphysical inversion as can be seen for instance from *Norham Castle* 1840-45 and the colour beginning from around 1840 shown here. Although they often have been given a title – the latter is called *A sunset* – these works do not have a subject, a *motif* in the strict sense of the word. They rather seem to be at one with what they express. 'Nature' here is not a specific entity: a landscape, a sun, a lake, but the very nature they awaken in the eye of the beholder. In this way one confronts oneself, one's own – not private, but objectively cosmic – nature in the shades of colour in the painting. Like in a mirror. In *Sun setting over a Lake* from around 1840, the sun literally seems to have become both a cosmic eye and a mirror-reflection of the observing eye of the painter – and consequently of the beholder. Perhaps this is what Goethe aimed at when claiming that the nature confronting the beholder of a landscape painting was not physical nature but the nature of the painter. Namely, one might add, the nature common to both the painter and its beholder.

Turner and Wordsworth

In the short span of years from 1798-1800 in his writing about the relation between mind and nature, Wordsworth took a position strangely analogous to the one Turner reached decades later. Let me list the key similarities allowing for the obvious differences between the art of colour and the art of words:

1) Like Turner, Wordsworth is concerned with the dialectical correspondence be-
    tween nature and mind.
2) Like Turner, Wordsworth in his artistical realisation of this correspondence sub-
    scribes to the tradition of the mirror of nature and secularises it.
3) Like Turner, Wordsworth considers reflection an inherent quality or process of
    cosmic nature, of which man – unknowingly or knowingly – is partaking, as
    opposed to reflection as an intellectual, analytical, and abstract contribution of
    the individual mind separating man from nature.
4) Like Turner, Wordsworth opposes the immanent danger of the metaphysical
    implosion: the solipsistic notion of the world as a projection of the individual
    mind. For both Turner and Wordsworth the human mind obeys universal phys-
    ical or psychological laws. The human mind thus is not an autonomous entity, a
    lamp. It is the creation or part of cosmic nature.
5) In this specific respect Abrams' dictum: the mirror turned lamp falls short of the
    matter. Neither Turner nor Wordsworth considers light to be the exclusive con-
    tribution of the artist's mind. The radiant light emanating from the human eye
    has an objective extra-human source or correspondent in cosmic nature. Thus
    the mind or eye of man is itself a creation of nature in an explicitly non-biolog-
    ical, non-modern sense.

Wordsworth's Turns

Leaving aside the similarities between the two, I shall now direct my attention to
Wordsworth and the change of his relation with cosmic – sublime – nature. When
Wordsworth utters the famous lines in the 1799-*Prelude:* 'An auxiliar light/Came
from my mind, which on the setting sun/Bestowed new splendour';[4] they must be
read in their proper context. In the narrow context the lines are part of the author's
portrait of a youthful mind that does not yet recognize the true limits of his powers.
In a wider context this wise author shows how inner light – or as Wordsworth also
names it: the inner eye – is impressed or shaped in early childhood by nature im-
printing itself on the mind of the young child. The auxiliary light of imagination
then is not a question of arbitrarily inventing but of finding and using what is
already there inside and outside the individual mind. This idea is based upon a
spiritual genealogical perspective reversing the traditional biological one as in the
phrase from 'My heart leaps up', 1802: 'The child is father of the man'. In other

words: the impressions of sublime nature in early childhood live in the mind of the grown up individual and consequently predispose it for the experience of sublimity whether it be found in the external or the internal, moral world.

Wordsworth's poetry in the decisive years, 1798-1800, displays this dialectic or correspondence between nature and mind. Its artistically most potent expressions are the recurring visions of doubled natural objects by way of their reflection in water. Related to these verbal pictures are phenomena like the rainbow ('My heart leaps up'), the echo, the call of the cuckoo ('To the Cuckoo'). In fact Wordsworth uses natural doubling or reflection to overcome the problems raised by the problem of reflection in the sense of analytical, intellectual power arising from the loss of the child's unreflected experience of nature and himself.

The division caused by self-awareness, self-reflection is visualised in doubled, mirrored landscape. But quite surprisingly it is also overcome by that very same configuration. As in Turner's case I shall confine myself to a few significant examples with relatively short comments on each, although they deserve to be analysed in depth and in a wider context.[5]

My first example is taken from 'Home at Grassmere' (March–April 1800).

> How vast the compass of this theatre,
> Yet nothing to be seen but lovely pomp
> And silent majesty (…)
> Behold the universal imagery
> Inverted, all its sun-bright features touched
> As with varnish, and the gloss of dreams;
> Dreamlike the blending also of the whole
> Harmonious landscape; all along the shore
> The boundary lost, the line invisible
> That parts the image from reality;
> And the clear hills, as high as they ascend
> Heavenward, so piercing deep the lake below.[6]

The most important feature in this image of a doubled, reflected landscape is the suspension of all visible boundaries not only vertically ('as high (…) so piercing deep') but also horisontally ('the boundary lost, the line invisible') creating a similar effect as when Turner erases the horisontal line in his paintings. In Wordsworth the ideological or hermeneutic consequences are made explicit: Image can no longer be parted from reality. Far from being a dangerous illusion this arch-typical manifestation of the Sublime represents a vision of true cosmic reality, emancipated from the solipsistic limitations inherent in intellectual self-reflection – 'that false secondary power' as Wordsworth names it in the 1799-*Prelude*.

By far the most complicated use of impressed, reflected landscape is 'There was a boy' (the fragment of 1798 and the added second part of 1800).[7] Here Wordsworth treats the very process leading from the child's unreflected perception of sublime nature to the reflected position of the grown-up poet recalling visually, what once was and never can be again – and yet is present as the very structure of the poet's visual imagination.

> There was a boy – ye knew him well, ye cliffs
> And islands of Winander – many a time
> At evening when the stars had just begun
> To move along the edges of the hills,
> Rising or setting, would he stand alone
> Beneath the trees or by the glimmering lake,
> And there with fingers interwoven, both hands
> Pressed closely palm to palm, and to his mouth
> Uplifted, he as through an instrument
> Blew mimic hootings to the silent owls,
> That they might answer him. And they would shout
> Across the wat'ry vale, and shout again,
> Responsive to his call, with quivering peals
> And long halloos, and screams, and echoes loud,
> Redoubled and redoubled – concourse wild
> Of mirth and jocund din. And when it chanced
> That pauses of deep silence mocked his skill,   ·
> Then sometimes in that silence, while he hung
> Listening, a gentle shock of mild surprize
> Has carried far into his heart the voice
> Of mountain torrents; or the visible scene
> Would enter unawares into his mind
> With all its solemn imagery, its rocks,

Its woods, and that uncertain heaven, received
Into the bosom of the steady lake.
    This Boy was taken from his mates, and died
In childhood, ere he was full ten years old.
Fair are the woods, and beauteous is the spot,
The vale where he was born; the church-yard hangs
Upon a slope above the village school,
And there, along that bank, when I have passed
At evening, I believe, that oftentimes
A full half-hour together I have stood
Mute, looking at the grave in which he lies!
(Prelude 1805. Book Fifth ll. 389-42)

It is possible to distinguish between three stages in the poem taken as a whole. *The first stage* is the boy's symbiotic unity with nature (the game with the owls), in which the boy is not conscious of any distinction between his own person and nature. *The second stage* constitutes the incipient schism between nature and the self, which is only registered by the narrator (nature surprising the boy). It is primarily in the actual structure of the final image in the first part that the hidden adult consciousness can be sensed. What the boy experiences as a sublime correspondence – because he has not yet consciously divorced himself from the surrounding world – is at the very same time the beginning of the division between the self and the surrounding world: paradise is no longer assured ('uncertain heaven'). The process leading to this division can be deduced from the order in which the narrator describes two stages in the boy's reception of nature: first the heart, then the mind. For this is no arbitrary order. The heart, i.e. feeling, represents an immediate stage and is also linked to sound, that is to say the child's earliest sense experience. The mind represents incipient self-awareness and thus the boy's approaching divorce from the close relationship to nature, linked to sight, which is the sense associated with distance.

Thereby the *third stage* is prepared: The fulfilled distinction between the (adult) consciousness and nature. This is marked by the silent, contemplating narrator at the boy's graveside and the picture of the landscape passed on by the narrator. On the slope above the school, where the young people congregate, the churchyard with the dead boy's grave is placed like a memento mori that silences the narrator. The boy's grave thus being emphasised as the central feature of the cultural landscape is, due to its being the interpretative core of the poem, the place from which all lines of sight secretly radiate and finally openly come together in the narrator's reflections. From this contemplation emerges the vision: the poem about the dead boy and the world that was his.

Although the poem evolves from the poet's meditation on the boy's grave, the poem itself is not created at the grave but literally beyond it. The scene with the poet at the grave is not only a recurring one, it is also seen or recalled from a distance in both space and time. In lines like 'I *believe* (…) I *have stood'* or 'Pre-eminent in beauty is the vale', the poet is obviously not only recalling his former meditations at the grave but also placing these contemplative moments within a larger frame – the actual valley as it lies before him at the very moment of writing.

So, whatever may be the relationship between the narrator and the boy and the time that has been lost – and on this very point the poem's narrator is silent – the grave is a reminder that only in death do we again become unambiguously one with nature. In the grave the dead boy has returned to the maternal earth from which he came. As the landscape sinks down, so, too, does the boy, sink down into the elementary, 'steady' bosom that is ready to receive him. Thus a boundary is established for any tendency to nostalgia or regression in the meditative narrator's relationship with childhood and the maternal, surrounding nature. What is lost is definitively lost in its original, sensual and physical manifestation. The grave is firmly closed around its contents, rejecting any meaningful intrusion or exchange. At this point the poem takes over. The boy's return to the earth, to nature, is the precondition for the inverse thrust of the poem.

For the narrator's silence does not only derive from the paralysing conditions of death. It also forms the logically second and final stage in a great articulatory thrust in the poem as a whole reversing the irrevocable fall. The first stage of the process belongs to the voice of nature, this language before language which was the boy's spontaneous expression or which impressed itself in him – partly in the *unarticulated sounds of nature* produced by the boy and the owls, and partly in the sovereign *non-human voice* of nature that penetrated into his heart. The second stage of this articulatory process appears when an individual personality emerges from his immediate relationship with nature and another language of a reflective, interior kind enters. The death of the unarticulated sounds of nature prepares the way for the growth of an articulatory potential associated with the mute narrator and his poem. In this sense a silent form of expression – the written word – takes over.

In other words, the spontaneous, unreflective experience of nature encompasses its own irrevocable catastrophe in that it is submerged, while the imprint of it remains. For this afterlife in the mind drags the retrospective and in that sense reflective, mirroring aspect along with it. This is given quite tangible expression in 'There was a boy' by the poet closing with a last glimpse of the valley in which he places both the grave and himself.

Read from the first to the last line, the poem thus moves from a spontaneously sensed and imprinted landscape to a recalled landscape picture, from passive reception to creative imagination, from the boy's spontaneous 'unreflective' reflection of nature – via its imperceptible submersion and reflection in the lake or the reflective surface of the mind – to its re-emergence in the narrator's vision of the beautiful valley in which the boy was born and grew up ('the vale/Where he was born and bred'). With this retrospective panorama and with the use of the past tense 'was', the picture of the valley reiterates the total range of the poem, confronting 'then' and 'now': the boy's past fate and the narrator's final position at the end of the story in the present.

The implication suggested above can be illustrated with the help of a diagram of the poem's symmetrical structure.

LANDSCAPE

HEAVEN
FOREST AND ROCKS
THE BOSOM OF THE LAKE
FOREST AND ROCKS
HEAVEN

REFLECTED
LANDSCAPE

If the upper triangle corresponds to the originally sensed landscape and the lower one to its impressed sublime form in the boy, then the overall rhomboid figure, where the borderline between the upper and the lower triangles is dissolved, corresponds to the sublime totality which is created in the grown man's imaginative use – his inversion, reflection – of the original sublime mental impression. The pattern on which the poem is composed thus emerges in a repetition and reduplication of the form which the boy's mind unwittingly received from nature.

In this context, the boy's death, the grave – the end of the childhood world – emerges as a necessary prerequisite for the creation of the poem and thus also for the Sublime as an *aesthetic* form. This is why the downward orientation from the upper to the lower triangle, the lake's embrace, represents a deepening understanding, the seeds of a mental transformation and in that sense also a fall from innocence preparing the way for a new consciousness. It can be illustrated if we view the sketch moving upwards from below. In an inverse movement of this kind – one that sublimates and crosses boundaries – the sinking movement is reversed, and what time has separated is gathered in a single dynamic image, a dual conceit.

If we read the sketch and the poem in this way, we can talk of a twofold reduplication, two kinds of mirroring, a passive and an active. On the one hand there is the one taking place in the boy's mind, where the landscape is spontaneously reflected on its surface (the lower triangle), on the other the recalling of this experience in the poem (the overall rhomboid sketch). In this special sense the downward movement of the boy (representing the loss of the world of the child) is the prerequisite for the emergence of the adult consciousness, whose sober acceptance of the conditions of reality and death makes it into not only a consciousness of loss, but a consciousness of a comprehensive process of necessary transformation determining consciousness itself. Thus the primal world of the child survives as the formative principle of sensuous and spiritual mature being.

Viewed from this angle the poem's final image – and thereby the Romantic paradigm of loss and restitution – appears in a new and deeper perspective. The landscape which the poet sees before him as he writes is the same as the landscape in which the boy grew up. The poem's beautiful valley with the boy's grave at its centre thus contains another, older, and yet radiantly young landscape which is buried in the landscape of the present as its invisible archetype. And what applies to the poem applies to the poet too: the child is present in the adult as the dynamic structural principle of his whole being. At once for ever lost and present.

The perhaps most simple expression of Wordsworth's idea of correspondence can be found in a 1798-fragment intimately related to the closing passage of the first part of the 1799-*Prelude*. To me it represents the very essence of Wordsworth's poetics in 'There was a boy': 'Those beauteous colours of my early years/Which make the starting-place of being fair /(…)/Those recollected hours that have the charm/Of visionary things, and lovely forms/And sweet sensations, which throw back our life/And make our infancy a visible scene/On which the sun is shining' (*Prelude* 493). What was once a physical sun has now become an inner source of light generating a poetical double-vision in which the past is present. Retrospection is not, then, looking back at – or reconstructing – the past, but the past presenting itself in the inner, creative eye of the poet in the present ('visionary things, and lovely forms', 'a visible scene').

This correspondence of nature and mind, past and present, however, does not survive in Wordsworth. In a passage in *The Excursion* (Book Ninth ll. 439ff) written in 1804, Wordsworth notes the potentially disturbing implications of respectively innocent and reflected (self-aware) mind in the beautiful scene of a snow-white ram reflected on the quiet surface of water:

> In a deep pool, by happy chance we saw
> A twofold image; on a grassy bank
> A snow-white ram, and in the crystal flood
> Another and the same! Most beautiful
> (…)
> The breathing creature stood; as beautiful
> Beneath him, showed his shadowy counterpart.
> Each had his glowing mountains, each his sky,
> And each seemed centre of his own fair world:
> Antipodes unconscious of each other,
> Yet in partition, with their several spheres,
> Blended in perfect stillness, to our sight.
> (*PW* 5.300).

The image of the mirrored ram is reflected, double in more than one sense. On the one hand there is the dumb animal which is the autistic centre of its own cosmos and in this sense an entire world. On the other there are the observers, the narrative we's sympathetic understanding of the ram's being unaware of its own reflection. They are not only aware of the ram's non-reflective, innocent form of unconsciousness ('each seemed centre of his own fair world'), but also of the infinitely wide world which that innocense excludes ('Antipodes unconscious of each other'). But in pointing to what is excluded, the observers also point to the reflecting, dual form inevitably resulting from being conscious of the infinitely great world as an entity apart from the sensing and thinking subject. What the ram has no sense of is appreciated by the observers: the reflection *as* a reflection, as a doubling of the phenomena of the world ('Yet in partition, with their several spheres,/Blended in perfect stillness to our sight'). Thus the observers are not only conscious of the animal and its world, in observing they are also conscious of themselves *as* observers, as the concluding words 'to our sight' confirm.

This particular mirror-image is a reminder of the inevitable dualisation of the world involved in the loss of innocence and subsequent growth of self-awareness, self-reflection already treated in 'There was a boy'. But contrary to this poem the beholders cannot themselves escape duplicity emanating from the knowledge of the self. The image of the ram reflected in the pool is a statement of their own self-reflective minds and the instability of their world compared to the one of animal innocence, which is undividedly one. In this particular sense the mirrored ram is a mirror image of the inevitable duplicity inherent in human reflective consciousness. The mirror-reflection, thus understood, surely represents an expanded consciousness, but at the same time also a dualisation of the world, which of course is only divided for the person who can stand back from himself in contemplation. In this respect the mirrored ram is the mirror-image of the observers' own selves. It reflects their way of sensing the world. They see in the ram what they are not any more, but once were: one with nature, unreflected.

Thus within the very idea of correspondence between mind and nature a disturbing dualism emerges here in 1804. In another manuscript from c.1805 the passage is supplied with a remarkable ending in which the observer has been changed into the first person singular:

A stray temptation seized me to dissolve
The vision, but I could not, and the stone
Snatched up for that intent dropped from my hand.
(*Prelude* 506)

It is not possible to decide whether the destructive drive aims at the vision as an image of innocent unity or an image of the duplicity inherent in self-awareness. Correspondingly it is uncertain whether the narrator goes back on his spontaneous urge because he cannot bear to erase the fond deceit or because he realises that the double image, being a mirror-reflection of his own way of perceiving the world, cannot be shattered by throwing a stone. The important point, however, is that in either case, the temptation arises in a mind far beyond the state of primal innocence – a mind unable to part with the recurring experience of duplicity as the basic condition of self-awareness: the spontaneous – animalisticly primitive – reaction of the beholder is immediately negated by the self-reflecting mind.

The conflict suggested by these lines about the snow-white ram is made manifest in a strikingly programmatic form in 'Elegiac Stanzas Suggested by a Picture of Peele Castle in a Storm Painted by Sir George Beaumont', 1805.

In this poem Wordsworth seems to write off the basic imaginative idea he subscribed to in his daring visionary poetry around 1798-1800. The picture of reflected landscape gives way to a picture of man's mind in permanent conflict with nature. Wordsworth sets out by creating a deliberate alternative to Beaumont's conventional description of the sublime:

> I was thy neighbour once, thou rugged Pile!
> Four summer weeks I have dwelt in sight of thee:
> I saw thee every day; and all the while
> Thy form was sleeping on a glassy sea.
>
> (…) Whene'er I looked, thy Image still was there;
> It trembled, but it never passed away.

But this harmonious mirror-reflection of the castle does not last.

> I would have planted thee, thou hoary Pile
> Amid a world how different from this
> Beside a sea that could not cease to smile
> (…)
> So once it would have been, –'tis no more;
> I have submitted to a new control:

A power is gone, which nothing can restore
A deep distress hath humanised my soul.
(PW 4.258-60)

It is no longer possible to uphold the image of the rugged pile reflected in the calm sea. Instead the sea reflecting the rugged pile becomes a roaring chaotic power literally breaking the mirror of the sea. At the same time the rugged pile turns into a man-made castle.

By this significant double change Wordsworth dissolves the sublime correspondence of mind and nature. Wordsworth separates the man made artifact, the castle, which has lost its natural appearance (rugged or hoary pile) from the inhuman, destructive powers of nature. In this way Wordsworth adopts Sir George Beaumont's painting of Peele Castle in a Storm in the classical sublime manner, but in an non-conventional way, interpreting it as a symbol of the irreconcilable division between mind and matter, art and nature.

And this huge Castle, standing here sublime,
I love to see the look with which it braves,
Cased in the unfeeling armour of old time,
The lightening, the fierce wind, and trampling waves.
(*PW* 4.258-260)

Wordsworth's imagery is no longer creatively reflecting impressed nature but impressive art, gallantly opposing nature's wild, uncontrollable forces. As the very title of the poem demonstrates, art is reflecting art. Art has become anti-nature.

NOTES

1. Quoted from Baltrušaitis 1986. Baltrušaitis argues that the widely accepted interpretation of St. Paul's words about the glass as signifying an imperfect image is incorrect. 'Die Alten haben ihre Spiegel übrigens nicht für mangelhaft und in ihnen abgebildeten Gestalten verdunkeld gehalten. Ganz im Gegenteil, man hielt gerade das für ein Symbol der Genauigkeit und Klarheit' (84). On the contrary the mirror was a means of divination. Thus Baltrušaitis quotes J. Filere (1636): 'Wenn der Heilige Paulus (…) sich der beiden Ausdrücke Spiegel und Rätzel bedient, um uns zu verdeutlichen, wie wir in der Dunkelheit dieses Erdenleben Gott erkennen können (…), dann kann es in diesen Zusammenhang nicht verkehrt sein, euch hier einen Spiegel in einem Rätzel und ein Rätzel in einem Spiegel zu zeigen' (85). 'Rätzel', then, does not imply that the reflection is imperfect, blurred or faint, but that the mirror displays an enigmatic sign enabling feeble earthly minds to grasp what is otherwise unintelligible to them. Thus imperfection rests not with the mirror but with man.

2. The notion (underlying the illustration to the *Nervus Opticus*) of the perceived sun being a reflection of a reflection is – like so many Christian notions – much older than Christianity itself. Baltrušaitis quotes the Pythagorean Philolaos' speculations on the nature of the sun (300 B.C.): 'Sie ist eine Glasscheibe, die das Leuchten des kosmischen Feuers empfängt und die uns das Licht sendet; so unterscheidet man im Himmel drei Teile: zunächst das himmlische Feuer, dann sein Leuchten und dessen Wiederspiegelung wie in einem Spiegel: und schließlich die Sonnenstrahlen, die durch diesen Spiegel auf unsere Erde gelenkt werden: eben diese Reflexion bezeichnen wir als Sonne, sie ist nur das Bild eines Bildes' (Baltrušaitis 1986, 80).

3. Quoted from Hirsch 1966, 204-5.

4. Second Part, ll 417ff in: William Wordsworth 1979. The *Prelude* in the text with references.

5. For this I refer to my *The Time of Unrememberable Being. Wordsworth and the Sublime 1787-1805*, 1998.

6. 'Home at Grassmere' ll. 560-62 in: William Wordsworth 1967-72. *PW* in the text with volume and page references.

7. The poem exists in three versions. A fragment from October 1798 with only one verse, a version included in the second edition of *Lyrical Ballads*, 1800, containing a number of important changes, and finally the version quoted here from *The Prelude*, 1805 (Fifth Book).

BIBLIOGRAPHY

Baltrušaitis, Jurgis 1986. *Der Spiegel.* Gießen.

Hirsch, E.D. 1966. *Wordsworth and Schelling.* New Haven.

Mortensen, Klaus Peter 1993. *Himmelstormerne* (The Titans). Copenhagen.

Mortensen, Klaus Peter 1998. *The Time of Unrememberable Being. Wordsworth and the Sublime 1787-1805.* Copenhagen.

Wordsworth, William 1967-72. *The Poetical Works of William Wordsworth, I-V.* (Eds. E. de Selincourt and Helen Darbishire). Oxford. (Abbreviated as PW)

Wordsworth, William 1979. *The Prelude 1799, 1805, 1850.* Authoritative Texts, Context and Reception, Recent Critical Essays. (Eds. Jonathan Wordsworth, M.H. Abrams, and Stephen Gill). London.

Carl Gustav Carus and Landscape Painting

Diana Behler

Carl Gustav Carus, friend of Goethe, Caspar David Friedrich, and Alexander von Humboldt, was one of the most versatile men of his times. Scientist, physician, administrator, psychologist, traveler, and artist, Carus saw his life as a constant striving for a balance of physical and psychic realities, the midpoint between material and spiritual existence to be achieved only by approximation.

Carus began his *Letters on Landscape Painting* in 1815, when he turned to a more aesthetic, holistic view of human nature to complement his scientific interests.[1] Competent in drawing and painting and immersed in anatomical studies, Carus continued to find linkages between the transitory and the universal, the human body and the psyche, in an aesthetic appreciation of nature, not only to heal his own personal melancholy, but to address the growing alienation of human beings from nature. Spurred on by Goethe's favorable impression of four paintings he had sent to him in February of 1822, he published the essays in 1830. While written in letter format, the self reflective style of the expositions betrays a strong element of the diary, the dialogue merely serving as a cover for an analysis of Carus' own views. Carus' thinking is centered in his linkage of science and art, a symbiosis of cognitive and aesthetic modes of contemplating life in its corporeal and spiritual dimensions. Following studies in chemistry, physics, zoology, geology, and anatomy, Carus obtained both a doctoral degree in medicine and a master's degree in the liberal arts. Professionally, he worked as a general practitioner and gynecologist, was an advocate of public health, and published books on comparative anatomy, physiology, the psyche, the symbolism of the human form, as well as the standard *Textbook on Gynecology of* 1820. As a pendant to the letters on landscape painting, Carus also wrote 12

'Letters on Earth Life', preferring the term 'Erdlebenbildkunst' ('Earth-Life-Picture-Art') to landscape painting because he sought to grasp the life of the earth and nature in his depictions. Like Goethe, he thought the artist could best understand and depict nature by studying natural phenomena with a well trained eye. In the 1820s, Howard's analysis and classification of cloud formations in his book The Climate of London that was to culminate in the science of meteorology fascinated Carus and Goethe alike. Carus even dedicated his tenth letter on 'Earth Life' to 'Cloud Life' and concluded it with Goethe's poem 'Howards Ehrengedachtnis' (*DE* 185-87).

Noting a 'true dissolation' or 'bogginess' in German art at the beginning of the 19th century, Carus credited the Dresden Academy of Art with having at least provided 'a certain elevating tone', and in Caspar David Friedrich, he found a new artistic genius (*DE* 75). Deeply aware of Friedrich's melancholy mood and dissatisfaction with his own artistic works, Carus nevertheless admired Friedrich's 'individualistic, deeply poetic, if often gloomy and harsh style of landscape' that seemed so typically German (*DE* 137). Especially significant for Carus were two aspects of Friedrich's painting, the affective experiential impulse producing the painting, on the one hand – ('Ein Bild soll nicht erfunden, sondern empfunden sein') – and the closed spaced necessitated by landscape depiction, on the other. Whereas the picture, 'das Bild', is a fixed observation, ordinary, habitual seeing is changeable and knows no such concentration of mass and light. Thus, while landscape painting begins with a potentially infinite projection of the subjective interior self, its artistic execution requires external, objective limitation, the 'closed-off room' (*DE* 139).

Landscape painting for Carus thus requires two movements, one towards specificity and concreteness, and the other towards abstraction and a sense of the whole, which together demand a closed space, the center of the point of viewing where the axes of the eyes join together. The 'picture' resides not in the painting itself, but somewhere between the canvas and its viewer, a self-conscious artistry reminiscent of the Early Romantic view of artistic creation as an ironic self-awareness and mediation between the desire for complete expression and the necessity for limitation. Whereas the 'natural' demands the cosmos in painting, the 'artificial' requires the concentration of an enclosed space. Furthermore, with Carus as with Friedrich, landscape painting requires raising the prosaic to the poetic, a movement from melancholic subjectivity to poetic lumination and expansion.

While Carus clearly attributed Schelling's 'world soul' ('Weltseele') with having inspired his own thinking about the interrelationship of the human spirit and nature, it was actually Fichte who had laid the cornerstone of his intellectual foundation: 'Already in my 14th year, I read about the unlimited freedom of the mind in Fichte's easier and more accessible writings, and this freedom became the ideal and center of my being' (*DE* 632-33). Novalis' *Heinrich von Ofterdingen,* particularly the figure of Klingsohr, mirrored 'a disposition reflected in the world and in humanity' for Carus, but Tieck's *Phantasus* was equally formative for his poetic world views (*DE* 189-90).[2] Yet it was in Schelling's text *On the World Soul* of 1798 that Carus found what he terms the 'cardinal point' of his thinking. This text with its subtitle 'A Hypothesis of higher Physics' found little resonance, since it was overshadowed by Schelling's other writings, especially the *System of Transcendental Idealism* of 1800 in which the principle of the philosophy of identity and the thesis that nature is visible spirit and spirit invisible nature is more sharply delineated. The essay on the world soul, however, emphasizes the life principle underlying organic as well as inorganic life, animate and inanimate existence, and this is what drew Carus' attention. For Schelling this 'world soul' is at once present everywhere and nowhere, and because it is everything, it can be neither definitive nor specific. Thus it finds 'no specific designation' in language, but has been transmitted in 'poetic representations' instead. In the passage 'On the Relationship of the Real and the Ideal', Schelling calls the 'world soul' the 'absolute bond, the copula', that joins together nature and spirit, world and human beings, object and subject. This is not a matter of an independent characteristic that is added to things as a 'doubled and different reality', but constitutes an inner connection among all things and thus an 'absolute identity of the infinite and the finite'. This unity especially determines the relationship between the inorganic and the organic world and annuls the 'opposition between mechanism and organism', which according to Schelling, but also Carus, 'has held up the progresses of natural science long enough'. According to this view, 'the individual parts of nature are not an unbroken or infinitely extending series, but rather a constant chain of life always reverting back to itself, in which each link is necessary to the whole'. Nature is no longer merely a 'product of an incomprehensible creation', but is actually 'this creation itself'. In this idea of the world soul, concepts of immanence and transcendence become irrelevant empty words, since the opposition between them is annihilated, 'everything flowing together to a divinely filled world'.[3] Another reason for Carus' interest in Schelling's the *World Soul* will certainly reside in the link of this text to Goethe, for whom the designation 'world soul' can be viewed as the 'solution to the riddle' of the secret laws of nature that Goethe seeks to convey in his poetic 'Metaphorphosis of the Plant'.[4] Schelling's theory of painting contains important analyses of landscape painting as well, but Carus could not have known these, since they are found in Schelling's *Philosophy of Art,* which appeared much later than Carus' *Letters.* His Jena lectures on the Winter Semester of 1802-03, however, already contain pertinent comments about linear perspective and the subject-object relationship of art to nature.[5] Goethe found an echo of his own ideas in Carus, noting that he possessed the same amalgamation of scientific and artistic talents. He esteemed the *Letters on Landscape Painting* in a letter of April 20, 1822 to Carus and warmly recommended that they not be withheld from the public.[6]

Working on his *Letters on Landscape Painting,* Carus also came into contact with the ubiquitous Weimar school director Karl August Boettiger, who confirmed his own conjectures about the emergence of landscape as a modern aesthetic phenomenon, for with regard to antiquity, 'there was nothing to be found there to deserve the designation "landscape" as we conceive of it'. In antiquity, everything in nature was transformed into the human form, and only a few indications of cities and gardens lacking perspective have been passed on to us (*DE* 191-92). Not until the 17th century was nature viewed in terms of aesthetic beauty, Carus notes, the painters Claude Lorrain and Poussin in the south, and Ruysdael in the north marking the breakthrough. The poets of antiquity praised the beauty of nature, but did not really know of a genuine art of landscape painting. Montaigne did not even mention the beauties of Roman and Neapolitan natural surroundings, and even now, there are enough people who would never think of nature's 'beautiful contours, charming hues, and strange light effects', but see only the material 'yield of the earth and the usefulness or destructiveness of climate'. Claude's landscapes differ from material ones in their emphasis on tone rather than colour and in his ability to convey atmosphere. Claude's second secret is his attention to detail, the 'almost ancient abstraction from the specificity of nature while adhering unconsciously to it on the whole'. Thus Claude accomplished in painting what the Greeks had done in the plastic arts: 'This is where the plasticity of the Greeks celebrated its highest triumph, in that only they succeeded in divesting the human form of all its accidentalities while still delineating the appearance of its idea, along with the will of nature, in the human frame', Carus remarks. Claude's trees are really trees, but transfigured into a higher concept: 'Look at these trees! They are real trees, but in a higher transfiguration; they fulfill the concept of tree, without presuming to try to present the tree itself (which it could never attain) (…). Everything is true and yet not real — just as we can say of nature, that it is real but not in and of itself the higher transcendental true lying behind it, the idea'. Yet Carus warns of excessive, dry abstraction and merely mechanical reproduction, maintaining the necessity for a balance of the unconscious and the reflective that constitute landscape depiction (*DE* 97-98).

Joachim Ritter has analyzed the ancients' neglect of the aesthetic aspects of nature, noting, however, that Jakob Burckhardt had already perceived some appreciation in Petrarch's description of climbing Mont Ventoux near Avignon.[7] Inspired by Livius' account of Philipp of Macedonia who had climbed the Thessalonian Haimon because he wanted to see if one could view both the Adriatic and the Black sea at once, Petrarch sought to experience firsthand the mountain he had seen afar from childhood. Uncanny, even to those living on its slopes, Mont Ventoux disappointed the climber Petrarch, who considered its heights incomparable to those 'that can be reached through the observation of the human being' (Ritter 143). Because Petrarch's attempt to climb Mont Ventoux arose from a freely conceived personal desire to enjoy the view from the mountain's peak and to participate in the entirety of nature and God, it had 'epochal significance' (Ritter 146). Practical considerations no longer came into play here, and nature as landscape now became 'the fruit and product of the theoretical mind' for Ritter. Citing Carus' *Letters on Landscape Painting* as consciously determining nature as landscape in concepts belonging to the 'tradition of philosophical theory', Ritter notes that 'heaven' denotes the 'visibility of the cosmos as 'word order' and its appearing presence' in the Kantian sense of a union of the starry skies above and the moral law within'. Alexander von Humboldt too had seen the sublime determination of the human being as grasping the spirit of nature, 'lying hidden beneath the cover of appearances' and deriving pleasure from nature as 'independent from the insight into the functioning of the powers' (Ritter 152). Ritter defines landscape as 'nature that in its observation by a feeling and sensitive observer is asthetically present'. It constitutes an enjoyment of nature without thought of a river as a navigation route or a problem for civil engineers. Carus is cited as having seen landscape as the 'eternally continuously operative world creation' at precisely that juncture when analytical science had gained the upper hand, and it became the providence of the free 'production and reproduction of the artistic genius' to express this world creation (Ritter 148). For Carus, poetry and art transmit nature aesthetically as landscape, a phenomenon Ritter considers inevitable following the loss of a philosophical, scientific grounding for nature. Yet as Schiller had remarked in his *Letters on Aesthetic Education* of 1793-94, this consciousness of separation from nature is not rued as loss and deterioration, but as freedom, as a reversal from man's passive enslavement to nature's control (Ritter 161).

Baudelaire in his essay 'The Painter of Modern Life' also rooted his concept of beauty in the present rather than some lost age, for while both eternal and transitory components constitute beauty, these can only be joined by the artist's imagination, his synoptic glance, a function of the present.[8] Baudelaire views the modern as 'ephemeral, the fugitive, the contingent, the half of art whose other half is the eternal and the immutable', the aesthetic experience evoking a symbolic congruence of the momentary and the eternal. Paul de Man, in in his essay on 'The Rhetoric of Temporality', has also detected an inherent contradiction among those critics who emphasized the analogy between mind and nature in Romantic literature, who see Coleridge, for example, as the 'great synthesizier' and 'take his dialectic of subject and object to be the authentic pattern of Romantic imagery'. While asserting the 'priority of object over subject implicit in an organic conception of language', de Man states, this critical stance gives priority to nature, 'limiting the task of the mind to interpreting what is given in nature'. It puts Romanticism into one of two traps, that of a solipsistic subjective idealism, or a return to the naturalism of a nostalgic, unreachable past. Thus De Man eschews the symbol 'as the outstanding characteristic of Romantic diction' where image coincides with substance (representation with nature) and presupposes simultaneity. Instead, he prefers the allegorical sign that always refers to a preceding sign, presupposes repetition and distance in time, and renounces nostalgia. Thus allegory is seen by de Man as the true Early Romantic voice that not only precludes identification with the non-self, but gives it full, albeit painful recognition, and renounces both nostalgia (Rousseau) and loss of self in death or error (Wordsworth).[9]

It is in this sense of a recognition of the separation of the human being and nature, body and soul, the temporal and eternal, that Carus' views about landscape should be appraised. Landscape is the mark of the alienation of man from nature, nature's aesthetization, whereby the artist's rendering of nature constitutes the link between the two realms in the present. Thus while Carus terms man's relation to nature 'symbolic', he does not use this to signify an identity of the two poles, but rather a complementary relationship analogous to that of science and art. And as he did not lament the separation of these two modes of cognition and their functions, but attuned himself to one or the other for varying purposes, he also did not regret that landscape was not really nature. One might say that Carus's letters display an ever-present enjoyment in landscape, in the subject's control and limitation of nature through artistic depiction rather than its mystical immersion in nature. With Carus, landscape marks the boundary between body and soul, the conscious and the unconscious residing midway between the physical and the psychic, and is seen as something dynamic to be contemplated in its potential for change and growth, a reflection of the continuous metamorphoses of human life (*DE* 14).

Scrutinizing the inner structure, external environment, and the illness that can befall human beings, Carus reflected upon destruction: 'This enormous question as to the 'why?' of all this change, all this constant destruction, this often burdens the young mind with the force of a ton', he remarked. But citing his healthy constitution and his reading of Kant and Schelling, Carus gained the assurance that within nature's spectacle of destruction, there indeed remained something free (*DE* 41-42). As much as one tries to transgress the border between consciousness and unconsciousness, and however related they are, he notes elsewhere, they nevertheless always remain estranged entities, for which reason 'conscious spirit always stands before the unconscious with a certain awe, whereas the unconscious itself receives the effects of the conscious never directly, but always only in a roundabout way, but never grasps it in and of itself' (*DE* 157).[10] Such reflections provide a framework of understanding for interpreting Carus' *Letters* and their conceptual development and warn the reader not to linger too long with one aspect of Carus' thought to the exclusion of others. Whereas the emphasis is on unity at one point, such harmony is disrupted again and again by his delineation of the separation of man and nature, a horizon that permits landscape to emerge as a dominant aesthetic form of expression. Yet Carus continued to maintain the preeminence of the artist, the vision of 'life as a work of art' and the individual's task of transforming one's life into art.

While time precludes any extensive discussion of Carus' *Letters on Landscape Painting,* there are a few essential points deserving mention here. First among these is Carus' insistence on the essential unity of the human being's rational and aesthetic capacities. Pure rationality, 'cold reckoning of contrasts and rational concepts', produces mere poetic cripples without a corresponding 'inner excitement of the soul', and artistic creations, while not truly living in reality, can nevertheless appear as living to us and authenticate 'the kinship of the human being to the world spirit' (*BAL* 13-14). Art creates the world anew and speaks a marvelous language of sun and moon, air and clouds, mountain and valley, trees and flowers, animals and human beings, elevating us beyond the ordinary 'through contemplation of the divine' for Carus, whereby art appears as the mediator of religion. It familiarizes us with a small portion of the power and soul of the world, which in its entirety is beyond our weak human perception (*BAL* 19). Landscape painting maintains a twofold impact, first in the nature of the object depicted, and second, to the degree that the work of art is a creation of the human mind. While reason dictates the distinction of art from science, Carus sees each as equally necessary to the production of the other, for neither alone can reach the unity demanded by human existence. There is a sharp distinction between the 'truth' of an actual landscape and the painting for Carus, however, the painting experienced as a whole, a microcosm of itself, whereas a glimpse of actual nature is torn out of its organic connections and pressed into unnatural limits when perceived. Thus the painting is closer to us as an 'enclosed creation', but never provides complete satisfaction, since it owes its existence to the creative power of the human mind (*BAL* 20, 26-27).

In questioning 'what is beauty', Carus insists on the function of the senses and perception for the phenomenon of beauty to emerge. Nothing lying outside of nature that is not available to the senses, such as the concept of a mathematical point or other abstraction, can thus be beautiful. Landscape depiction exhibits beauty when it fulfills its artistic goal of 'expressing the inner life through the depiction of one moment out of the entire natural life of the earth; where this has truly been accomplished, just through that, beauty is depicted'. For Carus true insight into nature is prepared and furthered by art: 'It is as if the infinite wealth of nature were written in a language that the human being first had to learn', he claims. Rejecting both the ancient utilitarian view of landscape as a mere background for human activity as well as a purely sentimental or symbolic landscape art, whereby nature becomes a mere chiffre requiring only that we grasp its symbolic meaning, Carus insists that true landscape art reflect a genuine harmony of 'reason and nature' permeating the universe (*BAL* 34-39). Such art is one of organic development reflecting periods of youthful flowering, perfection, and decline, and periods of artistic flourishing are seen as inevitably followed by a certain decline or false direction. Here Carus sees an emergent landscape art with Titian and Raphael, its maturity with painters such as Claude Lorrain and Ruysdael, as well as in the historically tinged works of Salvator Rosa and Nicolaus Poussin. Ensuing landscapes by Swanevelt, Friedrich, Poussin, and Berghem, mark a certain decline from which the early 19th century has not recovered, but the new landscape art, termed 'orphic' in a borrowing from Goethe, portends landscapes revealing the history of mountains and plant formations corresponding to the same development and dissolution within human life. And it should be noted that Carus' concept of landscape depiction is not restricted to drawing and painting, but includes Goethe's poeticized landscapes as well as Humboldt's descriptions of prairies and astounding waterfalls of America, for they draw images for the soul with words (*BAL* 55-59, 62, 67).[11]

Other interesting points include Carus' exhortations to art academies that emphasize copying, viewing nature 'through foreign glasses', rather than the scientific study of nature and the training of hand and eye. Furthermore, the public must be educated to appreciate landscape not as a practical asset exemplified in the proliferation of travel brochures and prints of well-known regions, weather reports, and assessments of the shade value of trees and hay production of meadows, but in terms of its poetic and aesthetic significance (*BAL* 77, 85-86). Finally, despite all attempts to fathom the significance of nature for humankind, to relate it to human perception, Carus remained dumbfounded by the sublime aura and power of nature, particularly during his travels through the Alpine and southern regions of Italy, the domiciles of antiquity in Capri and Ischia, as well as the austere coasts of the island of Rügen. His own drawing and painting evidence his continuing attempts to bridge the gap between the awesome grandeur and incomprehensibility of nature and the astute, perceiving subject. Landscape depiction, combining scientific accuracy, technical skill, and poetic imagination, was one way for Carus to telescope nature's vastness to encompass it within a frame of human comprehension, at least for a moment in time.

NOTES

1. Carl Gustav Carus. *Denkwürdigkeiten aus Europa,* 1963, 77. In the text as *DE* with relevant page numbers.

2. Carus was especially drawn to Tieck after the latter's move to the 'old market' of Dresden, where he drew Carus along with others under the spell of his 'astonishing and beautiful dramatic readings'.

3. *Von der Weltseele,* in: *Friedrich Wilhelm Joseph von Schellings sämtliche Werke,* 1856-1861, First Section, 2. 349, 361, 378.

4. Johann Wolfgang von Goethe, 'Die Metamorphose der Pflanze': *Gedenkausgabe* 1. 203-6.

    Alle Gestalten sind ähnlich, und keine gleichet der andern;

    und so deutet das Chor auf ein geheimes Gesetz

    Auf ein heilige Rätsel. O könnt ich dir, liebliche Freundin,

    Uberliefern sogleich glücklich das lößende Wort!

5. The Würzburg Lectures of 1803-04 on the philosophy of art appeared in 1859 in Schelling's *Sämtliche Werke. Erste Abteilung. Bd. 5;* the Jena first version of 1802-03 has been preserved in a transcript by Henry Crabb Robinson edited by Ernst Behler: 'Schellings Ästhetik in der Überlieferung von Henry Crabb Robinson', *Philosophisches Jahrbuch 83* (1976), 133-83.

6. Carl Gustav Carus, Zehn Briefe über Landschaftsmalerei mit zwölf Beilagen und einem Brief von Goethe als Einleitung 1815-1835. *Briefe und Aufsätze über Landschaftsmalerei,* 1982, 9. In the text as *BAL* with relevant page numbers. Goethe considered Carus' Letters on Landscape to be both 'well conceived and beautifully written' and thought that they would have a positive impact on the public, opening the eyes of artists and nature-lovers to the various harmonies of nature.

7. See Joachim Ritter 1974, 141-63. Ritter in the text with relevant page numbers.

8. Charles Baudelaire, *The Painter of Modern Life and Other Essays,* 13.

9. Paul de Man 1983, *The Rhetoric of Temporality,* 197-98, 207.

10. Carus investigates the relationship of 'psyche' and 'physis', the conscious to unconscious modes of existence in his book *Psyche* of 1846, which he termed an 'embryo of psychology' (377).

11. Carus anticipates a third stage of aesthetic production, much like G.E. Lessing's expectation of a third stage of moral fulfillment in his 'Education of the Human Race'. He thereby reveals his adherence to the eighteenth century ideal of perfectibility: 'but it will certainly come! There will soon be landscapes of a higher, more significant beauty than Claude and Ruysdael have painted', he exclaims. 'They will be pure nature depictions viewed through a spiritual eye and portrayed through an increasing technical perfection' (64).

BIBLIOGRAPHY

Baudelaire, Charles 1964. *The Painter of Modern Life and Other Essays.* (Trans. Jonathan Mayne). Greenwich.

Carus, Carl Gustav 1963. *Denkwürdigkeiten aus Europa,* conveyed by Carl Gustav Carus as a picture of life and compiled by Manfred Schlosser. Hamburg. (Abbreviated as *DE*)

Carus, Carl Gustav 1982. 'Zehn Briefe über Landschaftsmalerei mit zwölf Beilagen und einem Brief von Goethe als Einleitung 1815-1835'. In: *Briefe und Aufsätze über Landschaftsmalerei.* (Ed. Gertrud Heider). Leipzig and Weimar. (Abbreviated as *BAL*)

Man, Paul de 1983. 'The Rhetoric of Temporality'. *Blindness and Insight. Essays in the Rhetoric of Contemporary Criticism.* Minneapolis.

Ritter, Joachim 1974. 'Landschaft. Zur Funktion des Asthetischen in der modernen Gesellschaft'. In: Joachim Ritter, *Subjektivität.* Frankfurt. (Abbreviated as Ritter)

Schelling, F.W.J. 1856-1861. 'Von der Weltseele'. In: *Friedrich Wilhelm Joseph von Schellings sämtliche Werke.* (Ed. Karl Friedrich August Schelling). Stuttgart.

The Overgrown Space:
Romantic Imagination and Arabesque in
Søren Kierkegaard's *The Concept of Irony*

Isak Winkel Holm

In *The Concept of Irony,* Kierkegaard describes the Romantic poet as an addict of imagination who makes his life dissolve into hallucinations and illusions. This critique, however, is not a total condemnation of imagination but rather a transformation and existentialization of it. In a recent book, *Kierkegaard's Dialectic of the Imagination,* David Gouwens explains that Kierkegaard 'can take even the faults of the Romantic artist and transpose them into virtues of the subjective thinker'.[1] Thus, imagination plays a crucial role in Kierkegaard's later works as an indispensable capacity providing the individual with existential possibilities. The subjective thinker described in *Concluding Unscientific Postscript,* for instance, is allowed to make use of fantasy as long as it is 'directed to a concrete life, not a concrete work of art' (Gouwens 123). In Kierkegaard's own metaphor, imagination is legitimate if moved from the stage of paper to the stage of existence.[2]

I agree with Gouwens's thesis concerning Kierkegaard's existentializing of the Romantic imagination, but I am not sure that the treacherously simple distinction between stages of paper and existence is useful in dealing with Kierkegaard's complex relationship to Romanticism. After all, it is not possible for an author, as long as he is an author, to move from the stage of paper to that of existence. The subjective thinker – and Kierkegaard, for that matter – does not cease to write books on paper. For this reason, imagination not only appears as a capacity providing the individual with existential possibilities but also as an omnipresent textual phenomenon, in the shape of textual images or poetic mimesis.[3] In the following I shall examine Kierkegaard's discussion of literary images in the philosophical text in order to demonstrate the way in which he takes over and displaces the Romantic notion of imagination.

Plato's Supplements

Kierkegaard addresses the problematic mixture of philosophical concepts and literary images in his first book, *The Concept of Irony*. In an infrequently read chapter called 'The Mythical in the Earlier Platonic Dialogues as a Token of a More Copious Speculation', Kierkegaard discusses Plato's stylistic 'duplicity' or 'duplexity', by which he means his moving back and forth between dialectics and myth, between philosophical and literary textual strategies. This stylistic duplexity, Kierkegaard asserts, can be explained by the fact that Plato had a 'poetic temperament' that forced him to add a 'supplement' to socratic dialectics (*CI* 207). Since Plato wrote tragedies before he met Socrates, he is led to supply invisible thought by the sensuousness and visibility of textual images. As Kierkegaard explains: 'Thus the addition given to the dialectical movement by the mythical presentation (…) is that it lets the negative be *seen*' (*CI* 194).

From Kierkegaard's papers we learn that this duplexity of invisible concepts and visible images is not only a characteristic of Plato's philosophical style but also one of Kierkegaard's own. Apparently, Kierkegaard wrote this chapter in *The Concept of Irony* in order to make clear his own understanding of such a 'misrelation' between thought and its supplement, between understanding and productive imagination. Kierkegaard opens the discussion considering a variety of leading Plato scholars – Stallbaum, Baur, Ackermann and Ast – but this display of academic knowledge hides another conflict between two more important philosophers who are not mentioned in the chapter: G.W.F. Hegel and Friedrich Schlegel.

The point of departure for the whole discussion is an unmistakably Hegelian definition of the mythical as 'the idea in a state of alienation, the idea's externality – i.e. its immediate temporality and spatiality as such' (*CI* 189). Hegel's *Lectures on the History of Philosophy*, in particular, feature significantly in Kierkegaard's view of Plato. Here, Hegel categorically rejects the possibility that Plato's myths are more 'outstanding' than his abstract conceptual thought. When philosophy is able to walk on its own, it is no longer in need of images, Hegel explains. In some cases, however, the philosopher can use the 'superfluous adornment' of the mythical image as an aid for the slow-witted reader: 'Nach außen mögen jene Mythen freilich dienen; von der spekulativen Höhe geht man herunter, um leichter Vorstellbares zu geben'.[4] Kierkegaard recycles Hegel's metaphor when he sums up this view by saying that

Plato 'in the mythical descends to the listener' and uses the 'frame' of an image as a condescending 'accommodation'.

When Hegel attacks those who believe Plato's mythical images to be more important than his concepts, he is most likely to have Friedrich Schlegel in mind.[5] Indeed, Schlegel writes in *Athenäum* that poetic beauty in Plato's style is not only a means but a goal in itself.[6] Twelve years later, in his lectures on literary history, Schlegel repeats this theory and asserts that 'Plato treated philosophy entirely as art'. These lectures are important for an understanding of Kierkegaard's reading of Plato: just as Kierkegaard talks about a platonic 'misrelation' between dialectics and myth, Schlegel refers to a 'Zwiespalt', a split, between cool reason and enthusiastic poetic presentment (*KSF* 4.53). Furthermore, just as Kierkegaard talks about a 'negative dialectics', Schlegel states that Plato's dialectical reflections are only the 'negative part' in the dialogues leading step by step towards the mythical images. As Schlegel explains, Plato is closest to divine truth when he writes in an 'oriental manner' in 'Sinnbildern und Mythen', that is, in the visual allegories of the myths.

Compared to Hegel, Schlegel turns the hierarchy of thought and supplement upside down by claiming that only fantasy and not its rational supplement is able to reach divine truth. Schlegel and his fellow Romantics based the theory of a profound intuition on the Kantian notion of the 'aesthetic idea' and claimed that aesthetic intuition, thanks to its inexplicable horizon of 'Nebenvorstellungen', is able to function as an allegory of the absolute. Kierkegaard does not cite Schlegel in this chapter but contents himself with transcribing Ast's almost identical repetition of the sentence about Plato's 'Sinnbildern und Mythen'.[7]

According to Kierkegaard, the Hegelian position is a rationalist aesthetics that only accepts aesthetic intuition as a kind of packing of abstract concepts. Against this rationalist view of intuition Kierkegaard asserts that in Plato, 'the mythical has a far more profound meaning', namely as 'a presentment of something higher'. Thus, the rationalist and 'Hegelian' position is corrected in terms of the Romantic theory of aesthetic intuition. Later on in *The Concept of Irony*, however, Kierkegaard turns out to be a hard critic of the Romantic imagination. From Schlegel's novel *Lucinde* he cites the main character Julius's manifesto about poetry and love:

[in Poesie und Liebe ist] kein Zweck zweckmässiger, als der, daß ich gleich Anfangs das was wir Ordnung nennen vernichte, weit von [meiner Schrift] entferne und mir das Recht einer reizende Verwirrung deutlich zueigne und durch die That behaupte.[8]

The product of this stimulating and sensual confusion is the arabesque with all its entwined vines and leaves. Kierkegaard comments that a disorderly Romantic imagination of this kind only leads to 'confusion': 'as [Schlegel] abandons all understanding and lets fantasy alone prevail', he ends up with 'a simple, eternally moving image' (*CI* 362). According to Kierkegaard, Romanticism suggests an inversion of the Hegelian movement from art via religion to philosophy: what Schlegel says 'clearly means that when the understanding has reached its apex, its order should give way to fantasy, which now alone is to prevail'. The yielding of understanding to imagination must, of course, be a target for Kierkegaard's critique of the Romantic poet. In his reading of *Lucinde,* Kierkegaard reacts like a morally offended adversary of uncontrolled fantasy, and, in a rather Philistine voice, informs the Romantics that imagination should only be 'an interlude in the task of life', so that it does not turn real life into a dream.

Myth and Image

As we have seen, Kierkegaard criticizes both Hegel's and Schlegel's views of imagination. Instead, and unusually for him, Kierkegaard tries to mediate between these two positions by constructing a theory about 'the inner history of the mythical in Plato'. The problem is to be solved by introducing a temporal development in Plato's work: after all, both Hegel and Schlegel are right, because, in his philosophical writings, Plato moved from a Romantic type of image to a Hegelian one, or as Kierkegaard says: from *myth* to *image,* from 'Mythe' to 'Billede'.[9]

Kierkegaard's own guiding metaphor is a battle between spirit and body, between invisible thought and seductive visibility. For this reason, Plato's stylistic misrelation turns out to very similar to Kierkegaard's description of the battle between morality and wild, 'naked sensuousness' in Schlegel's 'obscene' novel, *Lucinde.* To use the concept put forward by Alice Kuzniar, the early works of Plato are characterized by a Romantic hypervisuality in which intuition seduces and 'overwhelms' the individual. Later on, however, the mature Plato 'masters' the imagination that is now only a humble servant of dialectic thought.

The development from myth to image – that is, from a Romantic to a rationalist image – is described in functional rather than stylistic terms. As a young man, Plato was influenced by Socrates' 'negative dialectics', which, according to Kierkegaard, is a kind of unsteady abstract thinking unable to attain the Idea towards which it is groping. Since the Socratic dialectics fails to 'clamber up to the idea', fantasy stops the restless movement of thought, lies down and begins to dream, and the Idea then becomes present in the static visibility of myth. By Idea, Kierkegaard apparently means individual life as a coherent totality, not far from what the Romantics called the absolute. Thus, mythical intuition is to be understood as a compensation for an impotent dialectics: When the concepts proves to be unable to grasp the individual life in its totality, the mythical 'gains more and more ground, accommodates more and more in itself, [until it] finally acquires such dimensions that all existence becomes visible in it' (*CI* 192).

This swelling of the mythical image from particularity to universality is strongly influenced by Hegel's description of Oriental pantheism.[10] For Kierkegaard, however, the important point is that mythical pantheism only procures an illusory totality. As Kierkegaard explains, the mythical 'discloses itself not as a completion of the inaugurated process but as a completely new beginning' (*CI* 194). Fantasy does not move in the direction of the philosophical totality but only creates an autonomous fragment of aesthetic *Schein* that is 'secterially self-contained' and in violent opposition to its dialectical context.

The mature Plato, however, has moved from Socrates' negative and jumpy dialectics to another kind of thinking that moves towards a *'terminus'* (*CI* 207). Since this type of teleological thinking is able to create speculative totality on its own it is in no need for mythical compensation. This also means that the hostility between dialectics and its supplement has been replaced by a mutual 'friendship' which is, to be sure, controlled by understanding: As *image,* intuition is no more the Other of dialectics but is 'taken up into the dialectical' and reduced to a 'secondary account for younger or less gifted listeners'.

Thus, Kierkegaard mediates between a 'Hegelian' rationalist and a Romantic view of intuition by saying that the Romantics rightly suggest that unmastered imagination contains something profound which cannot be reached by the concepts of understanding; but then adding that this dimension of depth is nothing but an 'Anticipation [of] authentic Platonism' (*CI* 209). It is merely a 'Token of a More Copious Speculation', as the chapter-heading asserts. In this way, Kierkegaard's Romantic theory of the allegorical meaningfulness in mythical intuition is incorporated into a strictly Hegelian narrative. At a certain stage of the spirit's development, understanding is allowed to step aside while imagination enjoys its freedom, but after a while the spirit must leave this kind of imagination behind. As Kierkegaard writes, the mythical has to be 'raised to a higher order of things' in a regular Hegelian *Aufhebung* subjecting the sensual flesh of imagination to the supersensual spirit of conceptuality.

Now and then, Kierkegaard formulates this spiritualisation even more rationalistically than Hegel had done. In the reflective modern world, he says, one has difficulties in even believing that once upon a time mythical images played such an important role. Today, images rather look like an 'antediluvian fossil reminding us of another kind of life that doubt eroded'. Apparently, the journey from pantheistic and muddled Orient to clear-minded Occident is a thing of the past.

Chaos

There are, however, certain features in the chapter that undermine the Hegelian narrative and contradict Kierkegaard's diagnosis of his own Romantic insights as an intellectual type of childhood illness. Hegel depicts the journey from myth to dialectics on the broad canvas of world history but Kierkegaard is clearly more intrigued by the fact that the mythical can 'affirm itself in an isolated individual' (*CI* 192). In *The Concept of Irony*, the milleniums of human history shrink to the story of a single human being, and even this ripening-process tends to vanish into a single moment. In the mythical 'condition', Kierkegaard says, 'there is at every moment a possibility that the mythical will undergo a metamorphosis' (*CI* 191). The development from myth to image is apparently not a development at all, but rather a kind of Kierkegaardian leap.

This foreshortening of the historical perspective transforms the antediluvian fossils of myth into a contemporary phenomenon. Indeed, Kierkegaard finds a 'retrograde movement toward the mythical' in the modern age, and his example is a 'grand and ambitious image' in a text by the Danish-Norwegian Romantic philosopher Henrich Steffens. In this Romantic image, it is possible to distinguish so many different particulars that mastering the multiplicity of sensual 'Nebenvorstellungen' becomes impossible; just as the fertile vines of the Romantic arabesque confuse the understanding and overwhelm the individual. Two pages later, Kierkegaard generalizes this insight, explaining that mythical regression not only befalls effeminate Romantics but threatens every philosophical author: 'Anyone who has anything to do with abstract thinking will certainly have noticed how seductive it is to want to maintain something that actually is not, except when it is annulled'.

Apparently, it is seductive to immobilize the movement of dialectics by means of illusory aesthetic imagery – 'but this is a mythical tendency', Kierkegaard hastens to add (*CI* 194).

This mythical tendency is not only an omnipresent temptation on the road to philosophy, it turns out, but is more than that: the mythical condition is a precondition for philosophical thinking in just the same way that ancient myth was a precondition for the birth of philosophy. Kierkegaard's description of the mythical as a state of mind is influenced by the traditional theory of poetic enthusiasm, as formulated by Plato and reformulated by the Romantics. This relation between myth and inspiration surfaces in one of more puzzling literary images in the chapter: 'the mythical is the idea's flourishing embrace. The idea descends and hovers over the individual like a beneficent cloud' (*CI* 191). The mythical philosopher ('the individual') is here transformed into an enthustiastic poet being inspired by the god. In an early draft of this passage, the individual is impregnated by a shower of gold,[11] but in *The Concept of Irony*, Danae is replaced by Io, whom Jupiter impregnated while disguised as a more ordinary cloud. This displacement from gold to a vague mistiness incorporates the poetic inspiration in an important metaphorical context. A couple of chapters earlier, oriental mysticism had been described as a 'foggy' condition in which 'one is chaotically scrambled and then moves with vague motions in a thick fog' (*CI* 159). Compared to the sky of Greece, the Oriental sky is 'flat and burdensome' and 'hazy and close', so that it 'anxiously sink[s] down', just like the fertile cloud that settles over the writing philosopher. The underlying metaphor – a sinking sky – can be found for the first time in a note from the diary of 1837. Here, Kierkegaard identifies 'Oriental mythologies' with the page in Mozart's *Figaro's Wedding*. In both cases, reflection has not yet been aroused, and this means that intuition dominates and 'multiplicity exerts a pressure' on the individual:

Just as in a room with a low ceiling (…) an extremely complicated and overcrowded painting on the ceiling seems to press down and gives one the feeling that it is sinking down, just so is the heaven of the Orientals, whereas the Greek's light drawings and beautiful forms produce harmony and serenity.[12]

In the terminology of *The Concept of Irony*, the ceiling of the Orientals is painted with overwhelming *myths,* whereas the light drawings of the Greek word are domesticated *images.*

In spite of Kierkegaard's Hegelian concepts and, we could say, his Hegelian intentions in *The Concept of Irony,* his view of textual imagery is heavily influenced by Romanticism. The sovereign spirit has not brushed off intuition on the journey towards self-consciousness, as Hegel puts it.[13] Instead, textual imagery is an uncontrollable but inevitable point of departure for philosophical writing.

The Overgrown Space

Even in Kierkegaard's later works, the mythical chaos of Romanticism functions as a precondition of philosophical writing. In his introduction to the posthumouly published *De omnibus dubitandum est,* Johannes Climacus gives an autobiographical account of the talents that could be seen as preconditions for his own personal approach to philosophical problems. Climacus narrates that he and his father walked around in the living-room in order to train his fantasy by imagining a walking tour around Copenhagen. The resultant kind of hypertrophic imagination creates a 'filled space' that is closely connected to the sinking ceiling of the overcrowded and pantheistic mythical image:

What had entertained him on the walking tours was the filled space into which he could not fit snugly enough. His imagination was so creative that a little went a long way. Outside the one window in the living-room grew approximately ten blades of grass. Here he sometimes discovered a little creature running among the stems. These stems became an enormous forest that still had the compactness and darkness the grass had.[14]

In Schlegelian terms, Climacus' outlook from his Biedermeier interior is an arabesque: an entanglement of organic stems which is so compact and dark that it cannot be penetrated by the clear logic of understanding. This arabesque character is, incidentally, even more evident in Kierkegaard's draft of this passage, in which the space of imagination is called 'the overgrown space' and is filled with lush grass and seaweed.

The relationship between Climacus' overgrown space and the products of Romantic imagination could be developed further. In this context, I must content myself with stating that Climacus does not condemn these compact windings of the imagination but, rather, sees imagination as a necessary condition for evolving philosophy in a better way than the hopelessly abstract Hegelians. A couple of pages later the figure of the grass reemerges in a portrait of himself as a young philosopher: 'everywhere where he had a presentment of a labyrinth, he had to find the way'. Face to face with this labyrinth he took pride in 'penetrating the windings of the difficulties with his will'.

What is wrong with the Hegelian philosophers is precisely that they do not discover the windings of difficulties: they can thus construct their easy system of glittering abstractions without ever confronting the opacity of real life. Therefore, the Romantic imagination with its organic windings is to be understood as a precondition of a more authentic kind of philosophy, not because it is an allegorical way of solving the problems (this is how the Romantics saw it) but because it provides a capacity for difficulty. In other words, imagination is not only an escape from real life but also an acknowledgement of its intractable opacity. This type of philosophical imagination, by the way, cannot be located on the stage of existence as opposed to that of paper, as David Gouwens suggests: it rather comes prior to any distinction between paper and existence.

NOTES

1. David Gouwens 1989, 120.

2. Søren Kierkegaard 1945, 381.

3. Søren Kierkegaard 1989, 189. In the text as *CI;* page references are from the first Danish edition of the dissertation since this pagination can also be found in the Hong & Hong translation.

4. G.W.F. Hegel, *Vorlesungen über die Geschichte der Philosophie,* in Hegel 1970, 18.109.

5. The same relation is emphasized in Christoph Jamme's research on Hegel's influences in 'Platon, Hegel und der Mythos. Zu den Hintergründen eines Diktum aus der Vorrede zur *Phänomenologie des Geistes'.*

6. 'Dem Plato hingegen ist die Darstellung und ihre Vollkommenheit und Schönheit nicht Mittel, sondern Zweck an sich. Darum ist schon seine Form, streng genommen, durchaus poetisch'. Friedrich Schlegel, *Gespräch über die Poesie,* in Fr. Schlegel 1988, 2.207. In the text as *KSF* with references to volume and page numbers. See also the *Athenäum* fragments no. 165 and 450.

7. Ast writes, and Kierkegaard cites: 'Man könnte sagen, daß in den platonischen Gesprächen die philosophischen Darstellungen nur den Zweck haben, den Geist auf die höhere Betrachtung hinzuleiten und zur Anschauung der in den Mythen sinnbildlich geoffenbarten Unendlichkeit und Göttlichkeit vorzubereiten' (*CI* 189).

8. Schlegel 1962, 5.9.

9. Hong and Hong translate 'Billede' with 'metaphor' but I prefer the less rhetorically precise 'image'.

10. Hegel 1970, 12.174.

11. Søren Kierkegaard 1968, *Papirer,* 1. C 124.

12. Kierkegaard 1975, 4.279.

13. Hegel 1970, *Enzyklopädie,* 10.277.

14. Kierkegaard 1985, 121.

BIBLIOGRAPHY

Gouwens, David 1989. *Kierkegaard's Dialectic of the Imagination.* New York.

Hegel, G.W.F. 1970. *Theorie Werkausgabe.* Frankfurt.

Jamme Christoph 1988. 'Platon, Hegel und der Mythos. Zu den Hintergründen eines Diktum aus der Vorrede zur "Phänomenologie des Geistes"'. In: *Hegel-Studien.* (Eds. Friedhelm Nicolin and Otto Pöggeler). Vol. 15. Bonn.

Kierkegaard, Søren 1945. *Concluding Unscientific Postscript.* (Trans. David F. Swenson). London.

Kierkegaard, Søren 1968. *Papirer.* (Ed. Niels Thulstrup). Copenhagen.

Kierkegaard, Søren 1975. *Journals and Papers.* (Trans. Hong & Hong). Bloomington.

Kierkegaard, Søren 1985. *Philosophical Fragments and Johannes Climacus.* (Ed. and trans. Hong & Hong). Princeton.

Kierkegaard, Søren 1989. *The Concept of Irony.* (Ed. and Trans. Hong & Hong). Princeton. (Abbreviated as *CI*)

Schlegel, Friedrich 1962. *Lucinde, Kritische Friedrich-Schlegel-Ausgabe.* (Ed. Ernst Behler). München, Paderborn, Wien.

Schlegel, Friedrich 1988. *Kritische Schriften und Fragmente.* (Eds. Ernst Behler and Hans Eichner). Paderborn. (Abbreviated as *KSF*)

The Romantic Other

William Blake and the Gothic Sublime

Ib Johansen

According to Thomas Weiskel in his classic study *The Romantic Sublime* (1976), William Blake 'offers all the advantages of a perspective truly outside the Romantic sublime'; furthermore, Blake's myth of the Fall – situated, as far as its structural position is concerned, at the very centre of the Blakean universe – may be read as 'an analytic critique of sublimation'.[1] But other scholars, e.g. Morton D. Paley and V.A. De Luca, have been tempted to offer an interpretation of Blake in the light of the poetics of the sublime.[2] V.A. De Luca stresses Blake's 'refusal to allow Nature a role in the propagation of the sublime experience' (239) – in that respect Blake differs from Kant as well as Wordsworth – and what the said critic focuses on in Blake is emphatically a *textual* sublime; in this context it is interesting to notice that De Luca refers to Piranesi and his *carceri d'invenzione* and their 'antihuman sublime' (229), for thus we approach another key-term in eighteenth- and early nineteenth-century aesthetic theory, i.e. the notion of the *Gothic* – a category conceptualized/-thematized in widely divergent ways by Blake's contemporaries, it goes without saying. In Blake's prose fragment 'On Virgil' (etched about 1820) the poet's own use of the term is clearly coloured by his *medievalism,* insofar as 'Gothic' to the eighteenth-century cultural élite came to be 'descriptive of things medieval – in fact, of all things preceding about the middle of the seventeenth century'.[3] 'Grecian is Mathematic Form Gothic is Living Form Mathematic Form is Eternal in The Reasoning Memory. Living Form is Eternal Existence' (Blake 267). Blake's perspective on the Gothic is definitely anti-classic, but to what extent is the Blakean version of the Gothic *sui generis,* and to what extent is it possible to read it in the light of other late eighteenth-century representations of these literary and pictorial codes and conventions?

In David Punter's view, 'Blake builds, with the help of Gothic tools, a universe of man/machine chimeras, of dehumanised men and women and of machines with a curious and malevolent mode of life. In this universe all is threat and violence, and the comfortably traditionalist features of the Gothic are pressed into the service of an all-embracing vision of the horror of the fallen world' (Punter 103-4). Furthermore, Punter regards Blake as a poet 'attracted by the potential political dimensions of Gothic', e.g. in such ballads as 'Gwin, King of Norway' (1783) and 'The Grey Monk' (ca. 1803?) (Punter 101-2). I shall discuss these two poems rather briefly, but besides I shall also focus on Blake's early prophecy *Tiriel* (written ca. 1789 or, possibly, some time between 1785 and 1793).[4] As far as the political dimensions of Blake's Gothicism are concerned, it might also be worthwhile attempting to come to terms with another early prophecy, i.e. *The French Revolution* (1791).

In a recently published critical study, Vijay Mishra's *The Gothic Sublime* (1994), the author makes the two key-terms we have focused on in the preceding paragraphs come together and theorizes them in a new manner, inasmuch as the Gothic sublime is represented as the (hidden, submerged, repressed) Other of the Romantic sublime. According to Mishra, 'The Gothic tropes the sublime as the unthinkable, the unnameable, and the unspeakable, always making it, the sublime, and its basic forms (the rhetorical and the natural) both incommensurable with each other and in excess of language'.[5] As we shall see, William Blake thematizes this self-same problematic in *Tiriel,* when he turns his blind protagonist into (what Deleuze and Guattari have called) *un Oedipe trop gros,*[6] making the latter exceed all established boundaries with regard to patriarchal power through his extravagant use of magical (or pseudo-magical) curses (struggling with his precursor text, Shakespeare's *King Lear*). And in *The French Revolution* the political sublime of the prophecy unseals 'the graves of arch-angels' (Blake 296), turning the events preceding the Fall of the Bastille into a truly apocalyptic scenario; at the centre of this text we once more become acutely aware of the overwhelming impact of that which is in excess of language, of 'the unthinkable, the unnameable, and the unspeakable'.

Two Gothic Ballads

According to David V. Erdman, Blake's 'Gwin, King of Norway', one of the longer *epic* poems (ballads) published in his *Poetical Sketches* (1783), 'is of considerable interest as Blake's earliest and plainest account of a revolution and as evidence of how far he entered imaginatively into the drama of civil conflict'.[7] But together with the ballad 'Fair Elenor' from the same collection of poems 'Gwin, King of Norway' also bears witness to Blake's early interest in the Gothic mode. Like the precursor text *par excellence* of the whole genre, Horace Walpole's *The Castle of Otranto* (1764/65), Blake's ballad is dominated by a 'terrorizing patriarch' (Mishra 54),[8] and furthermore the whole scenario of the poem reminds us of Angela Carter's characterization of the Gothic tradition, where 'Character and events are exaggerated beyond reality, to become symbols, ideas, passions'.[9] The characters are, literally speaking, larger than life, and the ghastly battle scenes of the poem are imbued with an authentically *apocalyptic* aura, inasmuch as the contagious terroristic effects appear to affect the cosmos itself at its very core:

> And now the raging armies rush'd,
>   Like warring mighty seas;
> The Heav'ns are shook with roaring war,
>   The dust ascends the skies!
>
> Earth smokes with blood, and groans, and shakes,
>   To drink her childrens' gore,
> A sea of blood; nor can the eye
>   See to the trembling shore!
> (Blake 410-11)

The war against the 'terrorizing patriarch', i.e. 'Gwin, the son of Nore' (Blake 410), is presented to the reader as a popular uprising, and Gwin is portrayed as a cruel tyrant, whose 'land is desolate' (Blake 409); furthermore, his 'palace' is depicted as an archetypal Gothic castle, whose 'signifying chain (…) draws into itself the human body, the ruthless father, the yielding mother, as well as the thematics of sexual transgression'.[10] Gwin's train of followers literally merges with the site of feudal power, i.e. with the *building* itself; actually, they are *turned into stone,* and in this connection it is interesting to notice that the figure they surround (or circumscribe) in this manner, i.e. the patriarchal ruler (Gwin), appears to have passed over already to *death's other kingdom:*

Like reared stones around a grave
    They stand around the King;
Then suddenly each seiz'd his spear,
    And clashing steel does ring.

(Blake 410)

Feudal power itself is hollow at the core – it is represented as an empty (?) *mausoleum* ('reared stones around a grave'). Nevertheless, it needs an apocalyptic 'sea of blood' (Blake 411) to bring about the *downfall* of this petrified power structure, and the ultimate outcome of such an extreme move (a popular uprising, here led by the giant Gordred) remains somewhat problematic, for Jan Kott's 'Grand Mechanism' cannot be left out of account when it comes to defining the historical scene (or determining what shapes the destinies of the individuals involved in these happenings).[11] Of course, this is the explicit point made by Blake in his poem 'The Grey Monk' (ca. 1803?), where the last stanza summarizes the narrative 'logic' of this 'Grand Mechanism': 'The hand of Vengeance found the Bed / To which the Purple Tyrant fled / The iron hand crushd the Tyrants head / And became a tyrant in his stead' (Blake 481).

Jan Kott in his *Shakespeare Our Contemporary* reads Shakespeare's chronicle plays in the light of the 'metaphor of the grand staircase of history': structurally speaking, according to this simile, 'There are no good and bad kings; there are only kings on different steps of the same stairs'; furthermore, Kott defines the inexorable logic of the 'Grand Mechanism' of history as 'A mechanism according to whose laws the road to power is at the same time the road to death' (32). In 'The Grey Monk' Blake appears, to a certain extent, to subscribe to a similar view when he comes up with the bleak prospect of the eternal return of the same in the final stanza of the poem (cf. above). On the other hand, the poem also foregrounds the main character's (the Grey Monk's) *imitation of Christ:* 'The blood red ran from the Grey Monks side / His hands & feet were wounded wide …', etc. (Blake 480). What Blake elsewhere terms 'intellectual war' appears to offer a viable alternative to the entropic pull of the forces of secular (feudal) history: 'For a Tear is an Intellectual Thing / And a Sigh is the Sword of an Angel King / And the bitter groan of the Martyrs woe / Is an Arrow from the Almighties Bow' (Blake 481). The warfare of the *miles Christianus* thus seems to be altogether different from the atrocities and the universal bloodshed thematized in the battle scenes in 'Gwin, King of Norway'. But on the other hand, the poetics of 'intellectual war' – and the glorification of medieval ecclesiasticism – is nevertheless, in the last resort, subordinated to the narrative rules of the Gothic mode, for the ultimate outcome of this spiritual confrontation, i.e. the confrontation between tyrant and martyr, is pointed out at the very end of the ballad where the bloody triumph of the 'Grand Mechanism' appears to be the last word on this controversial issue.

In some respects Blake is close to a kind of political quietism in 'The Grey Monk', or at least this is the case when he articulates in a rather clear-cut manner his *pacifist* message: 'The Hermits Prayer & the Widows tear / Alone can free the World from fear', etc. (Blake 481). But on the other hand, we must not forget that the very opening of the ballad touches upon forbidden or tabooed areas, where an erotic link appears to be established between the Monk on his stony bed and the desperate mother (his lover?), who makes her appearance in the first line: 'I die I die the Mother said / My Children die for lack of Bread / What more has the merciless Tyrant said / The Monk sat down on the Stony Bed…' (Blake 480). The dynamics of (narrative) desire is at least hinted at in this equivocal episode, where we are incidentally reminded of Ambrosio's hidden desires and overstepping of sexual taboos within the four wall of his cell in Matthew Gregory Lewis' *The Monk* (1796). Anyway, what is at stake here is still, in Vijay Mishra's words, 'the human body, the ruthless father (i.e. the tyrant), the yielding mother, as well as the thematics of sexual transgression'.

Tiriel's Quest

In the Longman edition of *The Poems of William Blake,* edited by W.H. Stevenson (with a text established by David V. Erdman, 1971), Blake's early prophecy *Tiriel* is explicitly related to the Gothic tradition: '(…) it seems that [Blake] was attempting to write a 'pure' but 'Gothic' tragic poem about aged tyranny'.[12] The protagonist of the poem thus appears to live up to his prototypical role as a 'terrorizing patriarch' (Mishra), and in this connection the prophecy itself also echoes its canonic precursor, i.e. Shakespeare's *King Lear* (written some time between 1604 and 1606) – a tragedy about 'the problematicalness and break-up of the feudal family' (Georg Lukács),[13] but also a play where the main character's *madness* is presented as an all-important thematic issue. In *Tiriel* there is a close parallel to Shakespeare's tragedy, inasmuch as the protagonist himself is aware of his lunacy: '(…) Did I not command you saying / Madness & deep dismay posses[s] the heart of the blind man / The wanderer who seeks the woods leaning upon his staff' (Blake 276). Tiriel, who is 'king of the west' (Blake 275), is both mad and blind, and thus the prophecy also establishes a link to the subplot in *King Lear*, focusing on the Earl of Gloucester and his two sons (Gloucester is blinded in an extremely cruel manner by one of Lear's sons-in-law and by Lear's daughter Regan).

The exact time when Blake wrote *Tiriel* has not been established, but according to the modern editor of the manuscript (who published it in a facsimile edition together with a series of drawings by Blake himself illustrating the epic poem in 1967), i.e. G.E. Bentley Jr., 'The agreed-upon date of 1789 seems satisfactory enough if we recognize that none of our evidence would very convincingly contradict a date as much as, perhaps, four years on either side of this one'.[14] However that may be, 1789 is certainly a decisive year in European history, i.e. the first year of the French Revolution, and insofar as Blake's *Tiriel* focuses on such political topics as the feudal/patriarchal family, the absolute power of the monarch, the relationship between master and slave, etc., etc., the historical context of the poem appears to be highly significant; inasmuch as Tiriel's sons have managed to bring about the downfall of their father already before the opening of the poem, we may perhaps trace an oblique reference to contemporary revolutionary events, but on the other hand the prophecy does not seem to offer a viable political alternative to the claustrophobic universe of the *ancien régime,* i.e. a social world governed by the iron hand of 'aged tyranny'.[15] With regard to its historical references, its web of allusions to contemporary political events, etc., etc., the precise date of the poem thus appears to be *undecidable.*

According to Ronald Paulson in his brilliant study *Representations of Revolution* (1789-1820), 'The gothic did in fact serve as a metaphor with which some contemporaries in England tried to understand what was happening across the channel in the 1790s [...and] if one way of dealing with the Revolution (in its earliest stages) was to see the castle-prison through the eyes of a sensitive young girl who responds to terror in the form of forced marriage and stolen property, another was to see it through the case history of her threatening oppressor, Horace Walpole's Manfred or M.G. Lewis's Ambrosio (...)'.[16] Paulson suggests that the popularity 'was due in part to the widespread anxieties and fears in Europe aroused by the turmoil in France finding a kind of sublimation or catharsis in tales of darkness, confusion, blood, and horror' (220-21). In this connection it is worthwhile bearing in mind that de Sade himself in his famous 'Reflections on the Novel' (1800) characterized works like Lewis' and Ann Radcliffe's Gothic romances as 'the inevitable result of the revolutionary shocks which all of Europe has suffered (…)'.[17]

The plot in Blake's *Tiriel* is structured as a quest: the protagonist (Tiriel) starts by leaving his western kingdom, apparently in search of his origin(s), i.e. his itinerary traces a route to an eastern quasi-paradisaical (or would-be-paradisaical) region, where he encounters his own parents, the aged couple Har and Heva, whose *senility* is obvious and who are therefore nursed by (what appears to be) their own mother, Mnetha, whose very name suggests that she may be regarded as a powerful feminine deity (cf. the anagrammatic allusion to Athena, the Greek Goddess of Reason), but who may also be associated with 'Mnemosyne or Memory', referred to later in Blake's 'A Vision of the Last Judgment' (1810), where her inferior ontological status, compared to 'Inspiration', is explicitly thematized (*Tiriel* 6-7).[18] Later Tiriel travels back to his starting-point (apparently following a different route), and after having killed (by means of his curses) most of his sons and daughters *at one fell blow,* he once more goes back to 'the vales of Har' in the East, this time with his surviving youngest daughter Hela as his guide or *psychopomp.* After he has cursed his own father Har as the 'Mistaken father of a lawless race' (Blake 282), Tiriel's own journey comes to an abrupt end, when he ceases 'outstretched at Har & Hevas feet in awful death' (Blake 282). The structure of Tiriel's quest is thus rather extraordinary, inasmuch as his search for his own (place of) origin appear to be a *double* failure: the first time he reaches the vales of Har, he realizes that the pastoral serenity of this setting disagrees with his preestablished ontological position in the scheme of things, but the second time his violent and destructive behaviour actually (and inevitably) leads to his *own* death, accompanied as he is this time by Hela, the (Nordic) Goddess of Death – making him *autodestruct,* as it were.

When he first visits the *hortus conclusus* of his senile ancestors (Har, Heva, and Mnetha), Tiriel becomes aware of the fact that he belongs to a *Gothic* rather than a *pastoral* universe: 'My Journey is oer rocks & mountains, not in pleasant vales / I must not sleep nor rest because of madness and dismay' (Blake 276). His quest is also a search for his own identity, but during his whole journey his surroundings invariably turn out to be mistaken with regard to this identity: Mnetha does not recognize him, inasmuch as she still believes that 'Tiriel is king of the west' (Blake 275) and not a homeless wanderer, Heva (his mother) first thinks that he is 'my Tiriels old father' (Blake 275), but afterwards calls him 'old Tiriel' (Blake 275), whereas his brother Ijim regards him as a *demon* who has assumed the 'form of Tiriel blind & old' (cf. Blake 277-78)! Like Lear he has become an outcast, and like his Shakespearean predecessor he has been turned into 'Tiriel's shadow' (cf. the Fool's answer to Lear's question in the first act, scene iv, in Shakespeare's *King Lear*: 'Who is it that can tell me who I am? / *Fool*. Lear's shadow', I, iv, 238-39).[19] Tiriel also 'dissemblingly' tries to *fake* a purely fictitious identity as a wanderer from the North (Blake 275).

Of course, the Gothic mode in itself may be said to thematize an inherent drift towards *madness:* from the frantic behaviour of Walpole's arch-villain Manfred in *The Castle of Otranto* (1764/65) to the psychopathological excesses of E.T.A. Hoffmann's and Edgar Allan Poe's fear-ridden and haunted protagonists this psychotic symptomatology certainly seems to be present as a structural element within the Gothic tradition. Thus David Punter in his reading of Poe's 'The Fall of the House of Usher' (1839) focuses on the word 'madman' as the key-word of the whole text: '"Madman" is the hidden word on which the story has throughout hinged (...)', i.e. a 'primal scream [breaking] up the webs of reason and superstition which, in their interlocking, have sustained the house's apparent coherence' (Punter 206).[20] Tiriel's madness functions in a similar way in Blake's prophecy, insofar as it turns out to be highly contagious, and in a certain sense 'characterizes the actions of all the principal characters in the poem' (*Tiriel* 15).

In the symbolic geography of the Middle Ages the East *(oriens)* is the place of origin: According to the medieval theologian Pierre Bercheur's famous *Repertorium, vulgo Dictionarium morale,* the sinner always plans 'to go to the East, i.e. to Paradise, and nevertheless he constantly goes to the West, i.e. to Hell (...)'.[21] In Shakespeare's *King Lear* the spiritual pilgrimage undertaken by Gloucester and Edgar towards the white cliffs of Dover is imbued with a similar allegorical significance, and in Blake's *Tiriel* the protagonist's triple journey likewise fits in with this cosmological symbolism, inasmuch as Tiriel seems to be unable to make up his mind where he should take up permanent residence: in the vales of Har in the East or in his own (former) kingdom in the West. Nevertheless, Har's and Heva's quasi-paradisaical garden plot may be said to represent a degraded version of its mythical prototype, where Tiriel's parents – like Adam and Eve – rather stand for what Blake has elsewhere called 'Unorganizd Innocence. An Impossibility' (Blake 763), i.e. what we are confronting is a terrestrial Eden *gone sour:*

And Har & Heva like two Children sat beneath the Oak
Mnetha now aged waited on them. & brought them food & clothing
But they were as the shadow of Har. & as the years forgotten
Playing with flowers. & running after birds they spent the day
And in the night like infants slept delighted with infant dreams
(Blake 274)

Vincent Arthur De Luca notices that the majority of Blake's travellers 'are a hapless lot – figures who either wander back and forth over the same stretch of land, like Tiriel, or who go nowhere at all as they yearn for the traveller's destination like the Sun-flower of *Songs of Experience,* or who travel vicariously through the self-repeating lives of others, or who are simply lost, like the dreaming Traveller "under the Hill" in the Epilogue to *The Gates of Paradise'.*[22] In their second childhood Har and Heva are certainly unable to come to terms with the reality principle, and Tiriel cannot possibly find rest in their would-be paradise. Furthermore, the protagonist's inability to leave this region for good suggests that he is somehow inextricably caught up in the family universe – a claustrophobic setting insofar as all the characters mentioned in *Tiriel* 'are members of one enormous family' (*Tiriel* 1). The mechanism that may be discerned behind the huge family tree in this prophecy appears to be what Deleuze and Guattari have called *oedipalization,* for 'It is obvious that when traditional psychoanalysis explains that the instructor is the father, and that the colonel too is the father, and that the mother is nonetheless the father too, it reduces all of desire to a familial determination that has no longer anything to do with the social field actually invested by the libido'.[23] It is obvious that there is an Oedipal – or quasi-Oedipal – conflict at the very centre of the plot in Blake's *Tiriel,* where the father kills most of his sons and leaves only one daughter out of five alive. In a truly Girardian manner all male relations in the prophecy are actually based on mutual violence![24] In this perspective the *plague* that Tiriel calls down upon the heads of his children after he has returned to his lost kingdom takes on a special significance. In Girard's words, 'The Plague is universally presented as a process of undifferentiation, a destruction of specificities (…) Social hierarchies are first transgressed, then abolished. Political and religious authorities collapse (…)'.[25] But this drift towards undifferentiation is also a trend that characterizes the Gothic as well as the grotesque: '(…) both gothic and grotesque focus on the moment of estrangement, the transition between this world and that [i.e. a world under the influence of demonic forces], when plant and human are in metamorphosis and in the process of growing indistinguishable'.[26]

We may notice this bias in one of the drawings illustrating Blake's *Tiriel* (Har and Heva Bathing, Drawing No. 2), where the undulating hair and beard of the two bathers take on a strange, plantlike quality and (almost) merge with the long white ripples of the darkened, but still translucent pool (*Tiriel* 37). But the drift towards undifferentiation may also be read in the light of Freud's emphasis on the (omni-presence of the) *death instinct*, for according to Freud in *Beyond the Pleasure Principle* (1920), the first instinct to come into being was 'the instinct to return to the inani-mate state', and 'If we are to take it as a truth that knows no exception that every-thing living dies for *internal* reasons – becomes inorganic once again – then we shall be compelled to say that '*the aim of all life is death*' and, looking backwards, that '*inanimate things existed before living ones*'.[27] When Tiriel curses his sons for the first time (before setting out on his initial eastward journey), he actually characterizes himself in terms that thematize the primordial importance of the inorganic world (cf. also the way Gwin's warriors are turned into stone in 'Gwin, King of Norway', cf. above): 'Look at my eyes blind as the orbless scull among the stones / Look at my bald head (…)' (Blake 274). At this moment Tiriel is standing in front of the gates of his former palace with his dying wife Myratana in his arms, and actually he uses her as a kind of Medusa's head to turn his surroundings (and himself) *into stone*. In this perspective monarchy itself is hollow at the core (an 'orbless scull') whereas its para-phernalia (the stones) represent a state of utter lifelessness, and in this context it is worthwhile bearing in mind that what distinguishes inorganic nature is that it lacks all the *tensions* that characterize organic life and contribute to establishing *vital differ-ences* within this extensive, *polymorphous* field.

What approaches Blake's *Tiriel* to the Gothic tradition is not only its focus on a 'terrorizing patriarch', its emphasis on the theme of madness, and the fact that the characters tend to become more and more alike in terms of their behavioural code and psychological make-up. In a different sense what the prophecy also thematizes is what Vijay Mishra in *The Gothic Sublime* has termed the *oceanic sublime,* where 'the death instinct is momentarily triumphant' (Mishra 37), and when Blake makes his irate protagonist let loose the plague among his hapless sons and daughters, the nar-rative itself reminds us of another version of the (Gothic) sublime, i.e. the apocalyp-tic sublime – a type of sublimity that bring us very close to the edge or (in Vijay Mishra's words) to 'that horrible Gothic metaphor that would image the end of the world itself' (Mishra 157). The primary example of this kind of romance in Mishra's study is Mary Shelley's *The Last Man* (1826) (Mishra 157), but the said critic's characterization of the genre (or mode) in question might equally well be applied to Blake's eschatological extravaganza, where 'all the sons & daughters of Tiriel / Chaind in thick darkness utterd cries of mourning all the night / And in the morning Lo an hundred men in ghastly death / The four daughters stretchd on the marble pavement silent all / falln by the pestilence…' (Blake 279): in Mishra's words, 'Gothic apocalyptic narratives portray a world exhausted and otiose, anxious about itself and wary of any further participation in the processes of life' (Mishra 157), and this certainly summarizes the prevalent feeling of imminent ruin and extinction that seems to dominate the whole narrative. And yet this oversized patriarch, who has outgrown all 'normal' proportions like his legendary forebear in Walpole's *The Castle of Otranto,* the arch-ancestor Alfonso, 'dilated to an immense magnitude',[28] this *Oedipe trop gros* (Deleuze and Guattari), has to follow an extremely sinuous route on his way towards death, for we must also have in mind Michel de Certeau's illuminating comment on the Oedipus complex (and original parricide):

The 'father' does not die. His 'death' is only another legend and his law remains. Everything takes place as if it were forever impossible to kill this deceased father, and as if 'taking account' of him (…) just meant that he is simply displaced once more, and that he is precisely where we do not yet suspect his presence, in this self-same knowledge [i.e. a modern, secular, demystified knowledge belonging to a disenchanted world] and in the 'profit' this knowledge seems to ascertain.[29]

Apocalypse Now

Blake's political prophecy *The French Revolution* (1791) – a poem apparently left unfinished by the poet, inasmuch as only one book out of the seven announced ever materialized – may also be read in the light of the tradition of the Gothic sublime. The setting actually contrasts a series of sinister, Piranesi-like exteriors (the Bastille, the Louvre, etc.) with the wide-open spaces of a revolutionary dawn, where 'There is a morning of reason rising upon man on the subject of government, that has not appeared before (…)'.[30] According to Michel Foucault in 'The Eye of Power' (1977), 'A fear haunted the latter half of the eighteenth century: the fear of darkened spaces, of the pall of gloom which prevents the full visibility of things, men and truths (…) During the Revolutionary period the Gothic novels develop a whole fantasy world of stone walls, darkness, hideouts and dungeons which harbour, in significant complicity, brigands and aristocrats, monks and traitors'.[31] In Blake's *The French Revolution* the seven (allegorical) towers of the Bastille constitute a gloomy Gothic *tableau vivant,* where the hopeless situation of the prisoners is elaborated in a series of terrifying snapshots:

> In the seventh tower, nam'd the tower
> 　of God, was a man
> Mad, with chains loose, which he dragg'd up and down; fed with
> 　hopes year by year, he pined
> For liberty; vain hopes: his reason decay'd, and the world of attraction
> 　in his bosom
> Center'd, and the rushing of chaos overwhelm'd his dark soul…
> (Blake 284-85)

However, even this dark region – culminating in the seventh tower, in accordance with the narrative logic of the Gothic mode, with the triumph of *madness* over Apollonian clarity – is somehow pried open by the new revolutionary forces and ready to burst, as it were, for 'the dens shook and trembled, the prisoners look up and assay to shout; they listen, / Then laugh in the dismal den, then are silent, and a light walks round the dark towers' (Blake 285).

In accordance with their Biblical precedent, the revolutionary events themselves are envisaged in apocalyptic terms as a cosmic harvest, while the Duke of Burgundy expresses the eschatological fears of the representatives of the *ancien régime:* 'Shall this marble built heaven become a clay cottage, this earth an oak stool, and these mowers / From the Atlantic mountains, mow down all this great starry harvest of six thousand years?' (Blake 286). Of course, this agricultural symbolism may be read in the light of Christ's parable of the good seed and the tares in Matthew, Chapter 13, where Jesus advises his followers to let both grow together 'until the harvest: and in the time of the harvest I will say to the reapers, Gather ye together first the tares, and bind them in bundles to burn them: but gather the wheat into my barn' (Math. 13,30). What the aristocratic élite (the Duke of Burgundy) actually fears in the passage just quoted, however, is precisely that the process of undifferentiation is going to result in the universal breakdown of the hierarchical principle as such – placing heaven and earth, high and low, and palace and cottage *on the same (inferior) level,* as it were. In this context the 'mowers / From the Atlantic mountains' remind us of the American revolutionaries, who had fought for their freedom in the War of Independence only a few years earlier (a political theme Blake actually takes up later in *America a Prophecy,* 1793).

According to Michel Foucault, the revolutionaries had a dream, i.e. 'the dream of a transparent society, visible and legible in each of its parts, the dream of there no longer existing any zones of darkness, zones established by the privileges of royal power or the prerogatives of some corporation, zones of disorder' (152). In Blake's *The French Revolution* what Starobinski has termed 'the solar myth of the revolution'[32] gradually takes over the rhetorical universe of the poem: at the beginning of the prophecy, 'The dead brood over Europe, the cloud and vision descends over chearful France…' (Blake 282), and 'the morning cloud' is pale in the King's 'visage' (Blake 283); but at the end of *The French Revolution* 'the morning cloud' no longer overshadows the landscape(s), for at this point the Senate, i.e. the National Assembly, 'in peace, sat beneath morning's beam' (Blake 296). However, the apocalyptic turmoil of the prophecy has not managed altogether to dispel the ghosts of the (feudal) past, where 'The dead brood over Europe…' (Blake 282). At the end of the first book of the poem the King (Louis the Sixteenth) and his satellites are still very active as far as their counterrevolutionary activities are concerned, and even if the cataclysmic events in France have shaken the ancient regimes all over Europe, the apocalyptic imagery used by Blake to articulate this historical conjuncture remains somewhat ambiguous and open to more than one interpretation: 'And the bottoms of the world were open'd and the graves of arch-angels unseal'd; / The enormous dead, lift up their pale fires and look over the rocky cliffs' (Blake 296). Does this imply that a senescent and moribund monarchy, based on patriarchal power, is finally terminated? Or are the 'enormous dead' actually the dead *kings* of Europe, who have somehow obtained a new lease of life, whatever may be the reason for this sudden turn? And why have these 'arch-angels' been buried in the first place? Is this the ultimate metaphysical outcome of the Fall of Man – or the Fall of the Rebel Angels? A Bakhtinian reading might see in the 'enormous dead' an allusion to the ancestral body of the common people or carnival crowd (celebrating the triumph of a popular uprising). But maybe this reading is a little too optimistic, and the 'pale fires' introduced at this strategic point should perhaps give us warning that Blake has borrowed his metaphorical weaponry in another poet's arsenal, for behind his imagery we may locate the bitter sarcasm of Shakespeare's misanthropic protagonist in his *Timon of Athens* (written some time between 1604 and 1608?), where Timon reflects on the universality of 'thievery': 'The sun's a thief, and with his great attraction / Robs the vast sea; the moon's an arrant thief, / And her *pale fire* she snatches from the sun', etc., etc. (cf. IV, iii, 439-41).[33] The French revolutionaries actually 'robbed' the classical world just as Blake borrowed (or stole) from Shakespeare. And just as the Jacobins and their followers dressed up in Roman togas, Blake raids the poetical repositories of his precursors – and blows wide open the political firmament as well as the Gothic castle-prison. His pale fires (like those of his latter-day descendent Nabokov) are nonetheless capable of illuminating some of the most remote and obscure recesses on the metaphysical map – even if political correctness still demands that you should always already be sitting stock-still somewhere in the neighbourhood with an umbrella and a sewing-machine 'beneath morning's beam' and wait for the appropriate signals from Urizen's train in the sky, i.e. from your invisible masters!

NOTES

1. Thomas Weiskel 1986, 65 and 68. The references to Blake are to *The Poetry and Prose of William Blake,* edited by David V. Erdman. In the following Blake with page references in the text. Furthermore, I have made use of William Blake: *Tiriel.* Facsimile and Transcript of the Manuscript, Reproduction of the Drawings, and a Commentary on the Poem by G.E. Bentley, Jr. In the following notes simply referred to as: *Tiriel.*

2. Morton D. Paley 1970, 1ff; V.A. De Luca 1986, 218-41. Cf. also Vincent Arthur De Luca 1991.

3. David Punter 1980, 5.

4. Cf. *Tiriel* 1967, 51: 'The agreed-upon date of 1789 seems satisfactory enough if we recognize that none of our evidence would very convincingly contradict a date as much as, perhaps, four years on either side of this one.'

5. Vijay Mishra 1994, 23. In the following Mishra with page numbers in the text.

6. Cf. Gilles Deleuze and Félix Guattari: *Kafka. Pour une littérature mineure* 1975, 17-28 (Chapitre 2: 'Un Oedipe trop gros'). Cf.Vijay Mishra, *op. cit.,* 40: '(...) the sublime castrates, it humiliates by its (phallic) grandeur.' Mishra also regards the Gothic sublime as 'a collective disempowerment under the sign of patriarchal power' (*ibid.* 40).

7. David V. Erdman 1969, 20.

8. On the *personage régnant* of Walpole's precursor text: 'Manfred, the terrorizing patriarch, is presented as an agitated and high-strung occupant of a castle that he cannot contain within his consciousness – so much so that the castle will begin to have an independent existence'.

9. Angela Carter: *Fireworks. Nine Stories in Various Disguises,* New York , 1982 (originally published in 1974), Afterword, 133.

10. Vijay Mishra 1994, 52: 'The castle is a signifying chain that draws into itself the human body, the ruthless father, the yielding mother, as well as the thematics of sexual transgression (…) For "castle" is a *mise-en-scene,* a nightmare house, a site of sexual, genealogical and psychological struggles (…)'.

11. Jan Kott 1965, 7 ff.

12. *William Blake* (Ed. W.H. Stevenson) 1972, 74.

13. Cf. Georg Lukács: *The Historical Novel,* Harmondsworth 1976, 106-7.

14. Cf. note 4.

15. David V. Erdman finds allusions in *Tiriel* – characterized by Erdman as 'a kind of satiric drama we might call the histrionic grotesque' – to 'the first prolonged mental illness of King George, which lasted from the spring of 1788 to the spring of 1789 with a middle period of considerable violence' (David V. Erdman: *Blake: Prophet Against Empire, op.cit.* 131, 134). Tiriel's madness thus parallels the madness of George III, and the English King had likewise lost vast territories in the West (the American Colonies)! However this may be, Erdman's reading of the prophecy as a historical allegory seems to offer a somewhat *narrow* perspective on *Tiriel,* for such allusions to contemporary events – to the extent they may be discovered in the text – may not always provide us with relevant historical details/materials.

16. Ronald Paulson 1983, 217-18.

17. The Marquis de Sade: *The 120 Days of Sodom and other writings,* New York 1966, Reflections on the Novel, 109.

18. According to Bentley Jr., 'Mnetha is clearly, in the context of *Tiriel,* memory and conventional wisdom, and her charges Har and Heva have nothing of Inspiration about them (…)' (7). Cf. E 545 on the beginning of the Iron Age, begot by Jupiter on 'Mnemosyne or Memory' (!). But *Mnetha* may *also* contain an oblique reference to 'Lethe', the river in the Greek underworld that brings about *oblivion.* Thus a narrow-minded focus on 'Mnemosyne or Memory' may result in a fatal, Heideggerian *Seinsvergessenheit* ('forgetfulness of Being')!

19. William Shakespeare: *King Lear.* (Ed. Kenneth Muir). London 1961, 48 (I, iv, 239-29).

20. Cf. also my article on Poe, 'The Madness of the Text. Deconstruction of Narrative Logic in "Usher", "Berenice" and "Doctor Tarr and Professor Fether"'. In: *Poe Studies. Dark Romanticism: History, Theory, Interpretation,* Vol. 22, No.1, June 1989, 1 ff.

21. Pierre Bercheur: *Petri Berchorii…Opera omnia,* Vol. 3 (Coloniae Agrippinae: apud Joannem Wilhelmum Friessem juniorem, 1692), 325. (My translation).

22. Vincent Arthur De Luca 1991, 58.

23. Gilles Deleuze and Félix Guattari 1977, 62: *Anti-Oedipus. Capitalism and Schizophrenia.*

24. René Girard 1972, pp. 76. Girard notices on the Oedipus myth (complex): 'Si Oedipe finit par tuer Laïos, c'est Laïos, le premier, qui s'est efforcé de le tuer…' (!).

25. René Girard 1988, 136-37.

26. Paulson 1983, 237.

27. Sigmund Freud 1920, 32. Inasmuch as Tiriel is represented as an emissary from death's (other) kingdom, who carries with him the deadly germs, as it were, it is interesting to notice that a similarly negative portrayal of the lethal qualities of various royal characters may be found in *The Compendious History of Foolish, Wicked, Wise and Good Kings…,* Printed by order of the Long Parliament, 1641, 2nd edition (London: Printed for J. Baker, R. Burleigh and A. Dod, 1716), where evil kings have likewise been turned into carriers of death, insofar as the text refers to 'a Man that hates Peace, and *loves Death'* (x), and the moral is summarized in the following manner: 'Behold *Death* and *Evil* is set before us in the following examples of the Kings, who, though dead, yet speak much to the Instruction of the Living' (xii).

28. Quoted from Peter Fairclough 1979, 145.

29. Michel de Certeau 1975, 307-8. (My translation).

30. Thomas Paine: *Rights of Man,* Harmondsworth, Middlesex: Penguin Books, (reprinted 1971), 230.

31. Michel Foucault: 'The Eye of Power. A conversation with Jean-Pierre Barou and Michelle Perrot'. In: Michel Foucault 1980, 153-54.

32. Jean Starobinski 1979, 31-37: 'Le mythe solaire de la révolution'. Starobinski characterizes this (universal) metaphor as 'une image apollinienne, indéfiniment répétée' (31). Cf. in this context also my reading of *The French Revolution* in 'The Fires of Orc. William Blake and the Rhetoric of Revolutionary Discourse'. In: Anders Iversen 1990, 55-61.

33. William Shakespeare: *Timon of Athens.* (Ed. H.J. Oliver). London 1965, 115 (IV, iii, 439-41, my italics).

BIBLIOGRAPHY

Blake, William 1970. *The Poetry and Prose of William Blake.* (Ed. David V. Erdman, commentary by Harold Bloom). New York. (Abbreviated as Blake)

Blake, William 1972. *The Poems of William Blake.* (Ed. W.H. Stevenson; text by David V. Erdman). London and New York. (Originally published in 1971)

Blake, William 1967. *Tiriel.* Facsimile and Transcript of the Manuscript, Reproduction of the Drawings, and a Commentary on the Poem. (Ed. G.E. Bentley, Jr.) Oxford.

Certeau, Michel de 1975. *L'Écriture de l'histoire.* Paris.

Deleuze, Gilles and Félix Guattari 1977. *Anti-Oedipus. Capitalism and Schizophrenia.* (Translated from the French by Robert Hurley, Mark Seem, and Helen R. Lane). New York.

De Luca, Vincent Arthur 1986. 'A Wall of Words: The Sublime as Text'. *Unnam'd Forms. Blake and Textuality.* (Eds. Nelson Hilton and Thomas A. Vogler). Berkeley, Los Angeles, London.

De Luca, Vincent Arthur 1991. *Words of Eternity. Blake and the Poetics of the Sublime.* Princeton, New Jersey.

Erdman, David E. 1969. *Blake: Prophet Against Empire. Revised Edition.* New York.

Fairclough, Peter (Ed.) 1979. *Three Gothic Novels.* With an Introductory Essay by Mario Praz. Harmondsworth.

Freud, Sigmund 1920. *Beyond the Pleasure Principle.* (Trans. and Ed. James Strachey). Standard Edition Vol. 18 (GW Bd. 13). London.

Foucault, Michel 1980. *Power/Knowledge. Selected Interviews and Other Writings* 1972-1977. (Ed. Colin Gordon; trans. Colin Gordon, Leo Marshall, John Mepham, and Kate Soper). New York.

Girard, René 1972. *La violence et le sacré.* Paris.

Girard, René 1988. *'To double business bound'. Essays on Literature, Mimesis, and Anthropology.* Baltimore.

Iversen, Anders (Ed.) 1990. *The Impact of the French Revolution on English Literature.* (*The Dolphin*, No. 19). Aarhus.

Kott, Jan 1965. *Shakespeare Our Contemporary.* London. Reprinted 1965.

Mishra, Vijay 1994. *The Gothic Sublime.* Albany. (Abbreviated as Mishra)

Paley, Morton D. 1970. *Energy and the Imagination. A Study of the Development of Blake's Thought.* Oxford.

Paulson, Ronald 1983. *Representations of Revolution (1789-1820).* New Haven and London.

Punter, David 1980. *The Literature of Terror. A History of Gothic Fictions from 1765 to the present day.* London and New York.

Starobinski, Jean 1979. 1789. *Les emblèmes de la raison.* Paris.

Weiskel, Thomas 1986. *The Romantic Sublime: Studies in the Structure and Psychology of Transcendence.* Baltimore and London. (Originally published in 1976)

Schelling and the Unconscious of a Work of Art

Cecilia Sjöholm

Poetry and Difference

Romanticism is a paradoxical and contradictory movement: acknowledging the productive forces of differences, including sexual difference, whilst carrying a quest for identity; acknowledging an existence that is characterised by loss, absence and conflict whilst carrying a vision of its reconciliation. The concept of reconciliation has all too often come to summarize what Romanticism stands for alone. Here, I would rather like to stress its worrying anti-thesis. The recognition of finitude, limits and boundaries has provoked the desire to transgress these boundaries.

To some extent this can also explain why male Romantics have a complicated relation to the feminine other. Romantic authors tend to revere or exclude, worship or denigrate her. The feminine in male Romanticism often becomes a symptom of a lack or split which makes Romantic poetry painfully self-conscious. Representing the good, woman turns up in the guise of nature, mother-figure, muse, goddess, or some other mythical being. Representing the bad, she comes in the guise of death, of the prostitute, of chaos and night. Torn between these split images of the good and the bad, the male Romantic subject makes woman a cause rather than a symptom of his torments. The reason for this lies in the logic of how the male, specular subject of Romanticism maps itself as self-consciousness.

The specular subject of Romanticism, as Paul de Man has shown, reflects a consciousness of death that it is trying to move away from. Death, in fact, uncovers itself in the very moment that the text is striving towards: the experience of God, the truthfulness of an idea, or of an absolute presence. The Romantic text stages the moment when man, incomparable with the infinity of nature, becomes mortal.

Consciousness of finitude, or of death, shows its face in the Romantic text as a specular, or spectral reflection: in the experience of the sublime, the flight of the titanic moment, visions of a lost paradise. Romanticism is not other-worldly. It is the period when men become gods for each other, René Girard has said, quoted on this by Paul de Man.[1] The titanic moment of godliness lingers in the text, but its absence dominates the Romantic project as such.

God has become man, we are told. Reading the romantic text, however, it often seems closer at hand to state that God has become woman. That which is reminiscent of death, of loss, and of lack, which prevents that godly moment from fulfilling itself, often has a feminine face. Woman has come to represent finitude, she is the flesh, the bodily shape that haunts the male ego. This is the case in Johan Erik Stagnelius, a Swedish Romantic, who made the figure of 'Amanda' for his deadly twin soul: in her most perfected form, she represents his ego-ideal, beyond the desire of the flesh, signifying the purity of his own soul. But should he succumb to the worldly representation of the woman with the name Amanda, he is surely doomed to a terrible death, to be devoured by worms under the ground. In Wordsworth, the figure of Lucy reads as a signal from beyond the beautiful, while the prostitute meets in town. And in Schlegel's egalitarian love-tale of *Lucinde* the beautiful dying female heroine fulfills the well-structured dialectic between two complementary sexes. The task of woman is to show the secret of love, and this she does at the end of the novel. The beloved of the male hero appears in his feverish hallucinations, in the guise of a wonderful goddess of death, upheaving sexual difference and the suffering of loss in an erotic vision.

In all these cases, it is possible to read woman as a double figure: as death, on the one hand, but also as the silvered glass of the mirror which makes reflection possible. She gives birth to a self-conscious male poet, the Romantic 'ego' or 'I', the subject of Romantic mythmaking. His privileged access to hidden truths is linked to his discovery of the feminine.

Schelling and Poetic Productivity

The example of Friedrich Schelling shows that we must be wary of regarding the male Romantic or Idealist as someone who is merely trying to consolidate the notion of identity, and likewise, where the deadly woman disappears. Schelling's *System des transcendentalen Idealismus* (1800) is often referred to as a paradigm of Romantic poetics. Schelling was a radical revolutionary in his youth, and later became a philosopher of religion. Compared to Hegel, who was his student, Schelling has been considered as philosophically inconsistent, a prodigy à la mode in the neurotic circles of doomed intellectuals, caught in the feverish pangs of dying feudalism.

It would perhaps be possible to read Schelling's notion of the unconscious as a post-Kantian feminization of matter. In Irigaray's account, Kant's copernican turn from the thing-in-itself to the transcendental subject has created a philosophy of distance and exclusion. Male philosophical discourse is a specular construction, and places woman outside of the field of speculation. Woman is *nothing* where man is *being,* she is *difference* where man is *identity,* she is beyond the one, the similar, the visible. Luce Irigaray reads the metaphors of speculative philosophy as projections of the male will to extinguish sexual difference – the mirror reflects the same, sun and fire are images of male power, Plato's cave reflects the feminine inside in a vision of shadows, illusions and lies. The feminine is the hidden representative of a fear of death which shows itself through the extinction of sexual difference.

Schelling, as a speculative philosopher, tends to use metaphors from the pre-Socratics: the Schellingian world is one of earth, wind, water and fire, of shining things, of mirrors and fluids. He does, however, present us with an alternative vision to the kind of speculation Irigaray deconstructs. In Schellingian imagery, the world of forces is not eliminating sexual difference. They take part in a grander vision of polarities, where sexual difference is one. Certainly, this is not valid only for Schelling. In his writings, however, the ego does not find itself distanced from the world of forces, of matter, and of the unconscious. Rather, Schelling's subject, just like the psychoanalytic subject, is a subject of drives.

Two aspects of Schelling's philosophy of art and poetry deserve to be stressed in this regard. First of all, difference is productive, and his universe can never become fully identical with itself. It can only, perhaps, contain splits in a final vision of the absolute. This account of productivity gives primacy to the notion of difference, rather than identity. Secondly, Schelling's notion of productivity is strongly attached to the function of organic life. A work of art, for Schelling, is not only conceptual or reflective, it is a product in which nature takes on weight. It has an excessive, sensual quality which we experience as its necessity, as its compelling quality of poetry.

For Schelling, art is a space where the productive forces of attraction and repulsion gather to carry the weight of nature, a space which will never fully enlighten us through sublation or reconciliation but rather carry the force of the unknown, as he puts it. Going beyond the text-book formulas of 'nature is unconscious spirit, spirit conscious nature' we find that artistic productivity for Schelling is a drive bordering between the somatic and the psychic – body, nature, natural sensations and inclinations are all part of the organic life which gives rise to poetry.

Sexual Difference as Finitude

Some literary historians have suggested that male Romantics annexate or annihilate the feminine.[2] In this context I would like to suggest a different perspective on gendered concepts: the writers of the Romantic movement, male and female alike, explore sexual difference. And this perspective lends itself to an interpretation of the trope of woman-as-death which does not necessarily mean that she has come to carry the mark of an aggressive patriarchy cutting the edges of its monolithic boundaries. Rather: sexual difference as such has become a mark of desire, but therefore also of limitation and finitude. A mark of castration, in psychoanalytic terms.

The metaphors of sexual difference inscribed in the philosophy and literature of German Idealism and Romanticism are contradictory terms which, in their turn, derive from mythological representations in ancient religions. Speculation has shaped the metaphors of sexual difference after the pythagorean quadrate of oppositions, presented by Aristotle in *Metaphysics*: finite and infinite, singular and plural, male and female, good and evil, light and dark (1/986a). Thinking in oppositions is applied on the project of liberation and equality between the sexes that is declared in the Romantic salon, in terms that undermine the ideal of equality. On the one hand woman represents the low principle: she is passive, unconscious, the part that provokes a dangerous, corporeal attraction. On the other hand, woman is idealized beyond the limit where she is still visible as an individual: she is the muse, the spirit of poetry, love and faith. Women authors from the same period complain about their own 'unfeminine' desire to write as being a failure to comply with this image. In this regard Karoline von Günderrode confesses to be attracted only by 'the wild, great and glimmering' and considers it to be an irrevocable personal fault. She is a woman with 'the desires of a man' whilst lacking, she feels, in masculine powers.[3] Sexual difference is seen as a productive force for male and female authors alike, and the desire to write is a derivative of something bordering between spirit and nature. Both Friedrich Schlegel and Günderrode make the other sex into a motive for writing, although in different ways.

The Nature of the Poetic 'I'

Günderrode, like most of her friends, was a dedicated reader of Friedrich Schelling. *System des transcendentalen Idealismus* is a history of self-consciousness where man rises above the unconscious through morals, language and art, cultural manifestations of the freedom inherited by the human subject as a result of God's gift of freewill. The split in consciousness and the unconscious are not described as two simple symmetrical dimensions, the limit between them is mobile in a way that corresponds to the concepts of necessity and freedom. For Schelling, poetry originates in the unconscious, a bluntly stated hypothesis which sounds more banal than it should. This unconscious could be called nature, negativity or matter. It is a force that is both productive and resistant, the limit where necessity meets freedom and engenders ideas, thoughts, feelings, and poetry as its epitome. The force cannot exhaust itself. It will always be there as a kind of resistance on which consciousness can expand. It is a motive of desire, rather than an object of desire, and therefore, it cannot be fully integrated into consciousness. In a passage which is strongly reminiscent of the discussion of the struggles of the tragic hero Oidipus to freely assume his own destiny in *Philosophy of Art,* Schelling compares the identity between the conscious and the unconscious 'which radiates towards us from the work of art' with fate. In principle, the productive force of the creative genius operates in a way that corresponds to the workings of destiny in the symbolic actions of the tragic hero, namely as 'a dark unknown force which provides the element of completion or objectivity to the work of freedom'. It operates without our knowledge and even against our will, towards goals *that we have not been able to predict*.[4] Through acting in the world we manifest our freedom, necessity is that which acts upon our freedom. Schelling describes it as 'other intelligences', our own freedom is restraint through that of other subjects. Necessity, in short, seems to be adamant to the limit of difference constituted by other beings, as well as of a nature that perhaps lies closer to Merleau-Ponty's concept of 'flesh' than the image of a Romantic landscape. Art becomes a synthesis of freedom and necessity where the dark unknown force that carries this necessity is the very force which engenders the freedom to create:

(…) it can only be the opposition between the conscious and the unconscious in the act of free will, which sets the artistic drive in movement: just as, on the one hand, only art can satisfy our eternal strivings, and resolve the last and utmost contradiction within us.[5]

In spite of the fact that the last phrase talks about reconciliation, a certain tension will always remain in the poem between the intention of the artist and what is actually shown. Poetry is a product of conflict; eternity is just another name for transgression of those boundaries that difference sets up. The rift between consciousness and the unconscious is a work of art described in terms of *art* and *poetry:*

If we must look in one of these activities, that is, the conscious activity, after what usually is called art, but which only constitutes a part of art, namely the part which is practised through consciousness, intention and reflection, which can also be taught and learnt through others, and which can be achieved through tradition and practise, then on the other hand we have to look into the unconscious, (which also shows itself in art), after that which cannot be taught or achieved through practise in any another way, but which can only be inherent through nature's free gift, and which is what we with another word call the poetry of art. [6]

Poetry is a concept which in Schelling seems to connote the metaphoric qualities of art. It can neither be identified with the artist or his object, it can only be seen in the work of art itself as that which transcends the limitations of the object, or the artist, and takes on a life of its own. Art is unconscious boundlessness, *bewusstlose Unendlichkeit,* a 'synthesis between nature and freedom' (3/10.225). The metaphoric qualities of art, however, can only be achieved through a sublation of nature which manifests itself in artistic form. The weight of nature blends with the reflection of the artist, and is transformed into a poetic form which supersedes both.

Schelling relates artistic creation not to an intellectual domain but to a dimension between the physical and the spiritual, just as psychoanalytical accounts of artistic creation would have it. In *System des transcendentalen Idealismus,* art belongs to a sphere beyond a specular construction of the subject. It is not the ego that mirrors itself in nature, but nature that haunts the ego. In the Schellingian universe, the specular subject is not a sovereign hunter of shadows. Rather, it is the passive, the unconscious and nature, all those concepts which belong on the side of the feminine in the staples of antinomies, which have come to inhabit a subject who can no longer believe himself to be truly in control of his own boundaries.

The 'Drives'

In a criticism directed towards Hegel, Schelling says that thought manifests the splitting of the subject rather than abstractions: '(…) It thinks in me, it is thought in me, is a pure fact, just as I would be equally justified to say: I dreamt, and: it dreamt in me.'[7] 'Wo es war soll Ich werden', Freud wrote a hundred years later. Schelling postulates a connection between nature and self that is described as 'drive'.

'… I am not at the place where I am the plaything of my thoughts; I think that I am at the place where I do not think that I am thinking', is Lacan's rewriting of the cartesian cogito-phrase.[8] Lacan, as Manfred Frank has pointed out, continues the tradition from Schelling over Freud: where 'it' was, 'I' will be.[9] But Lacan makes the gap between 'I' and 'it' into a linguistic question. In Schelling the ego is a limitation of strife. Strife or desire becomes posited in the shape of an ego through a necessary limit to its workings. What is important here, however, is the analogy that can be made between the model of the ego versus the unconscious dreams, and the intentions of the poet and the actual poem. Poetic imagination continues to enact the strife between contraries. But in the creation of a poem, in its expression, boundaries are put on the unbound, the drive, if you like. The poem does, however, also contain its own excess: the poet creates something that goes way beyond his own intentions. The unconscious is a concept indicating how poetry surpasses the poet's own, limited faculty of understanding. But it is also a concept which previsages the psychoanalytic conception of the unconscious as dominated by the drives.

A distinction between the concepts of desire, drive and power is useful, since they are applied in a different way in Schelling than in psychoanalysis. *Begierde* corresponds in *Die Weltalter* to eternal desire, while *Trieb* is the unconscious movement of nature. Nature, Schelling writes, is 'the abyss of the past' (Die Natur ist ein Abgrund von Vergangenheit), hiding an original power of attraction in living bodies (8/10.243). In opposition to Hegel's conceptual dialectics which he considers to be dry and unsatisfactory, Schelling discovers something which surpasses, without upheaving, the differences between body and soul, subject and object. This is a power, *Kraft,* which expresses itself in attraction and repulsion. These are two modes of an original life-power which exists in everything, and could be compared to the libido.

In *System des transcendentalen Idealismus* (1800) nature and the unconscious strives towards realisation in art. But the unconscious is not to be mistaken for a wholly 'spiritual' category, identical with concepts such as eternity, or infinity, a mistake that has sometimes been made. Our body is part of nature. Through the movement of our limbs, we manifest our freedom. Our body connects us with matter, and makes it possible for us to enact our freedom in a material world. It makes us into beings between natural inclinations and freedom. In order for me to appear as free, there must also be a part of my corporeality over which I do not have any control: a natural inclination, objective necessity, the resistance in front of which our freedom takes form.

The presumption that the ego is founded in nature, that it is linked to the unconscious, makes the poet an extra sensible being, with a power to symbolize, to give expression. When the poet experiences a conflict between ideal and reality which 'springs from the feeling without reflection' then this is a manifestation of the drive.[10] The drive is there *before* consciousness and directs the human subject towards an external object, aiming to recreate a lost identity, to overcome the gap between outer and inner reality. The drive is neither nature nor poetry, but the connection in between.[11] In *Ideen zu einer Philosophie der Natur* (1797 and 1803), Schelling, influenced by the universe of magnetism in Romantic thinking, talks again about the contradictory powers dominating nature: attraction and repulsion. These powers are not independent of the human mind. Rather, they surpass the difference between the psyche and the external world. They are magnetic powers, not psychoanalytic drives. But they fill the same function of surpassing the difference between thought and matter, between word and body.[12]

If the goal of activity in Schelling's universe was to be achieved, this universe of attraction and repulsion would also extinguish itself. The drive has to restrain itself at some point through an unconscious limitation.[13] The gap between the conscious and the unconscious is the key to the power of creativity. Nature cannot realise itself, but it can give birth to philosophy, and poetry, the queen of arts. This figuration of events precipitates the freudian hypothesis of sublimation, where the drives are reformed and displaced into socially acceptable forms of expression.[14]

The drives participate in poetic expression, poetry being the epitome of a grander scheme of conflict. So, unlike the case with the specular subject, who maps his own reflection onto his understanding of the world, sexual difference is mapped onto the understanding so that which is outside of reflection is given a metaphorical place in discourse. Nature is the passive, and the feminine, the resistant Other which can never be spoken, only shown through the symbolic work of art. Nature is not the aim of desire, but its motive. As such, nature in Schelling is not to be read as feminine passivity that could be conquered, taken over, annihilated. It is rather the Other as such, the limit of our being.

The Unconscious of a Work of Art

Desire in Schelling is not so much directed towards reconciliation in the future, as it traces a fulness that has been lost. In Schelling the subject exists only as lack. What was whole in the beginning is now spreading out 'piece by piece', he writes. Against the vision that man should have acquired an immediate knowledge about nature as a whole, Schelling puts emphasis on the tool, art, poetry or philosophy:

We do not live in the vision; our knowledge is a quilt, that is, it must be produced piece by piece in a fragmentary way, through judgements and gradations, that cannot be created without reflection.[15]

For Schelling it is impossible to speak 'immediately from perception', a vain attempt to 'express the unsayable'. Words are subordinated an inner knowledge about the unconscious origin of perception, language created under a metaphysical principle of wholeness – but it can never itself catch this wholeness. What can be said will always remain incomplete in relation to its origin. That is, the whole can never be spoken.

(...) 'if art is brought to its completion through two distinctly separate activities, then genius cannot be found in neither the one nor the other, but in that which is above both of them.[16]

The poetic image works through a surplus of the unsayable – poetry manifests an instinctual knowledge of nature's movements, aesthetic intuition. The latter could perhaps be described as the moment when nature carries weight, a pre-meditated meaning, intentionality. Schelling talks of it in terms of beauty, an experience of calm where contradictions are resolved in the object. But art can also be an experience of absolute excess, of the sublime. It is significant that Schelling here talks about the unconscious in the same way that Kant talks about nature in *Critique of Judgement*. Whenever an object is talked about as sublime, it gives rise to the experience of an absolute magnitude which it is impossible for consciousness to accept and for understanding to treat. This is the overwhelming impact of the unconscious on the mind:

> (…) the sublime (as opposed to what is merely strange, and in a similar manner confronts imagination with a contradiction, but it is not worth the trouble trying to solve it) puts all our power of the senses in motion, in order to dissolve the contradiction which threatens all of our intellectual capacity.[17]

In the same passage, Schelling equates the beautiful with the resolution of the eternal conflict between the conscious and the unconscious. This resolution, however, can only take place in a metaphorical manner. Attempting to return to itself, spirit escapes itself: the return of nature to itself can never be completed, but only imagined through poetic sensibility:

> What we talk about as nature is a poem which lies wrapped in a mysterious and wonderful manuscript. And yet the riddle would dissolve if in it we saw the odyssé of spirit, which, wonderfully transformed, searches for itself, and during this search escapes itself; because through the world of the senses we can only see a glimmer, as through the words their meaning, only through curtains of mist can we see the land of imagination which we are looking for.[18]

The riddle would dissolve in that final return to itself, as would the fog that clouds our imagination. Spirit is wrapped up in organic life, the meaning of the words glimmer through the world of senses. It is in the nature of poetry to live in the shades and the shadows of imagination. It cannot be reduced to any dialectic of reason, which is to say that is closer to the nature of organic life itself than philosophy. Nature is a poem, that is what decides the imagery of the sequence. But the chiasmatic structure of Schelling's thinking makes us see that poetry, at the same time, is this sensual surplus in which spirit has wrapped itself up in the foldings of poetic expression, allowing for a sensual experience of nature's weight.

Why Conflict is Poetic

Schelling is fully aware of the tension between the symbol, the artistic means which helps to build up reflection, and the sensual dimension inherent in poetic language. In the lectures on 'Philosophy of art' held from 1802-1803, Schelling discusses the means by which the 'infinite' in a work of art can be represented. These lectures

were not published until after his death, but point both to the transcendental philosophy and philosophy of nature. Art is, on the whole, according to Schelling, symbolic (5/10.411). That is, it creates a meaning which aims to surpass the limits of the
aesthetic figure, while carrying an irreducible dimension that is related to the condition of finitude, of the limits that condition our experience.

The symbol gives to the work of art its 'infinite' status. When we give the symbol meaning, it ceases to be visible for us. But the strength of the symbol lies in the
fact that its meaning is repesented in a shadow-like dimension beyond its physical
presence. It is a *Sinnbild,* in German both 'meaning' and 'figure of the senses'. Poetry, in Schelling, is imbued with a surplus, a dimension which exceeds the limits of
art as craft: the *poetry* of art.[19]

The poem is a 'symbol for intellectual intuition'. Words like symbolism and
identity indicate that there is something beyond the limits of language, which literature can accommodate. It does not mean that differences are eliminated, but confronted. That the poem is the genre of 'reflection' *per se* means that the ego looks for
transcendence, but the eye can only see what it is separated from: this gives poetry
its weight, in the sense of the unconscious excess of the artwork. This is where the
question of the 'infinite' or unconscious of poetry can be posed.

Schelling's view of the unconscious is, naturally, not to be immediately conflat-
ed with a Freudian view of the unconscious. But the links are certainly there to be
found – Freud being a reader of Schelling in his youth. Schelling previsages ideas
that later have been integrated in psychoanalysis. Ideas that have to do with the
drives as being sublimated into poetic language, and with sexual difference as a creative conflict, embedded in a work of art. The subject of poetic intuition is, the way
Schelling puts it, not superior to the philosopher because it intuits reconciliation. It
is superior not only to the philosopher but also, paradoxically, to itself because it
reaches beyond itself. It surpasses the very same conditions of finitude that it uses,
creating a work of the senses, of the *Sinnbild*. The poet becomes a subject of transgression *per se*. Poetry is a space that does not deny the other, or annihilate the
other, but rather, that poetry is a space *of* the Other.

Schelling's interest in sexual difference and the interest which this subject has for
philosophy can be compared to the thinking of Fichte. Johann Gottlieb Fichte demanded the same civil rights for women as for men.[20] He is, however, not interested
in the sensual experiences and desires that Schelling investigates, but stays with the
reflective ego as an epistemological base. Fichte's introspective, abstracting and spirit-

ual ego has been characterised by Madame De Staël as 'le grand célibataire du monde.'[21] With Fichte, in the eyes of Madame de Staël, the great bachelor of the world enters the philosophical scene: Fichte's idealism disregards the problem how the ego can relate to other human beings. Fichte's transcendental self also demands a repression of nature's 'naturalness' and of sexuality. Schelling on his part maps nature as creative difference. Schelling makes it possible for this other, the hidden, to come to life.

The displacement of interest from the ego to nature and a 'natural' unconscious is a decisive step towards Freud. According to Odo Marquard, the radicality of Schelling lies in the fact that he departs from an idealism built around an ego of the same, towards a selfconsciousness that does not build upon rationality, but on irrationality, which Marquard equates with nature.[22] Perhaps such concepts as rationality and irrationality need not be used here since they were not part of Schelling's own vocabulary. His philosophical language, however, is gendered. Schelling's universe of activity, productivity and drives gives sexuality and the feminity connected with sexuality an ambivalent but powerful status. Sexual difference becomes creative.

Schelling, as opposed to Fichte, the bachelor of the world, gives place to the repressed, to nature and to the feminine which is connected with nature, as passive but productive principles. In Schelling's philosophy of nature, as later in Freud, passivity and activity are dynamic concepts.[23]

It has often been said that poetry gives room to that which cannot be simply expressed, that it provokes what is beyond the limits of language, that the true experience of literature lies in the shades of the unknown rather than in the comfortably familiar. It has more rarely been commented upon that this view of poetry can be related to the notion of drives, to a conflict that is mapped on the borders between the spiritual and the physical, and that these borders are intrinsically intertwined with sexual difference. Sexual difference is the conflict at the centre of the economy of the drives. Schelling figures poetic creation on that very border. His poetics allow for notions such as the body and the drive to enter into the experience of poetry — although, strangely enough, with a few exceptions such as Merleau-Ponty, these notions tend to have been cast out in the phenomenological and hermeneutic tradition after Schelling.

For Schelling, man is not just a produced creature, but a creature of production. Thus, Schelling makes poetry, paradoxical as it may seem, into a priviliged space of the non-identical, the not-I, the non-symbolisable, or the unsayable. What is poetic in art is more than its reflective potential. It is also the sensual image which carries the metaphorical capacity of language, the weight of the physical representation which points to a signification beyond its own boundaries. In a universe of contraction and expansion, attraction and repulsion, then, the poet becomes an advocate of desire, reaching for a spectral identity that turns to difference, and a form, that takes on the body of the other.

NOTES

1. 'Romanticism represents the moment of maximum delusion when the mediator who up till then had occupied a transcendental status at a godlike distance from man, is secularized and placed in man himself' – when, in Girard's terms, 'men will be gods for each other (les hommes seront des dieux les und pour les autres).' Quoted from René Girard 1961, in de Man 1993, 16.

2. See, for instance, Ross 1989, 49: 'Poetry motivated and shaped by the desire for self-possession, determined by the poet's aggressive relation to his fellows is not *intrinsically* masculine, but it is *sociohistorically* masculine'.

3. Letter to Gunda Savigny, August 29, 1801: 'Schon oft hatte ich den unweiblichen Wunsch, mich in ein wildes Schlachtgetümmel zu werfen, zu sterben – warum ward ich kein Mann! Ich habe keinen Sinn für weiblichen Tugenden, für Weiblichglückseligkeit. Nur das wilde grosse, Glänzende gefällt mir. Es ist ein unseeliges, aber unverbesserliches Missverhältnis in meiner Seele; und es wird so bleiben, denn ich bin ein Weib und habe Begierden wie ein Mann, ohne Männerkraft. Darum bin ich so wechselnd und so uneins mit mir' (Ed. Christa Wolf 1981, 140).

4. Fr. Schelling 1856-61, 3.613. References to volume and page numbers in the text. Translations from this work are mine (CS).

5. 'Es kann also nur der Widerspruch zwischen dem Bewussten und dem Bewusstlosen im freien Handeln seyn, welcher den künstlerischen Trieb in Bewegung setzt, sowie es hinwiederum nur der Kunst gegeben seyn kann, unser unendliches Streben zu befriedigen und auch den letzten und äussersten Widerspruch in uns aufzulösen' (3/10.617).

6. 'Wenn wir in den einen beider jenen Tätigkeiten, der bewussten nämlich, das suchen müssen, was insgeheim *Kunst* genannt wird, was aber nur der Teil derselben ist, nämlich dasjenige an ihr, was mit Bewusstsein, Überlegung und Reflexion ausgeübt wird, was auch gelehrt und gelernt, durch Überlieferung und durch eigne Übung erreicht werden kann, so werden wir dagegen in dem Bewusstlosen, was in die Kunst mit eingeht, dasjenige suchen müssen, was an ihr nicht gelernt, nicht durch Übung, noch auf andere Art erlangt werden, sondern allein durch freie Gunst der Natur angeboren sein kann, und welches dasjenige ist, was wir mit einem Wort die *Poesie* in der Kunst nennen können' (3/10.618).

7. '(...) Es denkt in mir, es wird mir gedacht, ist das reine Faktum, gleichwie ich auch mit gleicher berechtigung sagte: Ich träumte, und: Es träumte mir' (1/10.11-12).

8. '(...) je ne suis pas, là où je suis le jouet de ma pensée; je pense à ce que je suis, là où je ne pense pas penser' (Lacan 1966, 223). Lacan demonstrates his thesis of the split subject: the subject of the unconscious is to be found where the signifier of the ego is left out.

9. Manfred Frank has repeatedly remarked upon this relatedness between Schelling and Lacan (Frank 1980, 126; Frank 1984, 376-80).

10. '(...) einerseits frei, und doch anderseits unmittelbar und ohne/ alle Reflexion aus einem Gefühl entspringt' (3/10.559).

11. 'Jener Trieb, der in meinem Handeln Kausalität hat, muss objektiv erscheinen als ein *Naturtrieb,* der auch ohne alle Freiheit wirken und für sich hervorbringen würde, was er durch Freiheit hervorbringen scheint' (3/10.571).

12. See for instance 3/10.445-47.

13. '(...) dafür ist durch den Mechanismus des Empfindens, dadurch gesorgt, dass der Akt, wodurch alle Begrenztheit gesetzt wird, als Bedingung alles Bewusstseins, selbst nicht zum Bewusstseyn kommt' (3/10.409).

14. The similarity between Freud's and Schelling's figure of sublimation has been analysed by Marquard 1986, 162-64.

15. 'Wir leben nicht im Schauen; unser Wissen ist Stückwerk, d. h. es muss stückweise, nach Urtheilungen und Abstufungen erzeugt werden, welches nicht ohne alle Reflexion geschehen kann' (*Die Weltalter.* 1811-13, 1815, 8/10.203).

16. 'Wenn nun ferner die Kunst durch zwei voneinander völlig verschiedene Tätigkeiten vollendet wird, so ist das Genie weder die eine noch die anderen, sonder das, was über beiden ist' (3/10.619).

17. '(...) indem das Erhabene (ganz anders als das bloss Abenteuerliche, was der Einbildungskraft gleichfalls als einen Widerspruch vorhält, welchen aber abzulösen nicht der Möhe wert ist) alle Kräfte des Gemüths in Bewegung setzt, um den die ganze intellektuelle Existenz bedrohenden Widerspruch aufzulösen' (3/10. 621).

18. 'Die Ansicht, welche der Philosoph von der Natur künstlich sich macht, ist für die Kunst die ursprüngliche und natürliche. Was wir Natur nennen, ist ein Gedicht, das in geheimer wunderbarer Schrift verschlossen liegt. Doch könnte das Räthsel sich enthüllen, würden wir die Odyssee des Geistes darin erkennen, der wunderbar getäuscht, sich selber suchend, sich selber flieht; denn durch die Sinnenwelt blickt nur wie durch Worte der Sinn, nur wie durch halbdurchsuchtigen Nebel das Land der Phantasie, nach dem wir trachten' (3/10.628).

19. The definiton of the symbol is that it brings the so-called schematic concept and allegory together (5/10.407). The schematic, in Schelling, is first and foremost language referring to the

world of the senses, while allegory is a figure of conceptual meaning *(Philosophie der Kunst).*

20. Fichte 1796-97, *Grundlage des Naturrechts.*

21. '(…) la nature et l'amour perdent tout leur charme par ce système; car si les objets que nous voyons et les êtres que nous aimons ne sont rien que l'oeuvre de nos idées, c'est l'homme lui-même qu'on peut considérer alors comme *le grand célibataire du monde'* (de Staël 1814, 3.85).

22. Marquard 1986, 158-59.

23. In 'Triebe und Triebschicksahle' Freud discusses three pairs of antinomies working together in the development of sexuality and love, as well as hatred and destructivity: subject (ego) and object, pleasure and displeasure, activity and passivity (*GW* 10.229). From *Drei Abhandlungen zur Sexualtheori* (*GW* 5) and onwards, masculinity and femininity in Freud are discussed as if they correspond to the active and the passive, positions in relation to one another and theoretical constructions rather than biological concepts. See 'Die endliche und die unendliche Analyse' (*GW* 16.96-99) and 'Über die weibliche Sexualität'. Here, Freud describes sexual identity in terms of polarities such as activity and passivity (*GW* 14.537).

BIBLIOGRAPHY

de Man, Paul 1993. *Romanticism and Contemporary Criticism. The Gauss Seminar and Other Papers.* London.

de Staël, Germaine 1814. *De l'Allemagne.* Uppsala.

Fichte, Johann Gottlieb 1796-97. *Grundlage des Naturrechts.* Jena und Leipzig.

Frank, Manfred 1980. *Das Sagbare und das Unsagbare.* Frankfurt.

Frank, Manfred 1984. *Was ist Neostrukturalismus.* Frankfurt.

Freud, Sigmund 1905. *Drei Abhandlungen zur Sexualtheori. Gesammelte Werke* in 18 Bänden. London 1940-52. (Abbreviated as *GW*).Vol. 5.

Freud, Sigmund 1915. 'Triebe und Triebschicksahle'. *GW* 10.

Freud, Sigmund 1931. 'Über die weibliche Sexualität'. *GW* 14.

Freud, Sigmund 1937. 'Die endliche und die unendliche Analyse'. *GW* 16.

Lacan, Jacques 1971. *Ecrits.* Paris.

Marquard, Odo 1986. *Transzendentaler Idealismus, Romantische Naturphilosophie, Psychoanalyse.* Köln.

Ross, Marlon B. 1989. *The Contours of Masculine Desire.* Oxford.

Schelling, Friedrich 1856-61. *Friedrich Wilhelm Joseph von Schellings sämmtliche Werke* in 10 Bänden. (Ed. Karl Friedrich August Schelling). Stuttgart.

Wolf, Christa (Ed.) 1981. *Der Schatten eines Traumes.* Berlin.

The Erosion of Romantic Love:
From Friedrich Schlegel to E.T.A. Hoffmann

Chenxi Tang

Love is a form of communication which seeks to negate communication. Communication, according to Niklas Luhmann, is that which emerges from the interaction between systems of consciousness. It is an emergent reality, a condition *sui generis*. Because of the irreducible intransparency of consciousness-systems, communication is inexorably contingent and precarious. The possible failing weighs on every single act of communication. Understanding always implies mis-understanding.[1] However, modern society, constructed through the highly improbable acts of communication as it is, has an alternative form of communication at its disposal, which suspends the very structure of communication and constitutes itself in spite of, indeed because of, the intransparency of consciousness-systems. This form of communication is called love. A lover defiantly disregards the closure of his and his beloved's consciousness, and passionately insists on the fusion of the two disparate consciousness-systems. Love as passion presupposes stalwart repression and denial of the contingency of communication.[2] Yet to elude contingency is an impossible enterprise. Love emerges against the horizon of disguise, insincerity, deceit and betrayal. The baroque semantics of love was characterized by the incessant lamentation of the instability of love. The baroque thinker of our time, Jacques Lacan, proclaimed in his *Encore* that there is no love relationship, and one was better to call 'l'amour' 'la mur'.

Suffused with its own structure of contingency as it is, love nonetheless represents an alternative form of communication. The idea of passionate love intersects with and complements the general semantics of social interaction in modern society. The alternative character of love was nowhere so emphatically insisted upon and so systematically exploited than in Romanticism. The semantics of 'Romantic love' seeks to aggrandize and elevate love to the predominant form of communication. It aspires to monopolize communication in general and thereby institute society anew.

In this ambition, Romantic love merges into another form of communication privileged by Romanticism, namely aesthetic communication.

In its uncompromising denial of the contingency of communication, the semantics of Romantic love has an implacably paradoxical character. For this reason, no sooner was it articulated around 1800 than it started to crumble, that is, within the period of Romanticism itself. The rapidity of its erosion is a startling and illuminating fact. To a certain degree, the semantics of Romantic love still impinges upon the contemporary notion of intimacy. One may still speak of Romantic love today, but always *cum grano salis*. This is because its paradoxicality has been laid bare in the intervening times. The love-semantics of modern society oscillates between Romantic affirmation and post-Romantic skepticism. One does not have to give up the illusion of the ethereal Romantic love. Yet one is also taught to face bitter disillusionment. In the following, I shall trace the rise and fall of the notion of Romantic love in the early nineteenth century by reading two texts of German Romanticism, Friedrich Schlegel's *Lucinde* (1799) and Hoffmann's 'Elementargeist' (1821), belonging to Early and Late Romanticism respectively.

'Der Elementargeist', a novella written by E.T.A. Hoffmann in 1821, does not count among the author's most widely read texts, at least it has not created a research industry as did the legendary 'Sandmann'. Yet possibly more than any other fantastic tales − we know there are many of them − 'Der Elementargeist' brings into relief late Hoffmann's disenchantment with a wide range of Early Romantic credos. First and foremost, we can observe the collapse of the notion of Romantic love and along with it, the disintegration of the philosophical and poetological matrix in which this notion is embedded. In fact, the semantics of love conveyed by this text does not only index the ironic reversal of the established semantics of Romantic love, but also portends the erosion of the whole edifice of Romantic poetics. Thus, a reading of 'Der Elementargeist', this modest text unobtrusively tucked away within the vast *oeuvres* of its prolific author, holds the promise of revealing at least certain aspects of the dialectics of Romanticism.

The semantics of Romantic love was arguably codified by Friedrich Schlegel's novel *Lucinde* (1799), although we should bear in mind that the time around 1800 as an age of intellectual fermentation displayed such a variegated pattern of discourse formation that the privileging of a specific author is necessarily partial and unjustified. In his study of the codification of intimacy *Liebe als Passion,* Niklas Luhmann comments on the Romantic age in such a way:

Man hat insgesamt den Eindruck, daß die Unterschiede von Autor zu Autor in dieser Zeit größer sind als die Unterschiede zwischen den historischen Epochen. Keine Leitdifferenz kann sich durchsetzen. Die Semantik der Intimität wirkt vorübergehend wie ein strukturiertes Chaos, wie eine gärende, sich selbst anheizende Masse.[3]

The scope of this study disallows an extensive study of the Romantic ideas of love. For the purpose of argument, I will take *Lucinde* as the exemplary text in which the concept of Romantic love gains its archetypal form. After spelling out the various semantic levels of this concept, I shall demonstrate how Hoffmann's 'Der Elementargeist' collapses this concept and how the strategy of fantastic storytelling is deployed to salvage it, albeit without sustainable success. Based on the reading of this text, I shall at last make a brief observation about the post-Romantic concept of Romantic love.

Lucinde

Schlegel's *Lucinde* was published in 1799 and triggered an outcry of indignation, although the apologetic defense was not less vociferous. The concept of love in this quintessential text of German Early Romanticism has at least four semantic levels:

1) Romantic love is conceived as the imbrication of sexuality, marriage and friendship;
2) Romantic love thus conceived correlates with the Romantic program of progressive universal poetry;
3) Romantic love presupposes a normative notion of subjectivity and gender identity; and
4) Romantic love requires a specific narrative strategy for its articulation.

Firstly, in Romantic love, love, sexuality, marriage and friendship are imbricated with each other, that is to say, an individual's sexual experience, his status as a link in the social nexus and his ethical relation with the Other are supposed to blend into one harmonious whole. Julius, the protagonist of Schlegel's novel, wrote to Lucinde: 'Ja! ich würde es für ein Märchen gehalten haben, daß solche Freude gebe und solche Liebe, wie ich nun fühle, und eine solche Frau, die mir zugleich die zärtlichste Geliebte und die beste Gesellschaft wäre und auch eine vollkommene Freundin.'[4] Romantic love insists on the experience of absolute unity. In terms of sexuality, the notion of Romantic love hinges upon the persistently accentuated idea of the merging of the self and the other in the sexual union of man and woman. Schleiermacher parallels the experience of the moment of sexual union with the experience of absolute unity in religion:

Ich liege am Busen der unendlichen Welt: ich bin in diesem Augenblick ihre Seele, denn ich fühle alle ihre Kräfte und ihr unendliches Leben, wie mein eignes, sie ist in diesem Augenblick mein Leib, denn ich durchdringe ihre Muskeln und ihre Glieder wie meine eignen, und ihre innersten Nerven bewegen sich nach meinem Sinn und meiner Ahnung wie die Meinigen.[5]

The possibility of the ecstatic yet infinitely repeatable and even enhancible moment of sexual union rests on the presumption that the psychic system is constitutionally capable of transcending its symbolic overdetermination.[6] It is exactly this presumed capacity for transcendence that warrants the claim of the sexually united couple to be able to assume social and ethical responsibilities. Love can develop into marriage as a social institution because the two psychic systems engaged in the act of sexual union are able to shake off all the possible symbolic constraints and create a new social order. Marriage and hence society on the whole are founded by love. Furthermore, love can be identified with friendship as an ethical stance because the loving couple is endowed with the capability of obliterating all contingencies of communication and reaching the highest degree of compatibility or understanding. The friendship cult prevalent among educated men in the late eighteenth century was thus submerged in the cult of Romantic love and the institution of marriage. *Liebesehe* and loving companionship came into common currency.

Secondly, Romantic love thus conceived correlates with the Romantic conception of progressive universal poetry. In Romantic love, man and woman fuses together into an absolute unity without, however, forfeiting their respective individuality. They mirror each other and potentiate each other *ad infinitum*. This figure of love corresponds to Romantic poetry on various levels:

a) Love is analogized to a piece of organic work of art, while the lovers are likened to the parts which constitute the work of art as a whole. In love, as well as in a work of art, each part is a miniature of the whole. In his essay on Goethe's *Wilhem Meister,* Schlegel writes:

Der angebohrene Trieb des durchaus organisierten und organisierenden Werks, sich zu einem Ganzen zu bilden, äußert sich in den größeren wie in den kleineren Massen. Keine Pause ist zufällig und unbedeutend; und hier, wo alles zugleich Mittel und Zweck, wird es nicht unrichtig seyn, den ersten Theil unbeschadet seiner Beziehung aufs Ganze als ein Werk für sich zu betrachten.[7]

b) Love is isomorphous to aesthetic communication. Julius and Lucinde's relationship is no less of a 'symphilosophische' conversation than that which unfolds among the seven participants in the 'Gespräch über die Poesie'. In fact, love is nothing but aesthetic communication.

c) In love as in poetry, subject and object fuse into one entity. Romantic poetry can 'am meisten zwischen dem Dargestellten und dem Darstellenden, frei von allem realen und idealen Interesse auf den Flügeln der poetischen Reflexion in der Mitte schweben, diese Reflexion immer wieder potenzieren und wie in einer endlosen Reihe von Spiegeln vervielfachen'.[8] Love is homologous to the progressive universal poetry.

More examples of the correlation between Romantic love and Romantic poetry can be adduced. At this juncture, it is not possible for me to dwell on Schlegel's complicated philosophy of Romantic poetry. For brevity's sake, suffice it to say that a Romantic lover is necessarily a Romantic artist and the consummation of Romantic love is equivalent to the consummation of Romantic poetry. Julius' artistic creativity reaches its pinnacle in his love for Lucinde. The ability of the psychic system to transcend its symbolic overdetermination, which gives birth to Romantic love, corresponds to the artistic creativity which appears under various names in Schlegel's theory of Romantic transcendental poetry: fantasy, wit, irony and transcendental – poetic self-reflection – all these interrelated notions were used by Schlegel in different ways, but all of them refer to the idea of progressive universal poetry.

   Thirdly, Romantic love presupposes a normative narrative of the constitution of gendered subjectivity. It is no accident that the centerpiece of *Lucinde* is called

'Apprenticeship of Manhood/Masculinity' *(Lehrjahre der Männlichkeit)*. Indeed, a long process of maturation and preparation precedes the realization of Romantic love. Not only physical growth and successful socialization, but first of all sexual experiences are essential for the constitution of male subjectivity. Only after experiences with seven quite different women does Julius become mature enough for Romantic love. At the beginning, Julius' psychic world is a complete chaos. It is a long and torturous journey of quest and experimentation, at the end of which stands the encounter with Lucinde, that makes Julius into a real man. After he finds Lucinde, Julius at last finds the center of his self. He becomes a sovereign subject contributing toward the building of a 'free society' and a 'big family' (*Lucinde* 57). Alongside the normative notion of male subjectivity, the semantics of Romantic love also implies a 'theory of femininity'.[9] While the Romantic narrative of the constitution of subjectivity, which has as its telos the reflexive self-control or the creation of a transcendental imaginary, revolves invariably around a man, it also necessarily involves a woman: a compatible woman is needed for the constitution of male subjectivity. The transcendence to Romantic love is in the last resort predicated upon the union of a man and a woman. Schlegel conceived femininity as complementary to masculinity. Whereas man is characterized by a philosophizing impulse, woman is informed by natural poetry. Both philosophy and poetry are deficient in themselves. They need each other in order to reach absoluteness:

Nur sanfte Männlichkeit, nur selbständige Weiblichkeit (ist) die rechte, die wahre und schöne. Ist dem so, so muss man den Charakter des Geschlechts, welches doch nur eine angeborene, natürliche Profession ist, keineswegs noch mehr übertreiben, sondern vielmehr durch starke Gegengewichte zu mildern suchen, damit die Eigenheit einen wo möglich unbeschränkten Raum finde, um sich nach Lust und Liebe in dem ganzen Bezirke der Menschheit frey zu bewegen.[10]

The love between Julius and Lucinde is a union between masculine philosophy and feminine poetry. Julius' philosophical seriousness is initially 'frightening'. '(Seine) Gemälde blieben bei aller Gründlichkeit und Einsicht steif und steinern' (*Lucinde* 50). However, by combining his philosophical austerity with the poetical impulse embodied by Lucinde, he reaches perfection. Clearly, the semantics of Romantic love, whether coded as religion or art, envisions a normative gender identity for both man and woman.

Lastly, Romantic love requires a specific narrative strategy for its articulation. Romantic love has to begin with narration. One of the prerequisites for love is that two lovers tell each other about their lives. After Julius met Lucinde, she tells him about her life and 'Auch er erinnerte sich an die Vergangenheit und sein Leben ward ihm, indem er es ihr erzählte, zum erstenmal zu einer gebildeten Geschichte' (*Lucinde* 53). The narrative of the constitution of subjectivity gains its contour in the process of its being told by the lover to his partner. Staged as an exchange between a lover and his beloved, the telling of the life story forms an integral part of Romantic love. This life story assumes the form of the Romantic novel as defined by Schlegel, namely 'ein romantisches Buch'. For the Romantic novel, the most important thing is not a dramatic plot structure, but instead the discursive self-amplification and self-potentiation of ideas.

Der dramatische Zusammenhang der Geschichte macht den Roman im Gegentheil noch keineswegs zum Ganzen, zum Werk, wenn er es nicht durch die Beziehung der ganzen Composition auf eine höhere Einheit, als jene Einheit des Buchstabens, über die er sich oft wegsetzt und wegsetzen darf, durch das Band der Ideen, durch einen geistigen Centralpunkt wird.[11]

In a word, the narrative form requisite for Romantic love is the transcendental narration of the Romantic novel.

'Der Elementargeist'

In E.T.A. Hoffmann's 'Der Elementargeist', all these four semantic levels of Romantic love undergo an ironic reversal. In order to provide a point of reference for the textual analysis, I shall first of all recount the story in broad features.

On the 15th November 1815, when the Prussian army was *en route* from France to Germany after the hundred-day-campaign against Napoleon who was defeated on the 18th June, 1815 at Waterloo, the Prussian officer Albert von B., seized by a mysterious restlessness and absorbed in thoughts about past battles in which he had participated, rode on the road from Lüttich to Aachen. He had a vague sense that something exciting and important awaited him in Aachen, although he could not imagine what it might be. However, when he unexpectedly bumped into the groom of his friend Viktor, a Prussian officer as well, Albert established that he had actually contemplated visiting Viktor, an intention of which he had not been conscious. Then the groom Paul Talkebarth led him to the castle of Baroness von E., where Viktor was staying. The arrival of Albert and Paul, accompanied by the ravaging of the hennery, was felt as an annoying intrusion by the Baron, while Viktor avowed that he had telepathically known that Albert would come to visit him on this day. In the course of the evening it dawned on Albert that something was going on between Viktor and the Baroness. At the same time, it seemed that Albert himself had also succumbed to the coquettish charm of the plump and plain baroness who was at once flirtatious and domestic. The affective relationship had actually been established from the first moment he saw her with those dangerously seductive eyes, small feet in the dainty silk shoes and the very pretty bonnet which reminded him of a grisette he had been with in Paris. Vaguely sensing the sexual peril, he was seized by a fit of panic. Albert felt increasingly discontented with the uncomfortable, 'uncanny' atmosphere. The urge to talk with his bosom friend Viktor appeared in this circumstance to be an attempt to liberate both of them from a certain sexual anxiety and even latent rivalry.

Then followed Viktor's long story about his coming to the castle and the experiences in his young manhood. In terms of length, this framed narration takes up about three-fourth of the whole text. To Viktor's confession that he had really fallen in love with the Baroness, Albert replied: 'nun, das alles will ich am Ende auch noch für eine Krankheit halten'.[12] The narration is concluded with the following dialogue:

Du bist recht krank gewesen, denn die Kopfwunde, die du erhieltest, war bedeutend genug, um dein Leben in Gefahr zu setzen; doch jetzt finde ich dich soweit hergestellt, dass du mit mir fort kannst. Recht aus innigen Herzen bitt ich dich, mein teurer, innig geliebter Freund, diesen Ort zu verlassen und mich morgen nach Aachen zu begleiten. 'Meines Bleibens', erwiderte Viktor, 'ist hier freilich länger nicht (…)'. ('Elementargeist' 749)

At the end of Viktor's narration, a point is apparently reached where the illness of his being in love with the Baroness is regarded as cured. The act of narrating, punctuated with the narratee's responses, has succeeded in curing the illness. This narration would seem to be like a successful psychoanalytical session ending with the cure of the patient.

Before his departure on the second morning, Viktor went to see the Baroness for the last time. While the Baroness tried to stage a sentimental farewell scene, Viktor hurled a magic oath at her, and upon hearing this the Baroness fell to the ground. Albert and Viktor left for Aachen, without waiting for the Baron to return from hunting. The text ends with a coda, in which the reader is told that Viktor remained unmarried.

This text betokens the deep and disconcerting crisis of Romanticism. The notion of Romantic love stands on the verge of collapse and the entire poetological matrix of Romanticism threatens to break down. Schematically speaking, all the four aspects of the semantics of Romantic love are fundamentally unsettled:

1) The unity of love, sexuality, marriage and friendship degenerates into fetishistic sexual obsession;
2) The great expectation of progressive universal poetry gives way to the anxiety of influence and artistic impotence;
3) The affirmative male subjectivity is replaced by a decentered subjectivity which can be affirmed only in fantasy;
4) Along with the critical revision of the conception of subjectivity, the narrative strategy of the Romantic novel as envisioned by Schlegel is replaced by the fantastic storytelling.

Firstly, the unity of love, sexuality, marriage and friendship degenerates into fetishistic sexual obsession. All through this text, the motives of sexuality and marriage are drawn into an extremely comic light and the Romantic idea of *Liebesehe* is thus ironically dismissed. Baroness Aurora is plump and plain, combining jarringly domesticity and coquetry. But first of all, Viktor's relationship with her is adulterous. The feeling of cuckoldry is repeatedly expressed by the Baron himself, albeit always in the metaphorical guise. The marital life between the Baron and Baroness is at its best just boring, with the Baroness playing the dominating role at home. Friendship is coded as a relationship between Viktor and Albert, that is two men. With the establishment of the semantics of Romantic love, enthusiastic emotional expressions about the same-sex friendship is not only anachronistic, but also suspicious. In terms of sexuality, Viktor's infatuation with the Baroness is fetishistic. Viktor talks about her gaze (the mysterious fire that flashes from her eyes), her skin (the pressure of her hand), her feet and so on, all this hardly in the Romantic vein. I will come back to the problematic of fetishistic sexuality later in conjunction with the constitution of male subjectivity. We will see that this non-Romantic sexuality makes the vocabulary of Lacanian psychoanalysis the appropriate tool for its description.

Secondly, the great expectation of progressive universal poetry gives way to the anxiety of influence and artistic impotence. Just like every other Romantic hero, Viktor has a passion for poetry. Even though hampered by the austerity of military life, he indiscriminately devours all the poetic works he can possibly get hold of. Yet Viktor's entry into poetry turns out to be an entry into the shadows of the pre-existent, already canonized writings, especially Goethe and Schiller. At a certain point, he comes to the painful conclusion that he indeed does not possess 'den Homerischen Geist', that is poetic spirit. However, in spite of this insight, he cannot suppress the longing for poetic transcendence. In his fantasy, Viktor created the uncanny figure O'Malley who promises him to gain access to the sphere of 'der Homerische Geist'. But now the poetic spirit has metamorphosed into a poetic ghost (Hoffmann apparently puns on the German word 'Geist'). If the poetic spirit is identical with the creative power of a genius, the poetic ghost can only be conjured up by a grammar book. At the conjuring ceremony organized by O'Malley who uses a French Grammar book as the magic aid, Viktor saw the ghost appearing as a 'formless form' (*eine gestaltlose Gestalt*) and then fainted. Romantic transcendental poetry has become a ghost, a 'formless form', that is, an oxymoron. In front of this logical impossibility, the subject has to disconnect himself form consciousness. Viktor relinquished his belief in the impossible *Homerische Geist* and relegated it to narration: the whole course of O'Malley's conjuring ceremony and the appearance of the ghost conjured forth were later narrated to Viktor by another person.

Thirdly, Viktor's relation to the poetic spirit reveals the tension between the subject's subordination to the symbolic and his yearning for transcendence. The same tension also weighs on the constitution of the gendered subjectivity. In 'Der Elementargeist', the affirmative male subjectivity as conceived by Early Romanticism is replaced by a decentered subjectivity which can be affirmed only in fantasy. On the one hand, Viktor is unwilling to have his sexuality tamed by the symbolic order, but on the other hand, the overcoming of symbolic overdetermination as realized in Julius' relationship with Lucinde cannot be achieved either. He has to come to grips with the fact that the fundamental condition of subjectivity is the symbolic castration, the lack of being. The subject, the *je* is a pure lack and the desiring structure characterizing the subject is a 'desire for nothing'.[13] The subject desires, but he does not desire anything, because there is nothing capable of definitely slaking the desire which is caused by the ontological lack. The subject seeks, however, to fill in this lack and in fact he does possess a psychic mechanism which is capable of 'plugging the hole of symbolic castration or lack by positing a particular object as the cause of desire'.[14] This mechanism is fantasy. That means, fantasy is the psychic faculty pre-destined to substitute a particular object – what Lacan terms the *objet a* – for the for-ever lost phallus.[15]

Through fantasy a special sort of object (*objets petit a*) is created for the funda-mentally a-objectal desire. In consequence, an object-relationship can be estab-lished, although only in fantasy. The relationship thus established is therefore not one between a man and a woman as a person, but a woman as an assemblage of ob-jects to which the man is related in fantasy. Insofar as the man is related to these ob-jects, which are detached bodily parts in his fantasy, rather than to a human Other, the male desire is inherently fetishistic. The second part of the framed narrative in 'Der Elementargeist' chronicles Viktor's fascination with various objects or fetishes evoked by his fantasy. The space available here does not allow me to provide more textual evidence for this general observation, but it should be pointed out that the fetishistic desire structure implies that male subjectivity is essentially decentered, that is, a lack to be plugged by *objets a* in fantasy.

Lastly, along with the critical revision of the conception of subjectivity, the nar-rative strategy of the Romantic novel as envisioned by Schlegel is replaced by the fantastic storytelling. If Romantic love is reduced to a fetishistic relationship with *objet a* created by fantasy, and if male subjectivity is a lack to be plugged by the fan-tastic objects, then the narrative of love and male subjectivity is predestined to be *fantastic*. I have already analyzed the structure of fantasy as a psychic mechanism which enables the subject ruptured by the symbolic to establish an otherwise im-possible relationship with what lies outside the symbolic by connecting himself with imaginary objects, the *objets a*. Viktor's liaison with Baroness Aurora is struc-tured by the same mechanism of fantasy. Given this structural constellation, the question of how to tell a life story becomes actually a question of how to narrativ-ize fantasy. That is to say, life story is bound to turn into a fantastic tale. If anything in 'Der Elementargeist' appears fantastic, it is Viktor's narrative which recounts the constitution of his 'fantastic' relation with Aurora. At this juncture, we can in fact sense a new way of defining the Romantic fantastic in the offing.

But what is most interesting about the text 'Der Elementargeist' is the fact that Viktor's fantastic narrative itself keeps the fantastic under control and engenders Romantic normativity by its being narrated, that is to say, the narrating act succeeds in restraining the fantastic and restoring the normativity prescribed by the dominant semantic code of Romantic love and male subjectivity. At the beginning of Viktor's narrative, his affair with Baroness Aurora is ridiculed as an illness, a bad novel which has been repeated hundreds of times. But at the end of the narrative, the illness is considered cured and the poetic spirit restored. The act of narrating which produces the fantastic narrative proves at last to be really able to fulfill the function of a corrective: what deviates from the normative code – what is fantastic in this particular context – is held back, and immediately after the narrating ends, both the narrator and the narratee agree that what is at stake is finally dissolved. Viktor's narrative is in this sense comparable to a confession – and he does see it as a confession – in that in a confession a deviant deed is made harmless and even rendered null and void by its being narrated.

On the other hand, this narrating resembles a psychoanalytical session, in which the analysand's narrative, punctuated by the analyst's replies, gains insight into the genealogy of his psychic conflicts, thereby gaining the ability to solve these conflicts. In narrating, Viktor is confronted with the deviant, fantastic nature of his relationship with the Baroness, thereby acquiring the ability to relinquish it. But insofar as Viktor's narrative does not turn out to be a coherent life story, the resemblance obtaining between his narrative and the narrative of an analysand should not be exaggerated.[16]

After the fantastic is contained by the act of narrating, Viktor succeeds in returning to the normative code of Romantic subjectivity and poetic creativity. In 'Der Elementargeist', Albert's notion of spirit serves as this normative code. By acceding to it, Viktor relegates his former experiences into the realm of dreams, or rather, nightmares:

Ohne daß Albert sich jemals auf lange Widerlegungen oder Zweifel eingelassen, schien Viktor selbst sein mystisches Abenteuer bald für nichts höheres zu achten, als für einen langen, bösen Traum. ('Elementargeist' 750)

Viktor becomes reconciled to the normative code of Early Romanticism. But the reconciliation seems at last to be a little forced. The convergence of love and marriage is never reached in him. The last sentence of 'Der Elementargeist' reads: 'Der Obrist (Viktor) blieb unvermählt' ('Elementargeist' 751).

The above comparison between Friedrich Schlegel and E.T.A. Hoffmann brings to light the complex mechanism of the semantics of Romantic love. Hoffmann's text attests to the instability and vulnerability of the notion of Romantic love as crystallized in Early Romanticism. On the one hand, he poignantly depicted how easily Romantic love degenerated into obsession, perversion and anguish. But on the other hand, he evinced an embittered reluctance to renounce this notion altogether. In 'Der Elementargeist', Romantic love is actually rescued in the end. But the rescued love does not feel like the initial one. In it are impregnated fetishistic obsession, anxiety of the symbolic castration and tortuous nightmares. At the beginning of this article, I said that one could speak of Romantic love today only *cum grano salis.* It should be clear now why this is so. In the post–Romantic semantics of Romantic love, Julius and Lucinde's passion is encrusted with the gritty sediments of Viktor's experience with the elementary spirits.

NOTES

1. Luhmann's theory of communication, the centerpiece of his systems theory, is systematically expounded in his magnum opus *Soziale Systeme* (Luhmann 1984). For a laconic definition of the notion of communication, see Luhmann 1995.

2. Cf. Luhmann 1982.

3. Ibid. 171.

4. Fr. Schlegel, *Lucinde. KFSA* (5.1–92) 10. In the following Lucinde with page references in the text.

5. Schleiermacher 1970, 41f.

6. As we know, Lacanian psychoanalysis forcefully contests this presumption, but we will come to this later. In his *Seminar xx,* Lacan establishes that the code of Romantic love is based on the magic phrase: 'We are only one'. Lacan says: *'Nous ne sommes qu'un. Chacun sait bien sûr que ce n'est jamais arrivé entre deux qu'ils ne fassent qu'un, mais enfin nous ne sommes qu'un.* C'est de là que part l'idée de l'amour' (Lacan 1975, 46).

7. Fr. Schlegel, 'Über Goethes Meister'. In: *KFSA* (2.126–46) 131.

8. Fr. Schlegel, 'Athenäums-Fragmentev'. In: *KFSA* (2.165–255) 182f.

9. Schlegel's writings on women and gender are brought together by Winfried Menninghaus 1983.

10. Menninghaus 1983, 92.

11. Fr. Schlegel, 'Brief über den Roman'. In: *KFSA* (2.329–339) 336.

12. E.T.A. Hoffmann, 'Der Elementargeist'. Hoffmann 1992, 3. 724. In the text as 'Elementargeist' with page references.

13. Lacan 1988, 211.

14. Silverman 1992, 4.

15. In his unmistakable style, Lacan writes: '(the man) sets up dominance in the privileged place of jouissance, the object a of the phantasy (*objet petit a*), which he substitutes for the Ø (the symbolic phallus or the signifier of jouissance)'. (…) 'In its structure as I have defined it, the phantasy contains the (-Ø), the imaginary function of castration under a hidden form, reversible from one of its terms to the other. That is to say, like a complex number, it *imaginarizes* (if I may use such a term) alternatively one of these terms in relation to the other' (Lacan 1977, 320 and 322).

16. Hoffmann, however, did write a tale in which narrating assumes the psychoanalytical function of helping the analysand get rid of a psychic disturbance. See, 'Sanctus'. Hoffmann 1957, 134-52.

BIBLIOGRAPHY

Hoffmann, E.T.A. 1957. *Poetische Werke*. Vol. 3. Berlin.

Hoffmann, E.T.A. 1992. 'Der Elementargeist'. *Gesammelte Werke in drei Bänden*. Vol. 3. Essen.

Menninghaus, Winfried 1983 (Ed.). *Theorie der Weiblichkeit*. Frankfurt.

Lacan, Jacques 1975. *Encore*. Paris.

Lacan, Jacques 1977. *Écrits, A Selection*. (Trans. Alan Sheridan). New York.

Lacan, Jacques 1988. *The Seminar of Jacques Lacan*, Book II. (Trans. S. Tomaselli). Cambridge.

Luhmann, Niklas 1982. *Liebe als Passion. Zur Codierung der Intimität*. Frankfurt.

Luhmann, Niklas 1984. *Soziale Systeme*. Frankfurt.

Luhmann, Niklas 1995, 'Was ist Kommunikation'. In: *Soziologische Aufklärung* 6.

Schlegel, Friedrich 1958-95. *Kritische Friedrich Schlegel Ausgabe*. (Eds. Ernst Behler, Jean-Jacques Ansett, Hans Eichner). München. (Abbreviated as *KFSA*)

Schleiermacher, F.D.E. 1970. *Über die Religion. Reden an die Gebildeten unter ihren Verächtern* (1799). (Ed. Hans-Joachim Rothert). Hamburg.

Silverman, Kaja 1992. *Male Subjectivity at the Margins*. New York and London.

Dickinson and Whitman at the Crossroads: Perfection, Gender, and the Embryo of a Modernist Split Subject

Ide Hejlskov Larsen

In the appendix of Objective Knowledge Karl Popper introduces the idea that the mind is like a search light, not a bucket.[1] The mind has theories of what to expect to perceive, before it perceives anything. It searches for certain things leaving other things in the darkness, therefore the image of the search light. Applying the concept of the search light to literary history, I would like to propose that a literary American Romanticism existed in the mid-19th century – a period which has also been labeled the American Renaissance.[2]

Claiming that the writing of this period is Romantic usually means that one stresses the continuity with European Romanticism and thereby with several European ideas, one being that a new middle class held the sway in defining values and culture.[3] Furthermore, by calling the literature of mid-19th century Romantic, I intend directing the searchlight towards the Romantic urge to create unity between humans and nature, humans and divinity within literature.[4] As a foundation for this coherence the subject functions as an implied underlying unity. As Horace Engdahl sums up, 'The peculiarities of the Romantic works are all symptoms of the rise of the individual imagination to sovereign of the text'.[5] The Romantic texts most often have their center in an apparently autonomous subject creating its own coherent world. In order for this coherence to come true, as a beginning the Romanticists attempt to penetrate into all areas of the creating subject and strive for unity as well as understanding. From this urge for, and belief in unity, follows the realization that it is not always possible. This is where one finds the first suggestions of a modernist split or splintered subject.

My focus will be on the loci where the ideals of unity and autonomy fall apart and the deeper and darker aspects, i.e. the Freudian unconscious of modern humans

shows its face. Since the Romantic ideal is unity, the fact that a Freudian unconscious comes to the surface, undermining the unity, seems to create a fascination
with and a demonization of the unconscious. In America this may be more true
than elsewhere, since literary Romanticism or writing in the mid-19th century was
the beginning of an awareness of an American identity or, more precisely, the aspir-
ation to it, of American industrialization, of the blooming of American Adamic and
pioneer myths and their basic falsities. The new Adam represented a new civilization
opposed to earlier ones, especially the European civilization. The Adamic and pioneer myths were based on the concept of an autonomous, democratic, and innocent
American being without history, created out of the new and pristine American
nature, always, however, progressing into ever more perfection and thus creating a
perfect society – paradoxical ideas stemming from the Puritans of the 17th century.[6]

In the wake of the concept of the perfect societal construction and its potential
failure, followed the ideas of the Enlightenment of the perfectibility of human
beings. However, before the existence of this concept, social as well as other constructions had already preconceptualized what a perfectible human being was: White
Protestant man of the middle classes. To say this is not enough. One has to approach
the psychology of this White man. For the ideal of the Adamic or pioneer American
who was outlined for instance by Fenimore Cooper in the Leather Stocking novels,
had a relation with the wilderness that excluded heterosexual connections with
women. Women would transform the new Adam into a human and a sexual being
controlled by his sexual longings. The origin of the Adamic Leather Stocking is
never mentioned. For if he were to have been born of woman, the power to create
and take life would have been that of the woman. In the Adamic paradise there was
no female womb to conceive life. Therefore the hero could only relate lovingly to his
gun, the wilderness, and to his native American companion. The result being that this
'ideal' man had a latent and suppressed homoeroticism directed towards the man of
colour.

The need to suppress women and men of colour was not only part of the construction of a religious and moral hierarchy in which the White Protestant male
possessed the highest humanity. It was also a psychological need in the White man.
For suppressing the Native American or the African American meant both indulg-
ing in the slightly sadistic and clearly erotic fascination with 'him' and suppressing
the illegitimate emotions of homoerotic attraction and of sexuality in general within the White man. This ideal of a sinless American created a whole complex psy-

chology one of whose major features was repression (and destruction), projection and demonization of sexuality and of the wildness of nature. Double standards was another psychological feature.

This is the background of two major poets of the Romantic era, Emily Dickinson (1830-86) and Walt Whitman (1819-92) both of whom approach this complex of psychology, social and religious constructions, and ideals mixed with a concept of reality. While Walt Whitman seems to accept the paradoxes of this psychological and social complex, Emily Dickinson deconstructs it in many of her poems. However, in certain poignant passages of his poetry, like sections 24 to 29 of *Song of Myself* and in 'As I Ebb'd with the Ocean of Life', Whitman performs a 'destruction' or falling apart of his own ideal subject, the perfect Adam, and shows what lies hidden beneath: a fear of passive and uncontrollable homosexuality within himself connected with the Native American, a fear of the mother and of the Other maybe a God who is different from his own ideal self.[7]

Walt Whitman

In the idealizing passages of Whitman's poetry, which are almost all-pervasive, the lyric 'I' takes the role of a mythical and divine rhetorical subject.[8] Like Johan Hedberg I define the rhetorical subject as a timeless, autonomous function of the subject in language independent of the mimetic mortal subject. Both functions may be present in the same lyric 'I', though.[9] Throughout *Song of Myself* Whitman envisions the overwhelming abilities and properties of his mythical subject containing both the mimetic and the rhetorical function. He is not just part of nature, he *is* all of nature, 'Dazzling and tremendous how quick the sunrise would kill me,/ If I could not now and always send sunrise out of me' (section 25 of *Song of Myself*). The fact that he contains even the sunrise only prevents him from being killed by it. It is obvious that a power struggle is taking place which is rooted in fear. The mythical 'I' is afraid of being killed by the strength of nature. The fear, however, is a latent and unrealized feeling.

Most of the time the feeling of threat is removed from the surface. Thus, we are told that the mythical 'I' was there before the first humans, even before the creation of the world: (…) still I mount and mount. // Rise after rise bow the phantoms behind me, / Afar down I see the huge first Nothing, the vapor from the nostrils of death, / I know I was even there … I waited unseen and always, / And slept while

God carried me through the lethargic mist, / (…) / Immense have been the preparations for me, / (…) // For [my embryo] the 'nebula cohered to an orb' (section 44).

He seems part, or rather the origin, of some mythical past before cosmos was created out of chaos.

This mythical subject is not just an immanent, omnipresent being. When forgetting his latent fear, he is also a highly sensual one. His meeting and being with nature is generally shown in striking sexual imagery. At first it seems as though Whitman's encounter with nature is heterosexual. The night is called 'barebosomed' and 'We hurt each other as the bridegroom and the bride hurt each other' (section 21). But when scrutinizing the rest of the imagery in the same section and the following, it becomes obvious that both the Earth and the sea have male properties, 'Earth of the slumbering and liquid trees' – the trees having a fluidly phallic character. The Earth is also called 'Thruster'. The sea is asked to 'Dash me with amorous wet … I can repay you' (section 22). The lyric 'I' and the sea are one and the same element – and therefore male. For Whitman's mythical subject is always highly conscious of his masculine body.

In his attempt to incorporate everything, Whitman's mythical 'I' takes hold of the reader and depicts him in his own image. In so doing the lyric 'I' describes his own male physique in great detail, claiming 'it shall be you' (section 24). Since Whitman merges body and soul, humanity and nature, humanity and divinity, he thus creates a divine, natural human realm of masculinity only – at least as a subtext in his *Song of Myself*. In this realm there is no need of femininity since the new Adam possesses the power to create new life. For fertility is depicted like this: 'Sprouts take and accumulate, stand by the curb prolific and vital, / Landscapes projected masculine, full-sized and golden' (section 29). This is an enhancement of the procreational aspect of the Adamic myth in Cooper's novels where Leather Stocking has no origin in woman. He seems sprung from the womb of the wilderness. Leather Stocking is not, however, able to create new life. He is doomed to disappear along with the wilderness. Not so Whitman's mythical 'I'.

In section 28 of *Song of Myself* some of these values break down or fall apart. One might expect femity to break through since that is what has been excluded from the poem. What Whitman lets come to the surface, however, after having opened up to the depths of the psyche in section 24, is not femity – at least not in an ordinary sense of the word.[10] Until this point only pleasant sensuality has been displayed, but in section 28 the sensuality turns into an overwhelming sexuality which is out of his control. This makes the lyric 'I' uncertain of his identity, it situates him in a state of fear and anger. It is as if he is raped by a Native American, 'They have left me helpless to a red marauder' – red suggesting Native American and the male member. 'They' are creating the action and watching. A certain fearful exhibitionism is displayed in this section:

> Flames and ether making a rush for my veins,
> Treacherous tip of me reaching and crowding to help them,
> My flesh and blood playing out lightning, to strike what is hardly different from myself,
> On all sides prurient provokers stiffening my limbs,
> Straining the udder of my heart for its withheld drip,
> Behaving licentious toward me, taking no denial,
> Depriving me of my best as for a purpose,
> Unbuttoning my clothes and holding me by the bare waist,
> Deluding my confusion with the calm of the sunlight and pasture fields,
> Immodestly sliding the fellow-senses away,
> They bribed to swap off with touch, and go and graze at the edges of me,
> No consideration, no regard for my draining strength or my anger,
> Fetching the rest of the herd around to enjoy them awhile,
> Then all uniting to stand on a headland and worry me.
>
> The sentries desert every other part of me,
> They have left me helpless to a red marauder,
> They all come to the headland to witness and assist against me.
>
> I am given up by traitors;
> I talk wildly ... I have lost my wits ... I and nobody else am the greatest traitor,
> I went myself first to the headland ... my own hands carried me there.
>
> You villain touch! what are you doing? ... my breath is tight in its throat;
> Unclench you floodgates! you are too much for me
> (ll. 619-640).

But at the end (in section 29) the lyric 'I' realizes that it all originates in himself, therefore suddenly no problem exists. The implication is that only good emanates from Whitman's bodily and rhetorical subject. One could also claim that the mythical construction blinds the lyric 'I' to the contents of the un-conscious. For he is convinced, like Ralph Waldo Emerson, that the un-conscious is divine.[11] He does not seem to acknowledge that in his case the unconscious yearns for masochistic, exhibitionistic homosexuality which does not agree with the myth of the controlling and procreating Adam. Nor does it agree with the idea that the White Protestant man is a free and autonomous being. For such a man would not feel a need to be subjugated by other men.

It all started with a touch or something that felt like a touch: 'Is this then a touch? ... quivering me to a new identity' (section 28, l. 618). I will suggest that this touch is the touch of his Freudian unconscious, and finally it is the touch of dread at a change in terms of agents in language. All of a sudden there are other agents than the mythical 'I'. They are creating an action in which the subject becomes an object. All of these aspects are experienced as alien and alienating, splitting up the subject, but also in the end when they are subsumed under the mythical lyric I again, making him experience great sexual pleasure.

One could claim that for a brief moment Whitman realizes that the mythical construction of a subject containing the sensual and bodily aspects of a mimetic lyric 'I' and the immortal aspects of a rhetorical lyric 'I' is bound to fall apart. And then he lets this realization slip away, or rather, he gets a sexual kick from it and forgets about it.

The sections from 21 culminating in 28 is a pivotal part, quite literally, of the whole of the 52 sections of *Song of Myself*. For the long poem can be divided into seven major parts, and this is the fourth part, the exact middle. Thus the poem is structured symmetrically around this culmination or abyss.[12] Somehow the structuring poet must have realized the heavy and disruptive freight this section carries. But if he were to realize this fully, he would have to confront not only passive, exhibitionistic homosexuality, but also the separation of the mimetic from the rhetorical function and therefore the mortality of the mimetic lyric I. Death, however, is not present here or elsewhere in *Song of Myself*.

In 'As I Ebb'd with the Ocean of Life' the rhetorical subject has retired into the background 'the real Me stands yet untouch'd, untold, altogether unreach'd,/ Withdrawn far, mocking me with mock-congratulatory signs and bows' (section 2).[13]

Here the lyric 'I' has accepted his passive homosexuality. He clings to the father's breast, the shore, and hides from and fears the avenging mother sea. The Freudian and Lacanian Oedipal triangle has been turned around, the mother is the rival, castrator, and destroyer. However, the lyric 'I' is in death throes and the wreckage of the maternal sea seems to be himself and his poetry. Both of these crucial loci in Whitman's poetry might represent the subtext of the whole mythical American complex with which Whitman identifies, after all.

The mythical American hero with a latent homoerotic drive which is projected onto the African and Native American has in Whitman been transformed into a fear of a deep masochistic and exhibitionistic homosexuality that is related to a fear of being castrated by a woman Other. Whitman fears taking the traditional role of the woman, the passive one, while longing to position himself exactly there. When acknowledging this yearning, he feels the threat to his existence and thus to his divinity. A new and Other divinity and a new and Other nature is envisioned here. Nature is destructive and so is the Godhead, and death is close at hand. This poem is characterized by separation and distinction between many phenomena: namely the mimetic, mortal poet, the rhetorical subject, the mother sea, the father shore, the Godhead, all of which represent distinct aspects of the Freudian unconscious of the lyric 'I', except perhaps for the Godhead. Furthermore, they represent distinct entities in the external world. Whitman's lyric 'I' here acknowledges fragmentation in the world and in his subject. But it makes him feel depressive and without creative power.

Emily Dickinson

Unlike Whitman, Dickinson does not attempt to repress or remove fragmentation of the external world or of the subject. Nor does she feel depression as a consequence of the splitting up of the self and the world. At times her lyric personae experience euphoria because of the explosive but hidden powers of the unconscious. At times Dickinson just depicts the interrelationship between a fragmented personality and a fragmented society of double standards.

Even though no lyric 'I' is mentioned in Emily Dickinson's Poem 601 'A still – Volcano – Life –', it is obvious that references are made to the act or result of writing and therefore to a lyric consciousness.[14] So the volcano represents both an element in nature and the writer of the poem. What first is 'A still – Volcano – Life –', then 'A quiet – Earthquake Style –' in the third and last stanza turns into 'The lips that never lie – / Whose hissing Corals part – and shut – / And Cities – ooze away –'. Although the surface seems calm, an immense explosive force hides beneath. The lips seem to refer to both the female sex and to a phenomenon outliving a human life, since it is parallel to corals. Here we see a clearly aggressive, lethal, feminine power of the unconscious (the unconscious never lies) which is part of the unmentioned lyric 'I's creativity and therefore could be said to represent her rhetorical 'I'. As opposed to Whitman, Dickinson does not in her rendering of natural landscapes struggle with an idea of a divine human and natural unconscious. Nor does she see a threat to her lyric 'I' in nature. Instead she identifies with the disruptive aspects of nature. Her landscapes are in transformation or on the verge of transformation as are her lyric personae.

When Emily Dickinson deconstructs the complex social, religious, and psychological constructions, as she does in for instance Poem 443 'I tie my Hat – I crease my Shawl –', she shows how these constructions have become an ingrained structure in the female psyche of her persona and that they contradict the discovery of the persona's identity. The construction or growing awareness of her gender and her becoming mature is not a progress into a state of no change because one attains completeness, sinlessness, and harmony. The maturation is a marked change into instability of self, sexual identity, social, religious, and verbal meaning; an instability that creates despair, destruction, and creativity in the persona.

In Poem 443, what first seems to be the mimetic lyric 'I' cleaning and keeping order in the house, turns out to be an explosive rhetorical 'I', but the explosive force is no longer roaming free as in Poem 601.[15] As the explosiveness or the instability of the lyric 'I' has been acknowledged in the poem, the 'I' becomes a 'we'. Thus, having disclosed her being split or splintered she verbally and mentally turns into two subjects.

I tie my Hat – I crease my Shawl –
Life's little duties do – precisely –
As the very least
Were infinite – to me –

I put new Blossoms in the Glass –
And throw the old – away –

I push a petal from my Gown

That anchored there – I weigh

The time 'twill be till six o'clock

I have so much to do –

And yet – Existence – some way back –

Stopped – struck – my ticking – through –

We cannot put Ourself away

As a completed Man

Or Woman – When the Errand's done

We came to Flesh – upon –

There may be – Miles on Miles of Nought –

Of Action – sicker far –

To simulate – is stinging work –

To cover what we are

From Science – and from Surgery –

Too Telescopic Eyes

To bear on us unshaded -

For their – sake – not for Our's –

'Twould start them –

We – could tremble –

But since we got a Bomb –

and held it in our Bosom –

Nay – Hold it – it is calm –

—

Therefore – we do life's labor –

Though life's Reward – be done –

With scrupulous exactness –

To hold our Senses – on –

The fact that this 'we' holds a bomb in our bosom indicates that 'we' may be a combination of the rhetorical and the mimetic lyric 'I'. The realization that she is a poet and therefore has an autonomous existence within the poem has cut her in two. But this is not all there is to her explosiveness. Her bomb is loaded with instability of gender as well, 'We cannot put Ourself away / As a completed Man / Or Woman'. She is not certain whether she has become a man or a woman. This may be a realization of bisexuality since the sentence continues, '– When the Errand's done / We came to Flesh – upon –'. The errand may be the Puritan errand into the wilderness to transform evil into good. Thus, when she attempted to transform evil into good within herself, she encountered her flesh which led her to doubt whether she be a man or a woman. The errand may of course also be the chores of everyday life, which still leads to the same result as the first errand.

The errand is a negation of the body, however the body, or rather as I would claim the Freudian unconscious, cannot be suppressed. 'We came to Flesh – upon –' may imply that the rhetorical subject came into being as words that take on certain qualities like bodies. The Adamic myth suggests that a Christ-like figure comes into existence in America. That is how Whitman depicts his mythical, mimetic, and rhetorical subject. Dickinson's Christ-like figure, who is also partly her rhetorical subject, comes into being, into flesh, in a highly ambiguous way. Jesus was the word become flesh, Dickinson's persona may be the word become flesh, but a flesh that entails bisexuality and therefore sin. Thus, her divine rhetorical subject is rather a depressive and sinful demonic force.

The surroundings of the lyric 'we' scrutinize everything in scientific detail. Their interest therefore seems to be 'truth'. However, the truth they might encounter when realizing what goes on in the lyric I's mind, would be devastating to them. One can detect a criticism of the Puritan and scientific double standards that could not contain her experience of sexuality, creativity, and sin. As opposed to many American thinkers and writers of the time, Dickinson does not see the subject and its psyche as autonomous. Ralph Waldo Emerson saw society as an external and destructive force whereas human beings were seen as divine and autonomous beings in touch with nature.[16] Dickinson's persona participates so much in her culture that the scientific and Puritan double standards of her surroundings have become part of her own psyche. For the fact that her instability is depicted as a bomb which may explode when her surroundings tremble, makes it clear that the bomb is infected with the mentality of the surroundings. If the bomb explodes, she will be the first to die. Therefore she keeps a balanced surface.

What comes through in the poem 443 as well as in the other explosive ones, is the idea of a strong and castrating femininity. Yet, in the volcano poems (Poems 175 and 601), the complexity of Poem 443 is not present. For the reciprocity between the rhetorical subject and her surroundings does not exist in the other poems. In Poem 443 the complexity of the psyche and of the unconscious is shown, whereas in the volcano poems the singular destructive power of the unconscious is depicted. In Poem 443 it becomes obvious that were this creativity to open up completely and show its contents of aggressive femininity, it would destroy itself as well.

One sees woman as controlled by strong internal and external forces. As a rare phenomenon in Dickinson's poetry, an explanation of the persona's situation can be detected. This explanation can be found in the ideas of Puritanism and the Enlightenment, and in the Romantic transformations of these ideas. When going into the wilderness of nature and the mind to search for an ideal nature and for harmony, Dickinson's persona finds only bisexuality, evil or disharmony, and as a consequence depression, but also a potentially destructive creativity.

In Poem 754 'My Life had stood – a Loaded Gun –' Dickinson turns the relation between pioneer, gun, and wilderness upside-down by making the gun speak as a feminine persona. This persona is a rhetorical subject, for at the end of the poem, Dickinson writes, 'Though I than He – may longer live / He longer must – than I – / For I have but the power to kill, / Without – the power to die –' (ll. 21-24). Comparing the life of the hunter with that of the gun or her rhetorical subject, Dickinson creates a paradox. These lines suggest that the rhetorical subject will live for ever, whereas the mimetic subject, the hunter, experiences more life. The life of the gun is without quality. She can only kill. Dying makes a person vulnerable, makes it possible to hurt a person. The gun can neither experience pain, death, nor love. She can only experience a pleasure that is destructive in its autonomous narcissism, 'And do I smile, such cordial light / Upon the Valley glow – / It is as a Vesuvian face / Had let it's pleasure through –' (ll. 9-12). The hunter must experience pain, death, and love, therefore he must live longer. His life will be a real life.

Furthermore Dickinson offers a sadomasochistic interpretation of the relation between the gun, the owner, and nature in the shape of a doe. Again we see a power struggle between gendered objects. The feminine or rhetorical subject is imbued with masculine power by means of his shooting with her, which is her only aim in life. Sexuality and power are intertwined, and nature is part of the struggle for sexual power. If this struggle between divergent forces is seen as a struggle between various aspects of one personality, it seems obvious to suggest that the personality or consciousness is not only divided into separate, hostile forces, but also closely linked with the cultural code of the pioneer. The myth of the pioneer is turned into a demonic myth of destruction and narcissism, not divinity and love. And, it is seen as moulding the psyche into alienating self-destruction.

Conclusion

Thus, it can be said that Dickinson is working with the Freudian unconscious, and the consciousness in general, as interwoven with the norms of society and therefore with a subject and a nature in constant eruption, always threatening to change from one state to another, often its opposite, from calm to explosion. Her vision of the relation between the subject, a Freudian unconscious, and the natural landscape is always on the verge of turning upside-down: The volcano life may be subdued, but were it to explode, i.e. take over, cities would 'ooze away'. Whitman is concerned with a power relation between the subject and the natural landscape, too. The power relation underlying his oeuvre is however more like a stable hierarchical structure, and the few but significant breaches on that static structure are never fully adopted into his work, because he wishes to hold on to the mythical project of the divine Romantic Adam transforming evil and fragmentation into good and unity.

The power struggle between the sexes and sexualities, the struggle to acknowledge homo- or bisexuality, and the idea of hierarchy seems to be at the core of Whitman's and Dickinson's oeuvre, and it seems to be one major conflict within American Romanticism, at least the struggle between the sexes and the hierarchy underlying it. Dickinson seems to stand out in showing hierarchy to be never stable – or in Margaret Homans' words, 'Emily Dickinson as a woman poet enters in a non-traditional way into the ongoing dialogue in Western literature and metaphysics over the dualism of subject and object'.[17] She does it by indicating that the subject is not unified. A part of a psyche can be the subject in relation to other partial objects, and another part of the psyche can be object in relation to an aspect of itself or an aspect of another subject in the external world.

In American Romanticism the struggle of the sexes and the idea of hierarchy is so strong that either one gender is simply excluded from the context, as in Melville's *Moby Dick,* or it means the death of the other, often the woman, as in certain of Hawthorne's short stories, for instance 'Rappacini's Daughter', and as in many of Poe's short stories on women, for instance 'Berenice'. As in Whitman the hierarchy between subject and object is endangered by the fear of the sexual power of femininity.

Karl Popper argues that we always have presuppositions about the world before we make observations. Literary history and interpretation are also created by means of presuppositions. I have attempted both to clarify my preconceived ideas about

American Romanticism and to make readings in the light of these presuppositions. The result of this process has been positioning Whitman – which is not so surprising – and Dickinson at the center of American Romanticism from which, thus, a tentatively modernist gender, identity, and societal debate arises.

NOTES

1. Popper 1976.

2. See Matthiessen 1941. Matthiessen only included Emerson, Thoreau, Whitman, Melville, and Hawthorne in his study. Later treatments of the period have included Dickinson and Poe, see Reynolds 1988, and Fuller and Poe, see Steele 1987. The concept has been criticised a great deal for its exclusion of a great many writers, including almost only white men. See for instance Warren (ed.) 1993. However, no new concept for the period has been created – besides Romanticism – and I still consider Melville, Hawthorne, Poe, Whitman, Dickinson, and Emerson major writers of the period.

3. The idea that European Romanticism is a period of middle class culture can be detected for instance in Aarseth 1995.

4. Ralph Waldo Emerson is one Romanticist who conceived of an Over-Soul circulating through nature as well as human beings. He believed this spirit to have its origin in the (American) subject, not in nature. See Emerson, 'The Over-Soul' in: Emerson 1989, 973-84.

5. See Engdahl 1986, the English Summary, 5.

6. For a presentation of the Adam myth see for instance Lewis 1955. As to a connection between 17th century Puritanism and the Adam myth, see Miller 1956/64.

7. For an introduction of Whitman's use of the adamic and Puritan tradition and his relation to a modern American movie by David Lynch, i.e. *Blue Velvet,* see my article: Larsen 1994.

8. All my references to Whitman's *Song of Myself* are from the first 1855 edition of *Leaves of Grass.* (Ed. Malcolm Cowley), 1959/86. The titles like *Song of Myself* were chosen later by Whitman. Like Cowley, I employ those titles to simplify references.

9. Horace Engdahl mentions the performative function of language as opposed to that of the mimetic when interpreting a specific poem by the Swedish poet, Tegnér (Engdahl 1986, 263). Referring to Engdahl, Johan Hedberg employs the concept of the performative function in Edith Södergran's poetry, calling it an act in language (Hedberg 1991, 15). He extends the concept of the performative function to the lyric subject as well when it functions as an act in language and is conceived as existing there eternally, calling it the rhetorical subject as opposed to the experiencing or psychological, mimetic subject (ibid. 17). The idea of the performative is a concept from speech act theory. See Austin 1975.

10. The lyric 'I' orders, 'Unscrew the locks from the doors! / Unscrew the doors themselves from their jambs!' (ll.502-3).

11. See Ralph Waldo Emerson 'Nature' (1836). Emerson 1989, 926: 'God in the unconscious'.

12. Harold Bloom claims that *Song of Myself* is structured somewhat differently (Bloom 1976, 248-66). According to him the poem can be divided into six parts following his phases of the American sublime (ibid. 248). For Bloom the sections 31-38 are the culmination of the poem, the greatest instance of the American sublime (ibid. 259). However, they are not in the middle and they do not contain such massive symptoms of change as does section 28 with its fragmented syntax and with the use of negative words like 'prurient' and 'licentious'. The reason that Bloom does not see section 28 as the center of the poem is probably that he reads it as a masturbatory scene (ibid. 259).

13. This poem was first published as 'Bardic Symbols' in the *Atlantic Monthly,* April, 1860. The version I quote is the last one from 1881 in Whitman 1973.

14. All numbers of poems are in accordance with the numbering of *The Poems of Emily Dickinson.*

15. For a more detailed reading of Poems 443 'I tie my Hat – I crease my Shawl –' and 754 'My Life had stood – a Loaded Gun –' see Larsen 1995. Unlike Smith 1992, I see the last nine lines (ll. 25-33) of the poems as belonging to the poem. This is in accordance with Thomas H. Johnson's definition. Smith follows Franklin in *The Manuscript Books of Emily Dickinson.* Franklin claims that the lines 25-29 belong to Poem 1712 which is placed in the beginning of the fascicle as opposed to Poem 443 which is situated towards the end of the fascicle. For a closer argumentation as to why I follow Johnson, see my above mentioned article p. 83.

16. See Emerson 'Nature'.

17. Homans 1983.

BIBLIOGRAPHY

Aarseth, Asbjørn 1995. 'Forskyvninger i romantikkbegrepets funksjon – med særlig hensyn til norsk og nordisk litteraturhistorie'. *Litteratur og Romantikstudiers Skriftrække* 15.

Austin, J.L. 1975. *How to do Things with Words.* Cambridge, Mass.

Bloom, Harold 1976. *Poetry and Repression.* New Haven.

Emerson, Ralph Waldo 1989. 'Nature' (1836). In: *Norton Anthology of American Literature.* Third edition, Vol. 1. New York and London.

Engdahl, Horace 1986. *Den romantiska texten.* Stockholm.

Dickinson, Emily (1955). *The Poems of Emily Dickinson.* (Ed. Thomas H. Johnson). Cambridge, Mass.

Dickinson, Emily (1981). *The Manuscript Books of Emily Dickinson.* Cambridge, Mass.

Hedberg, Johan 1991. *Eros Skapar världen ny: Apokalyps och pånyttfödelse i Edith Södergrans lyrik.* Göteborg.

Homans, Margaret 1983. 'Oh, Vision of Language! Dickinson's Poems of Love and Death'. In: *Feminist Critics Read Emily Dickinson.* (Ed. Suzanne Juhasz). Bloomington.

Larsen, Ide Hejlskov 1994. 'Adam i den vilde amerikanske have - myter om amerikansk natur og identitet'. In: *Naturen som argument.* (Eds. Ide Hejlskov Larsen et al.). Odense.

Larsen, Ide Hejlskov 1995. 'Emily Dickinson Challenges American Myths: The Ritual Power of Words - to Re-create, Kill, and Make Sex'. In: *The Emily Dickinson Journal* 4.2.

Lewis, R.W.B. 1955. *The American Adam: Innocence, Tragedy, and Tradition in the Nineteenth Century.* Chicago.

Matthiessen, F.O. 1941. *The American Renaissance: Art and Expression in the Age of Emerson and Whitman.* New York.

Miller, Perry 1964. *Errand into the Wilderness.* New York.

Popper, Karl 1976. *Objective Knowledge.* Oxford.

Reynolds, David S. 1988. *Beneath the American Renaissance: The Subversive Imagination in the Age of Emerson and Melville.* Cambridge, Mass.

Smith, Martha Nell 1992. *Rowing in Eden: Rereading Emily Dickinson.* Austin, Texas.

Steele, Jeffrey 1987. *The Representation of the Self in the American Renaissance.* North Carolina.

Warren, Joyce W. (Ed.) 1993. *The (Other) American Renaissance: Nineteenth-Century Women Writers.* New Brunswick, New Jersey.

Whitman, Walt 1959. *Leaves of Grass.* (Ed. Malcolm Cowley). Harmondsworth.

Whitman, Walt 1973. *Leaves of Grass.* A Norton Critical Edition. (Eds. Sculley Bradley & Harold W. Blodgett). New York and London.

Poétique du rêve et théories de l'écriture dans l'Europe romantique

Alain Montandon

'Des récits décousus, incohérents, avec pourtant des associations, tels les *rêves',* demande Novalis.[1] Il existe de nombreuses théories à l'époque des romantismes européens: de *l'Athenäum* en passant par le *Prologue* de Wordsworth à celle de *Cromwell* de Hugo, on n'en finirait pas de dénombrer les fragments théoriques s'exprimant dans les préfaces, les essais. Ces efforts théoriques ne sont certes pas à négliger, mais ils nous renseignent sans doute moins sur l'écriture romantique que sa pratique même. L'effort spéculatif n'est jamais mieux pertinent que lorsqu'il se combine avec son déploiement esthétique. Le romantisme allemand qui sans conteste (je parle du premier romantisme, le romantisme d'Iéna, celui de *l'Athenäum,* tel que Novalis et Friedrich Schlegel le pensent au tournant du siècle) est l'une des formes les plus pures d'une telle spéculation, pose un principe fondamental qui veut que théorie et pratique ne fassent qu'un. C'est ce que développe admirablement un Friedrich Schlegel dans son roman *Lucinde.* Je voudrais évoquer ici la poétique du rêve comme théorie du romantisme[2] et de son écriture. Autrement dit montrer que le rêve dans son écriture est aussi théorie du rêve et théorisation d'une écriture romantique.

Songes, visions, rêveries et rêves

Pour ce faire, je rappellerai brièvement quelques caractéristiques concernant le statut du rêve au XVIIIe siècle. Le songe est avant tout un artifice formel[3] qui sert à faire passer des idées extravagantes, libertines, extrêmes. Discours symbolique ou allégorique dont le sens doit être explicitement et immédiatement décrypté par des références à un code de traduction établi, le rêve écrit apparaît surtout comme un artifice d'écriture servant à des fins très étrangères à toute prise en considération de la figurabilité onirique (pour reprendre l'expression freudienne de la 'Rücksicht auf Darstellbarkeit'). Le XVIIIe siècle a particulièrement insisté sur son inintelligibilité, faisant de lui la production chaotique d'une conscience délirante. Les représentants de l'Aufklärung chez Novalis comme chez Hoffmann seront porteurs d'une telle conception: 'Träume sind Schäume'! Pour Diderot 'nos rêves ne sont que des jugements précipités qui se succèdent avec une rapidité incroyable et qui, rapprochant des objets qui ne se tiennent que par des qualités fort éloignées, en composent un tout bizarre'. A peine quelques années plus tard ces mêmes caractères d'incohérence, de rapidité, de bizarrerie et de liaisons audacieuses entre objets vont constituer les éléments fondamentaux et positifs d'une activité onirique conçue non plus sur le mode de l'aliénation, mais de la révélation. Une telle rupture dans la conscience occidentale ne saurait être sous-estimée dans ses effets et il s'agit de comprendre comment s'est opérée cette radicale transformation du sens, qui donne à l'incohérence son statut, à l'étrange sa signification et au bizarre sa valeur esthétique.

La valorisation tout à fait nouvelle de l'onirisme et son entrée dans le champ du poétique sont étroitement dépendantes d'une transformation beaucoup plus large de la sensibilité, des idéologies, des pratiques d'écriture, qui est manifeste en France, en Angleterre et surtout en Allemagne à l'exclusion pratiquement de tous les autres pays européens. Une telle rupture avec la tradition est signifiée par Coleridge lorsqu'il écrit qu'il 'existe une espèce de poésie bâtie sur les fondations du rêve'.

Rêverie

L'une des premières étapes est représentée par l'épanouissement de la rêverie, activité qui offre les premiers éléments d'une telle poétique. Mais elle n'en est cependant qu'une esquisse fragmentaire et incomplète. Premier élément d'une chaîne dépressive (ennui, langueur, mélancolie), la rêverie a pris, surtout à partir des années 1760, l'aspect d'une rêverie-jouissance qui se développe et s'enrichit d'un nouveau contenu reposant sur un accord profond avec le cosmos. Pensée errante et indéfinie, suscitée par certains paysages, elle échappe à la maîtrise de la pensée consciente. 'Dans la rêverie, on n'est point actif. Les images se tracent dans le cerveau, s'y combinent comme dans le sommeil sans le concours de la volonté; on laisse à tout cela suivre sa marche et l'on jouit sans agir' écrit J.-J. Rousseau dans les *Rêveries du Promeneur solitaire*. Produit de la solitude caractérisée par une passivité fondamentale, la rêverie est comme le rêve, un monde détaché du monde, une conscience absente à elle-même, qui parfois se réduit au pur sentiment intérieur de l'existence ('rêver à la Suisse') ou bien se dilue dans l'identification extatique au monde: 'on oublie tout, on s'oublie soi-même, on ne sait plus ou l'on est' s'exclame Saint-Preux rêvant sur la montagne du Valais.[4] La métamorphose du paysage en lieu de l'imaginaire a pour corollaire la pénétration intime et totale de la subjectivité qui lui confère sa transparence, son unité et sa coloration affective. Si la sensation concrète est le point de départ, le 'vague d'une rêverie confuse', la 'libre succession des souvenirs' transforment la rêverie en un état quasi hypnotique, comme le sera pour les surréalistes l'écriture automatique selon la formule de Béatrice Didier. Cette confusion du rêveur et du monde, cette interpénétration libre de l'intime et de l'ouvert sont à l'origine d'une nouvelle poétique prenant en compte les tressaillements du cœur dans leur apparente incohérence. Par la suggestion de l'ineffable et de l'infini, par le jeu des impressions subconscientes, par la liberté anarchique de son développement, la rêverie est l'instrument et le lieu d'une nouvelle prose poétique répondant aux exigences que formulera plus tard Baudelaire, celle d'une 'prose poétique musicale sans rythme et sans rime, assez souple et assez heurtée pour s'adapter aux mouvements lyriques de l'âme'. Mélodique dans son mouvement, litanique par la répétition de mots, d'images ou de leitmotivs, l'écriture de la rêverie s'accompagne d'une régression au niveau du langage, où l'image devance la pensée et où la phrase même retrouve son 'origine' musicale et incantatoire.

'Comment définirez-vous la rêverie, ce frémissement intérieur de l'âme où viennent se rassembler et comme se perdre, dans une confusion mystérieuse, toutes les puissances des sens et de la pensée' écrivait Benjamin Constant. Chez René, c'est la 'surabondance de vie' dont le héros se sent 'accablé' qui fait jaillir la rêverie: 'Qu'il fallait peu de choses à ma rêverie! une feuille séchée que le vent chassait devant moi, une cabane dont la fumée s'élevait dans la cime dépouillée des arbres, la mousse qui tremblait au souffle du Nord sur le tronc d'un chêne, une roche écartée, un étang désert où le jonc flétri murmurait!'[5] Une poétique de l'indéterminé, de la liquidité qui dissout l'homme et le monde dans un même évanouissement, poétique de la mémoire qui creuse la distance.

Mais une telle poétique reste limitée, car elle ne fait qu'effleurer les ruptures de la conscience et l'on reste toujours en deçà d'une limite rarement transgressée. Rousseau, Senancour, Goethe, Chateaubriand sont de bien piètres rêveurs, soit parce qu'ils ne croient pas en la réalité authentique du message onirique, soit parce qu'une révélation dans laquelle la conscience perd ses droits et son pouvoir ne peut en être une. La succession rhapsodique d'images n'intéresse l'écrivain que dans la mesure où elle est saisie comme un phénomène de conscience.

La poétique du rêve, telle qu'elle est définie par le romantisme, est fondée justement sur la rupture de l'activité onirique avec la conscience. Par les 'fondations du rêve', Coleridge entend non seulement une nouvelle forme d'expression, mais aussi le jeu des activités inconscientes de l'esprit, celui de l'imagination la plus libre, ainsi qu'une certaine vérité ontologique, celle de l'unité de l'esprit et de la nature, exprimée par le rêve, qui se traduisent par la découverte d'un autre langage.

Visions et songes

Il existe cependant une autre forme d'écriture qui nous semble essentielle à la genèse de l'écriture onirique romantique: les songes et les visions, dont la tradition est ancienne, mais qui sont à nouveau au goût du jour, particulièrement avec un Sebastien Mercier dont on ne saurait sousestimer l'influence européenne. Dans la préface des *Voyages imaginaires, songes, visions et romans cabalistiques,* l'éditeur distingue le rêve du songe en voyant dans le premier un assemblage 'd'idées disparates, extravagantes et singulières', alors que le second se caractérise par 'un tour plus sérieux, moins déraisonnable' et donc finalement plus philosophique. Que ce soit les *Songes du Chevalier de la Marmotte* (1745) ou les rêves d'un quelconque philosophe pseudo-grec, le songe est un cadre facile pour l'exposé d'utopies ou d'idées morales. Sebastien Mercier avec ses *Songes philosophiques* (1768) et les *Songes d'un hermite* (1770), semblerait se situer dans une tradition bien établie, mais qu'il renouvelle cependant par des images fortes.

Mercier ouvre en effet un champ nouveau à l'imaginaire qui durera pendant tout le romantisme, faisant appel aux visions cosmiques, aux thèmes de la guerre, de la fin du monde, aux visions catastrophiques, aux images d'horreur (sang, cendre, mutilations, organes démembrés, etc.). Sans doute s'agit-il encore dans la tradition de Quevedo d'allégories, où la rhétorique de l'horreur est employée dans une perspective morale. Mais cette dimension n'est pas gênante, contrairement à ce que l'on pense généralement. Car la dimension allégorique, si elle est déplacée, n'en subsiste pas moins pendant le romantisme sous la forme de l'allégorie indirecte. Ce qui est très nouveau chez Mercier, c'est le fait que ce qui n'était qu'un moyen chez Quevedo, tend à prendre une place de plus en plus importante. La rhétorique de l'image onirique est de plus en plus au service d'elle-même. Si le cauchemar conserve généralement une leçon morale (importante pour Jean Paul, plus discrète chez Nodier), son centre de gravité se déplace vers une esthétique de l'horreur, celle de la 'beauté de la Méduse' (Mario Praz). Le rêve cauchemardesque est le cadre idéal pour la prolifération de ces 'belles horreurs'. Ainsi le cauchemar d'Oberman (Lettre LXXXV) débute-t-il par cette vision: 'Il y a quelques temps je vis une éruption de volcans; mais jamais l'horreur des volcans ne fut aussi grande, aussi épouvantable, aussi belle'.[6]

Ce qui est vrai pour les visions d'enfer l'est aussi pour les visions paradisiaques, même si les premières sont plus riches en thèmes et en images, comme l'a montré Jacques Bousquet. Les rêves de jardins merveilleux et paradisiaques sont présentés sous le signe du superlatif et de l'absolu: tout y est multiple, infini et pourtant uni par un mouvement liquide ou aérien qui enveloppe les apparitions dans un même élan. L'harmonie, synthèse de l'un et du multiple, suspend les qualités contradictoires des êtres et des choses. Heinrich von Ofterdingen est 'ivre d'extase, mais conscient de la moindre impression'.[7] Le rêve devient réalisation passive du désir: 'A l'instant mes souhaits furent exaucés: je me sentis porté doucement sur sa surface, je fus plongé dans une atmosphère embaumée'.[8] Si le rêve d'enfer est un drame dont le mouvement est une destruction progressive, celui du paradis est celui d'une pénétration fusionnelle, d'une dissolution qui se traduit par l'apothéose des sens chez Mercier et Novalis:

Une fraîcheur délicieuse tenait mes sens ouverts à la joie; une odeur suave coulait dans mon sang avec l'air que je respirais; mon cœur, qui tressaillait avec une force inaccoutumée, entrait dans une mer de délices, et le plaisir comme une lumière immortelle et pure, éclairait mon âme dans toute sa profondeur.[9]

(…) une sensation céleste inonda son cœur, d'innombrables pensées se pressèrent en lui avec une volupté profonde, images nouvelles, jamais contemplées, dressées comme pour se confondre et se transformer en créatures visibles. Et chaque vague de l'adorable élément se pressait contre lui comme une gorge amoureuse. Le flot paraissait fait de charmantes filles dissoutes dans l'onde, qui reprenaient leur forme dès que les effleurait le corps du jeune homme.[10]

Ou bien encore la dérive paradisiaque prend la forme d'une dématérialisation, par un cheminement de plus en plus incorporel chez un Jean Paul (la rosée devient larme, rayon de lumière, note de musique). L'imaginaire de l'infini débouche sur un monde indifférencié. Dans l'un et l'autre cas, les images ne sont que les traces symboliques du sentiment évoqué. Il y a donc un balancement continuel et une tension entre la fascination de l'image et sa dimension allégorique et symbolique.

On sait l'importance des songes de Mercier dans le romantisme européen, chez un Jean Paul, chez un Victor Hugo,[11] chez un Chateaubriand.[12] Celle-ci me semble double: d'une part elle réside dans la force des images, leur puissance sublime, leur intensité affective, d'autre part dans la puissance d'allégorisation qu'elles recèlent. Il s'agit moins de symbolisation dans le sens où l'image serait le symbole, clair ou confus, d'une idée qui transparaîtrait ou qu'elle porterait en elle-même que de la désignation du pouvoir allégorique du rêve, c'est-à-dire (et c'est là l'originalité de l'influence de Mercier qui a été trop peu notée) du pouvoir qui est moins celui de transmettre directement un message moral ou métaphysique que de signifier.

Intransitivité

Le rêve est le modèle paradigmatique d'une poésie qui trouve dans le fragmentaire des échappées d'éternité, dans la clôture le signe d'une totalité et d'une autonomie qui la constitue comme œuvre intransitive.

Le scénario de l'entrée dans le rêve marque un seuil, une coupure qui concilie l'exigence fragmentaire et celle de la totalité. L'hétérogénéité des splendides mosaïques du rêve est unifiée par l'intensité du sentiment qui accompagne l'aventure du rêveur dans sa pensée[13] mouvante. Ainsi le jeune Thomas De Quincey rêve-t-il le seuil, un dimanche de Pâques, à la porte de son cottage, celle d'une magnificence solennisée. L'entrée dans le rêve est marquée par de nombreux indices qui sont autant d'embrayeurs dans un mouvement qui conduit à un déplacement, un changement topique qui modifie la situation antérieure. L'instauration d'un scénario désigne ce déplacement dont le schéma le plus généralement suivi est l'entrée dans le rêve, l'apparition d'une figure (le guide) qui instaure un déplacement ou un voyage qui aboutit à une vision qui peut être une image harmonieuse et symphonique ou celle d'une désharmonie infernale. Un brusque réveil et un nouveau regard sur le monde concluent ce parcours.

Mais ce mouvement du rêve est plus la spatialisation d'une intensité affective qu'un parcours initiatique. Telle une arabesque il trace le déplacement comme automanifestation et autorévélation de soi. Il est le venir à soi du sujet par l'image et cette image qui se dérobe à la lecture allégorique ou symbolique est étrangement incohérente. Et pourtant 'quand quelqu'un ne parle que pour parler, il énonce alors les vérités les plus magnifiques et les plus originales' écrit Novalis, qui expose avec précision ce que doit être la nouvelle écriture:

Des récits décousus, incohérents, avec pourtant des associations, tels les rêves. Des poèmes parfaitement harmonieux tout simplement, et beaux de parfaites paroles, mais aussi sans cohérence, ni sens aucun, avec au maximum deux ou trois strophes intelligibles – qui doivent être comme de purs fragments des choses les plus diverses. La poésie, la vraie, peut tout au plus avoir un sens allégorique et produire, comme la musique, un effet indirect.[14]

Aussi l'écriture du rêve doit-elle être comme une algèbre, une œuvre d'art cohérente, non seulement parce que les signifiants sont aussi proches que possible du signifié, mais aussi parce que les signes tissent un réseau très dense de relations diachroniques et synchroniques. Diachronique, dans la mesure où le rêve est présenté comme une mélodie, 'dream-fugue' (De Quincey), variations sur un thème dont les écarts créent la pertinence. Et synchronique, par le réseau de correspondances entre les sens, les images, les thèmes, etc. L'incohérence devient cohérence supérieure par la métamorphose: si les asperges du jardin deviennent les doigts d'une main, les désœuvrés de la ville des hannetons bourdonnants (4ème et 24ème Songe de Mercier), les larmes des étoiles chez Jean Paul et la fleur un visage féminin chez Novalis, c'est que l'univers est animé et que toutes les images ne sont que des manifestations d'une idée ou d'un principe supérieur. Cette commune origine légitime les correspondances entre les différentes images.

Les critères formels de cette métamorphose du réel en symbole du surréel sont:

— *le démembrement:* les images sont libérées de leurs contextes familiers et utilisées, dans leur autonomie, avec la plus grande liberté.
— *Le changement de fonction,* qui est en un sens le corollaire du précèdent. Les images, les signes recoivent un nouveau sens. Ils sont même interchangeables. Tout peut signifier (presque) tout.
— *Instabilité:* les images naissent avec rapidité et disparaissent également.
— *Dissolution de l'individuel:* le rêve anime les images qui enlève aux objets leurs formes précises.

Le sens de ces métamorphoses n'est cependant jamais arbitraire et sous l'incohérence apparente (la pratique tend à restreindre fortement les théories extrêmes de Novalis) on découvre rapidement une logique des images très précise qui les regroupe par famille suivant leurs affinités symboliques. La métamorphose a également la fonction d'animer le matériel, de spiritualiser le corporel tout en donnant une forme concrète et un visage au spirituel. Ce double mouvement correspond à l'usage général de la métaphore qui selon Jean Paul 'transforme un corps en enveloppe d'un principe spirituel', 'et inversement, de même que (le poète) donne au physique, grâce au spirituel, des couleurs plus hautes au moyen de la métaphore, il en donne au spirituel grâce à la personnification'.

On ne saurait trop insister sur l'usage de la métaphore dont la fonction est de donner plus de relief à l'idée, de souligner le caractère affectif du discours figuré, de dire l'indicible en dépassant par le langage le langage lui-même. La métaphore, qui reprend au niveau de l'écriture l'écart du rêve (et son déplacement) opère sur la substance même du langage (et non sur la seule relation entre le langage et la réalité exprimée).

Le rêve est par excellence le monde des tropes et Novalis n'a d'autre projet, en voulant que le monde devienne rêve, que de les mettre à jour. Le rôle privilégié de l'imagination dans la métaphore est de donner l'impression d'identification de deux réalités étrangères. Albert Béguin a su parler avec un rare bonheur et une grande concision des rêves de Jean Paul, mais ce qu'il en dit est également valable et exemplaire pour tout rêve romantique:

Dans le flot chatoyant d'un style magicien, tout objet perd, sans la perdre, sa qualité première, pour signifier à la fois lui-même et autre chose. Un extraordinaire génie métaphorique efface si bien derrière lui la trace de son itinéraire, que les bonds les plus imprévus semblent aisés à sa démarche, et qu'il n'est jamais possible de marquer la ligne qui sépare la sensation immédiate de l'autre réalité, au cœur de laquelle on se trouve transporté. Et pourtant ce symbolisme universel n'est pas diffus; la vision reste singulièrement précise, la matière, qui se dissout en pure lumière ou se défait en musique, recompose un paysage de l'âme, une symphonie harmonieuse, un grand rêve continu et tout plein de certitude intérieure.[15]

Il est intéressant de remarquer que le processus de métaphorisation 'efface' en partie ses traces, les sèmes lui ayant donné naissance devant rester plus ou moins inconscients pour le lecteur, mais suffisamment prégnants pour que celui-ci devine ou sente les liens assez mystérieux qui sont tissés ainsi. Cette tension créée par un sens mouvant qui affleure et se dérobe en même temps, permet de préserver à la fois le caractère onirique du récit du rêve et son sens latent qui appelle une interprétation qui ne saurait être immédiate et univoque.

Une telle poétique engage le rêve dans un processus de métaphorisation généralisée. Si le caractère métonymique du rêve est premier (telle cette insolence du merveilleux si caractéristique de la dimension onirique du *Vase d'or*), avec son langage étrange, fait d'incohérence, d'accumulations, de ruptures, d'illogismes dans le déroulement d'une narration discontinue aux éléments hétérogènes, il appert que le métonymique se transforme inévitablement en métaphorique. Plus ou moins rapidement, car certains rêves restent parfois tout à fait métonymiques, résistant à tout processus d'interprétation et de métaphorisation. Mais cette résistance et la persistance du mystère ont pour fonction de retarder, de suspendre une élucidation dont la possibilité n'est cependant jamais mise en doute. Il existe un sens supérieur au rêve, mais celui-ci échappe parfois à la conscience humaine. Métonymie et discontinuité ont alors pour fonction d'accentuer le caractère fragmentaire d'une révélation dont le modèle reste la métaphore.

Prenons chez Jean Paul un exemple de ce type de transformation du métonymique en métaphorique. Dans le rêve de *l'Anéantissement,* l'Apparition pousse le rêveur sur un étroit sentier:

Le chemin traversait une mer sanglante, à la surface de laquelle on apercevait, comme les fleurs des plantes aquatiques, des cheveux blancs et des doigts enfantins – et le sentier était couvert de colombes qui couvaient, d'ailes de papillons humides, d'œufs de rossignol et de cœurs humains. Le fantôme sur son passage écrasait tout cela ...[16]

Dans un premier moment, et malgré le symbolisme sous-jacent, le lecteur ne sait que faire des éléments disparates de cette vision. Mais le sens général du rêve, la surdétermination des images infernales invitent à trouver des rapports d'analogie entre des objets apparemment fort étrangers l'un à l'autre. Il s'agit donc pour le lecteur de trouver les liaisons sémiques communes entre les différentes images. On s'aperçoit alors que la première séquence exprime une double métaphore, celle du temps (l'enfant et la vieillesse) et de la mutilation-castration (les membres épars). La seconde séquence, dominée par l'image de la naissance (les œufs, la chrysalide) développe l'idée d'une résurrection impossible, impliquant l'anéantissement des valeurs humaines les plus hautes (l'intériorité du Moi vécue sous sa forme morale et musicale). Ainsi les éléments présentés de façon métonymique, dans un texte où la contiguïté est signe de disparate et de désharmonie (procédé employé d'ailleurs très fréquemment dans tous les rêves d'enfer), sont-ils pris dans un réseau de métaphorisation générale que le texte entier appelle (par son allégorisme, son symbolisme et son réseau dense d'images).

Un autre caractère du rêve est ce que j'appellerai sommairement sa profondeur. Non pas seulement en raison d'une banale surdétermination, mais en raison même de son intransitivité d'une part, de son caractère autonome, total et organique. Les exemples sont certes nombreux, mais si j'en reviens au rêve des *Confession d'un mangeur d'opium anglais* je vois dans cette scène célèbre une superposition de niveaux qui en détermine le mouvement d'approfondissement: la scène de Pâques renvoie à l'idée de résurrection, appelle la série des images d'Ann qui elle-même appelle la série des images liées à la mort d'Elizabeth, la sœur de De Quincey, images qui appellent l'idée de l'Orient par la fenêtre ouverte sur le vide du ciel ensoleillé, lui-même ouvrant le champ de la lecture et des gravures de la Bible de l'enfance. Le rêve est un palimpseste, qui ouvre dans la conscience des espaces nouveaux, et ce caractère lié à la mémoire représente la structure même de l'esprit humain dans sa dimension symbolique. La structure en palimpseste du rêve a le grand intérêt de faire jouer les parties des textes entre elles. Cette circulation entre les différents niveaux, le jeu des échos, des reprises, des répétitions contribuent à un phénomène de résonance général.

Langage onirique

Le rêve a son propre langage, ce que Schubert exprime dans un paragraphe très célèbre de sa *Symbolik des Traumes* de 1814 pour avoir été repris par E.T.A Hoffmann dans les *Kreisleriana* que Baudelaire lui a ensuite repris:

En rêve, et déjà dans cet état de délire qui précède le sommeil, l'âme semble parler un tout autre langage qu'à l'ordinaire. Certains objets de la nature, certaines propriétés des choses désignent tout à coup des personnes, et inversement, telle qualité ou telle action se présentent à nous sous forme de personnes (…) tant que l'âme parle ce langage, les idées suivent une toute autre loi d'association qu'à l'ordinaire (…). Nous exprimons bien plus dans ce langage par quelques hiéroglyphes, parmi des images étrangement juxtaposées (…) que nous ne pouvons le faire pendant des heures avec les mots.[17]

Ce langage qui procède par associations secrètes obéissant aux lois de la sympathie, n'est pas linéaire, morcelé, discursif, mais totalisateur, continu et 'musical'. Intraduisible dans le langage de la veille, il est cependant entendu par le sentiment, 'cette merveilleuse confidence de l'inconscient au conscient' (Carus). La langue onirique se donne comme réminiscence du langage naturel, fusion du spirituel et du corporel, de la nature et de l'esprit, de la subjectivité et de l'univers sensible, langage d'un âge d'or dont le poète sait retrouver les traces enfouies dans la nature sous formes de signatures et d'hiéroglyphes. Les théories du langage romantique ont singulièrement marqué l'écriture du rêve (et inversement la langue du rêve a pu inspirer les théories du langage) ne serait-ce que dans sa forme synesthésique.[18] L'analogie, le symbole, la métaphore qui font surgir l'identité, l'unité, la cohérence du monde, permettent au poète au regard dessillé par le rêve de signifier 'l'invisible qui plane sur nos têtes'.

Pour Senancour, et bien plus encore pour les romantiques allemands, les caractères de ce langage qui ne connait pas l'arbitraire du signe, sont les traces d'une recollection à effectuer pour surmonter la dispersion du monde et en retrouver la profonde et originelle unité. Réminiscence, quête, voyage, initiation, autant de démarches qui de Jean Paul à Novalis tendent à libérer 'le chant qui sommeille en chaque chose' (Eichendorff) et à supprimer les limites du monde phénoménal, vécu comme dispersion des sens. La destruction de la finitude (envisagée sous les catégories kantiennes de l'espace, du temps et de la causalité) libère l'homme de ses pesanteurs. Le rêve d'envol et d'infini témoigne de cette nouvelle liberté retrouvée.

Ein Traum bricht unsere Banden los
Und sendt uns in des Vaters Schoss.
(Novalis)

La musique, non mimétique par nature, est un modèle pour ce nouveau langage, qui suspend les discours au profit d'une voix exprimant le sentiment. 'C'est dans les sons que la nature a placé la plus forte expression du caractère romantique' (Senancour), parce qu'elle substitue l'état (*Zustand*) à l'objet (*Gegenstand*). Ce qui retient donc l'attention des rêveurs n'est pas le caractère plastique de l'image, mais d'abord son caractère musical, sonore, c'est-à-dire son mélodisme, sa résonance et son harmonisme symphonique. Le rêve, 'Geistersprache des Gefühls' (Schubert) parle la langue de ce monde enfoui, celui de la 'grotte ou nage la sirène' pour reprendre l'image nervalienne.

Par son étrangeté, son absence de liaison logique apparente, par ses répétitions, son atmosphère affective, ses incohérences et ses ruptures, son décor instable à métamorphoses, son mélange d'indications réalistes et de traits irréalistes, sa succession d'événements insolites, sa temporalité contractée, ses 'effets d'irréel', ses signifiants incongrus ne recouvrant aucune signification fonctionnelle immédiatement déterminable et qui semblent n'être là que pour connoter l'onirique, le rêve déplace le monde, transforme le statut du rêveur et appelle l'interprétation.

De Quincey parle des 'splendides mosaïques du rêve'. L'image est intéressante puisque chaque élément n'est qu'une bribe, une miette, en soi étrange. Ce n'est que dans la saisie globale de l'ensemble que la vision prend son sens. Ceci implique également que les éléments en eux-mêmes, les images qui composent la vision, peuvent être les résidus du monde diurne ou l'héritage d'une tradition bien établie. C'est le travail du rêve et l'écriture du poète qui crée, par la composition, l'assemblage, l'unité. Jean Paul pense que les parties doivent être réelles, l'ensemble idéal. Cette méthode de composition est également suivie par certains peintres romantiques. C.D. Friedrich dans ses tableaux utilise des croquis fort réalistes, mais dans l'assemblage de ce qui n'est pour lui qu'un alphabet naturel, crée une vision idéale aux caractères oniriques évidents. Aussi la nouvelle poétique du rêve est-elle inséparable d'une théorie de l'imagination qui légitime sa pratique.

La nouvelle théorie de l'imagination, qui opère selon M.H. Abrams une rupture radicale, dans la tradition européenne, est contemporaine d'une découverte du monde intérieur du poète. 'La vie réelle de l'homme est en lui-même, celle qu'il reçoit du dehors n'est qu'accidentelle et subordonnée' (Senancour). Il faut donc fermer les yeux pour voir, pour reprendre l'expression de Joubert. Ce qui implique un rejet des doctrines de l'imitation et l'ouverture aux créations libres des 'caprices de la nuit'. 'Tout ce que nous imaginons ne peut être formé que de ce qui est; mais nous rêvons comme nous imaginons, des choses nouvelles et qui n'ont souvent avec ce que nous avons vu précisément, aucun rapport que nous puissions découvrir' (Senancour). La descente en soi est le chemin mystérieux qui mène à la création poétique. Rousseau écrivait déjà: 'Si je veux peindre le printemps, il faut que je sois en hiver'. Jean Paul pousse à l'extrême cette théorie de la création poétique. Pour lui, à la différence des arts plastiques qui idéalisent la réalité, l'art poétique est une 'realisierte Idealität'. La puissance totalisante de la *Phantasie* crée un monde en soi, vrai si le poète est un miroir intérieur, 'allwissend', faux si ce monde rêvé n'est qu'une illusion, mais de toutes façons d'une vérité supérieure puisque fondé ou non, il constitue un monde en soi, clos sur lui-même et possédant sa structure propre. Le rêve qui est 'la vallée de Tempé et la patrie de l'imagination' (Jean Paul) représente l'imagination à l'état naissant. On peut voir germer dans l'activité onirique le poétique, en observant la métamorphose des objets en symboles. L'imagination toute puissante et libre fait accéder l'homme à l'infini. 'L'idéal de la poésie n'est rien d'autre que le reflet de cet infini', écrit Jean Paul qui rapproche le 'dichten' du 'verdichten', pour montrer que le travail de création de l'imagination est la condensation et la concrétion d'un monde.

Un tel monde est d'abord l'expression du monde intérieur du poète. 'Poetry is the spontaneous overflow of powerful feelings' (Wordsworth). Si l'acte poétique est une descente au fond de soi (symbolisé par l'image de la grotte où sourd une eau féminine et eurydicéenne) l'œuvre poétique qui est l'intérieur fait extérieur, et qui est souvent représentée par l'image du volcan,[19] est l'expression naturelle du mouvement de l'âme. 'That if Poetry comes not as naturally as the Leaves to a Tree it had better not come at all' (Keats). Ceci ne signifie nullement que la production, inconsciente comme une croissance végétale ne fasse pas l'objet d'un travail d'écriture. Mais que le poète, qui est 'nightingale, who sits in darkness and sings to cheer its own solitude' (Shelley), obéit à sa propre musique sans souci d'un projet ou d'un public.

Le poème issu des ténèbres de la nuit constitue un monde en soi, d'une beauté désintéressée ('Zweckmässigkeit ohne Zweck', d'une finalité sans fin), un 'poem per se', parfois à la limite de l'intelligibilité comme la vision de rêve de *Kubla Khan*. La clôture sur soi définissant une nouvelle esthétique identifie beauté et totalité. 'Le concept d'un tout existant en lui-même est indéfectiblement attaché à celui du Beau' (Moritz). Aussi le rêve qui réalise plus que toute autre forme cette autonomie absolue se signifie-t-il lui-même par le jeu de ses parties. C'est dans cette *'intransitivité'* du beau (l'expression est fort heureusement employée par T. Todorov dans ses *Théories du symbole*), que le romantique voit l'expression finie de l'infini. Pour Jean Paul, l'imagination n'est rien d'autre que le sens de l'infini en tout homme, comme il est pour Blake[20] l'activité de Dieu lui-même dans l'âme humaine. Coleridge, Novalis et bien d'autres souscrivent, à quelques nuances près, à cette théorie. Hölderlin n'écrit-il pas : 'Ein Gott ist der Mensch, wenn er träumt'? Ce qui ne doit pas être entendu seulement dans le sens de la toute-puissance qui sert de refuge au poète fuyant le monde, mais dans son sens le plus plein, d'une authentique création démiurgique. Le travail de l'imagination définit les termes de la nouvelle poétique qui est d'abord une métaphorisation du réel, une métamorphose du sensible en spirituel, guidée par le sens de l'infini. Ce travail d'idéalisation caractérise toute la poétique onirique de notre période.

Dicté par l'inconscient, le 'poète caché' (Schubert, Hoffmann), le rêve écrit est un véritable 'art poétique involontaire' (Jean Paul), générateur de multiples tensions: tensions entre le rêve et tout ce qui n'est pas lui (le monde extérieur de la conscience diurne, l'œuvre dans laquelle il est inséré), tensions entre le rêveur et le rêve, entre l'image et son écriture.

L'identification tout a fait nouvelle et originale opérée par le romantisme du rêve à la création poétique répond à une théorie de l'inspiration pour laquelle la vérité vient de l'intérieur dans la passivité et l'absence d'effort. Reçu comme une révélation, le rêve qui est 'comme la poésie (…) d'une signification sans règle, absolument libre' (Novalis) est l'expression d'une transcendance. Autonome, il est juxtaposé à l'écriture romanesque chez Jean Paul, sans rapport à l'intrigue, comme une fenêtre romantique ouverte sur un autre ciel, à l'intérieur de l'univers 'romanesque' de la prose du monde. Absolu et totalisateur, il peut envahir le roman en suivant l'épanchement progressif du songe dans la vie réelle, comme dans le roman de Novalis, *Heinrich von Ofterdingen*.

Le rêve est poésie involontaire; il montre que le poète, plus qu'aucun autre homme travaille avec son cerveau physique. Pourquoi personne ne s'est-il étonné encore de ce que, dans les scènes détachées du rêve, on prête aux personnages, tout comme si l'on était Shakespeare, le langage le plus individuel, les paroles les plus révélatrices de leur nature (…) Le véritable poète, de même, n'est en écrivant que l'auditeur et non pas le maître de langue de ses caractères, c'est-à-dire qu'il ne compose pas le dialogue en cousant bout à bout les répliques, selon une stylistique de la psychologie péniblement apprise; mais comme dans le rêve, il les regarde agir, tout vivants, et il les écoute (…) dans le rêve, la conscience de l'effort fait défaut.[21]

L'étrange dialogue du rêveur avec son rêve ouvre une perspective et une profondeur fécondes. 'Et comme en songe, nous découvrons dans ces contes notre double moi: celui qui rêve et l'esprit qui contemple le rêve, le narrateur et l'auditeur (…). C'est un merveilleux pouvoir accordé à l'homme que cette poésie involontaire et autonome des contes et des rêves' (Herder).

Le dialogue, poursuivi par Heinrich von Ofterdingen avec le sens mystérieux de sa vision de la fleur bleue, de Gérard de Nerval avec ses rêves, du vieux marin de Coleridge avec son aventure, permet au rêve d'être revécu, multiplié par ses répétitions et en même temps poursuivi dans ses métamorphoses. Il relie l'image à son interprétation et à la quête d'un sens qui interpelle le lecteur. L'anonymat d'un narrateur s'exprimant à la première personne rend possible l'identification et la participation du lecteur à l'expérience existentielle si singulière que peut représenter par exemple le rêve *Du haut de l'édifice du monde, le Christ proclame qu'il n'y a point de Dieu,* l'étrangeté ou le caractère horrible du rêve, autrement dit le pouvoir de provocation de son exagération, de la transgression de certaines limites, créant d'autre part une distance suffisante pour interroger le rêve sur son sens et dépasser le stade de la fascination immédiate.

L'écriture du rêve est prise dans la tension entre l'instant de la vision et la temporalité et la linéarité de l'écriture, entre l'image et son scénario. Lichtenberg disait: 'Der Traum ist dramatisiertes Besinnen' (le rêve n'est qu'une prise de conscience dramatisée). Il est en effet patent que de nombreux rêves se développent autour d'une image-mère. Le roman de Walpole, *The Castle of Otranto* (1764), n'est-il pas, d'après son auteur même, le développement romanesque de la vision du heaume? Et le *Dit du Vieux Marin* n'est-il pas la mise en scénario du fameux 'skeleton ship'? On peut suivre dans les différentes versions d'un même rêve de Jean Paul comment l'image première s'enrichit peu à peu pour se constituer en scénario. C'est dans une telle élaboration progressive que l'on perçoit avec le plus d'acuité les caractéristiques du rêve et les procédés d'onirisation par emphatisation, symbolisation et enrichissement thématique (cf. les trois variantes du rêve du *Christ proclamant qu'il n'existe point de Dieu*). Toutes les comparaisons entre rêve noté et rêves re-rêvés (nachgeträumt) montrent à l'évidence le travail de stylisation et d'écriture qui métamorphose une impression vécue en une création littéraire. Il faudrait bien entendu faire une différence entre les notes prises au réveil, les rêves narrés pour leur curiosité à des correspondants dans des lettres privées et le rêve composé, qui correspondent à trois types d'écriture différents. Ainsi les rêves de Coleridge des années 1800 publiés depuis 1957 dans les *Notebooks,* qui sont des textes intimes, non élaborés, répondent, comme ceux de Jean Paul ou de Novalis à un premier jet d'écriture. Naturellement, même dans l'écriture la plus spontanée, on trouve déjà une ébauche d'organisation et un tri inconscient qui répond aux préoccupations de l'époque. Il est intéressant de voir ce qui est éliminé, ce qui n'est pas retenu comme pertinent dans la composition plus achevée du même rêve. Les transcriptions fragmentaires et brèves, quasi expérimentales d'un Coleridge de rêveries hypnagogiques donnent naissance à une écriture vraiment novatrice, presque joycienne (monologue intérieur), mais qui reste sans conséquence sur le développement du rêve comme genre littéraire, puisque celles-ci n'ont pas été publiées et qu'elles n'ont pas été reprises dans les œuvres (je renvoie à ce qu'en dit C. La Cassagnère dans son introduction aux *Poèmes* de Coleridge). Aussi est-ce essentiellement dans les rêves publiés comme œuvres qu'il nous faut chercher les traits les plus pertinents concernant la poétique onirique de l'époque.

Une intensité passionnée: puissances de l'image

L'affirmation de la priorité logique (et chronologique) de la passion sur la raison, à travers diverses notions comme celles de l'enthousiasme, du génie, du sentiment, de l'extase, de l'illumination, a transformé profondément le champ et la structure du domaine poétique dans son ensemble, de 1760 á 1820, non seulement dans le rejet des règles et de l'imitation, dans la valorisation de la liberté du créateur, mais aussi dans son contenu même. Situé dans la perspective d'une problématique de l'origine (origine du langage, des passions, de l'art, de la fabulation), le lieu du poétique est l'image. 'Les sens et les passions ne parlent que par images, n'entendent que les images'.

Le langage du rêve est un langage régressif, entendu dans le sens le plus positif qui soit, c'est-à-dire comme retour à l'origine et qui, du conscient à l'inconscient, du pensé au vécu, de la notion à l'image, ramène le poète à la source de la création poétique. Dans son étude sur 'The Intentional Structure of the Romantic Image' Paul de Man observe que le statut de l'image comme dimension du langage poétique, a connu de singulières variations. A partir de la fin du XVIIIe siècle, on assiste de façon très générale à une redécouverte du pouvoir de l'image liée à la constatation de l'insuffisance radicale du langage pour exprimer le monde intérieur du poète. 'Dies mystische Erscheinen unseres tiefsten Gemüts im Bild [...ist] das Romantische (...) Die Romantik ist hohe, ewige Poesie, die im Bilde darstellt, was Worte dürftig oder nimmer aussprechen'.[22]

Sebastian Mercier est à bien des égards exemplaire par son programme poétique qui définit un véritable culte de l'image basé sur le langage, la néologie. Le pouvoir magique du mot n'est pas d'épuiser la réalité qu'il évoque, mais au contraire de la suggérer, de la créer, de déclencher l'activité du lecteur qui saisit le mot dans son jaillissement, et le langage comme force productrice et source de nouvelles énergies. 'Les mots frappent l'imagination plus que ne le ferait la chose même (...) Mettre en jeu l'imagination et ne point la rassasier, voilà l'art d'écrire'.[23] Et pour cela il faut des 'images fortes'. Morphologie et sémantique de l'image sont interdépendantes. Une image forte est une image qui évoque ce qui dépasse l'homme, qui touche au sublime dans l'horreur comme dans le beau. En cela le pouvoir et la fonction de transgression du rêve est affirmée hautement. Si l'on examine maintenant les procédés d'écriture du rêve, on s'aperçoit que le changement de proportions est l'une des premières marques du rêve, dont le début se traduit presque toujours par *l'emphatisation*. Cette démesure est marquée par la qualification apophatique (insupportable, infini, ultime, éternel, innombrable, immense, etc.). Cette caractéristique du rêve, semble être à l'origine même des architectures grandioses entrevues par De Quincey, Coleridge, Nerval, etc. Elle rend également compte de l'idéalisation du rêve (cf. *La Géante* de Baudelaire).

La seconde caractéristique est l'usage d'une *'prose passionnée'* (De Quincey) devant traduire le caractère affectif du rêve. Le modèle de cette prose sont les langues 'primitives': 'Les images, les métaphores, les inversions, les ellipses abondent dans ces langues que vous appelez barbares, et vont au devant de toutes les vérités par l'énergie du sentiment'.[24] Un tel programme trouve son achèvement dans l'écriture onirique. Certaines figures stylistiques font l'objet d'une prédilection particulière.

La *répétition* est un moyen pour créer les étranges impressions de fascination, liées aux compulsions de répétition propres aux fantasmes oniriques et à mettre l'accent sur le caractère indéfini et interminable des espaces rêvés. Ces phénomènes d'échos et d'abîmes sonores que l'on trouve chez De Quincey, Coleridge et plus tard E. Poe, sont également présents chez les écrivains français qui nourrissent leurs rêves des *Prisons* de Piranèse, tel Nerval et sa vision de couloirs ou de corridors: 'Des corridors, – des corridors sans fin! Des escaliers, – des escaliers où l'on monte, où l'on descend, où l'on remonte, et dont le bas trempe toujours dans une eau noire agitée par des roues, sous d'immenses arches de pont (…)'.[25]

L'antithèse, cette 'loi de succession et de contraire qui est le fond même de la nature' (Hugo) est l'une des marques de la 'vraie poésie' puisqu'elle permet 'l'harmonisation des contraires' (Préface de *Cromwell*). Il faudrait ajouter l'emploi plus général d'une image dans son contraire (l'eau qui flambe, le soleil dans la nuit, les montagnes liquides, etc.).

La figure de style la plus révélatrice de notre période est cependant, dans l'écriture du rêve, *l'oxymoron,* qui permet d'unir deux images incompatibles. De nature fondamentalement subversive, l'oxymoron court-circuite véritablement le langage dans son fonctionnement normal, en créant une réalité nouvelle sous la forme d'une image à la fois une et éclatée, qui exprime et concentre l'absolu d'une vision qui dépasse par son caractère infini et instantané la logique quotidienne, faisant entrer le rêveur dans un monde qui, bien que plein de tensions, ignore le principe de contradiction. 'Anéantir le principe de contradiction est peut-être la plus haute tâche de la logique supérieure' écrit Novalis. L'oxymoron est ce véritable opérateur magique. Nous le trouvons bien sûr dans les 'magnifiques horreurs' de Chenedollé et dans l'ʼhorribly beautiful' de Byron, mais surtout dans des images archétypales comme le 'soleil noir' de Jean Paul ou le 'sunny pleasure-dome with caves of ice' de Coleridge.

L'oxymoron (ou toutes les figures stylistiques assez nuancées qui s'en rapprochent) met l'accent sur l'une des caractéristiques les plus spécifiques du rêve romantique: *la dualité*. Le rêve apparaît de prime abord comme un miroir biseauté qui a pour fonction de déformer le monde et d'en révéler, par ses déplacements singuliers, les manques. L'opposition du supra-terrestre et du terrestre, de la réalité quotidienne dans sa médiocrité et sa carence et de l'idéal, est exprimée par le rêve, défini comme une 'seconde vie', double du monde, mais double déformant par décalage, transfert et métamorphose. Le rêve est un moyen de surmonter cette dualité et cette division, mais celle-ci est à nouveau jouée et mise en scène dans le rêve lui-même (par exemple dans la double postulation de l'enfer et du paradis).

On comprend l'importance des associations synesthésiques et des correspondances magnifiées par le rêve.

Ce n'est pas tant dans le rêve que dans cet état de délire qui précède le sommeil, et particulièrement quand j'ai entendu beau coup de musique, que je perçois une manière d'accord entre les couleurs, les sons et les parfums. Il me semble alors qu'ils se manifestent tous, de la même façon mystérieuse, dans la lumière du soleil, pour se fondre ensuite en un merveilleux concert. Le parfum des œillets rouge foncé a sur moi un singulier pouvoir magique: involontairement, je tombe en un état de rêve et j'entends alors, qui semblent venir de très loin, s'enflant et puis s'évanouissant, les sons du cor de basset.[26]

Cet 'inépuisable fonds de *l'universelle analogie*' selon Baudelaire, Swedenborg, Fourier, Lavater établit des correspondances verticales ou horizontales (que sont les synesthésies).

Tout vit, tout agit, tout se correspond: les rayons magnétiques émanés de moi-même ou des autres traversent sans obstacle la chaîne infinie des choses créées; c'est un réseau transparent qui couvre le monde, et dont les fils déliés se communiquent de proche en proche aux planètes et aux étoiles.[27]

Lorsque Baudelaire affirme que 'tout est hiéroglyphique',[28] il fonde bien une poétique sur le rêve et sur ce langage en image. 'Tout, forme, mouvement, nombre, couleur, parfum, dans le *spirituel* comme dans le *naturel,* est significatif, réciproque, converse, *correspondant'*. Je ne développerai pas plus cette théorie des correspondances qui spécule la totalité.[29]

> O métamorphose mystique
> De tous mes sens fondus en *un !*
> Son haleine fait la musique,
> Comme sa voix fait le parfum ![30]

La musicalité même est la forme lyrique de l'analogie et de la correspondance. Les figures musicales, fugues, échos envahissent le paysage contribuant à son onirisation.

L'hiéroglyphe et l'arabesque

Je reviens sur deux figures qui sont particulièrement signifiantes du langage onirique romantique que sont l'hiéroglyphe et l'arabesque. L'hiéroglyphe répond à l'attente d'un mode d'expression originaire, ignorant la séparation, l'hétérogène, l'autonomie des codes propres. A l'exubérance orientale, à l'insondable antiquité s'ajoute un véritable collapsus des significations et une hyperactivité des signifiants créatrice d'une opacité fantastique, inquiétante, douloureuse parfois, à la limite même du cauchemar. Les hiéroglyphes sont l'image d'un sacré qui échappe par la saturation de l'écriture, que ce soit chez un Thomas de Quincey ou un Théophile Gautier, image même du secret condensé et dérobé. On sait combien les romantiques allemands ont pu évoquer ce type d'écriture et combien les hiéroglyphes du rêve sont un modèle poétique. L'arabesque quant à elle a pu être considérée comme un hiéroglyphe en mouvement. Mais alors que le premier est généralement une écriture de la masculinité, de la puissance et de l'effroi, la seconde est une écriture de la féminité et de la séduction.

Avec l'arabesque, la ligne devient sa *propre finalité*. Cette autonomie esthétique qui figure la liberté et l'art pour l'art (et qui se rapproche de l'intransitivité symbolique propre au romantisme) est également propre à l'écriture littéraire comme on le voit dans le style digressif de De Quincey. Ce jeu de la ligne pour elle-même (voir *Le Thyrse* de Baudelaire), met en avant *la forme comme origine*. Et cette abstraction formelle[31] est signe du *spirituel* (chez Baudelaire, au sens de non-naturel), de l'imagination sans limite qui s'exprime par la ligne, le mouvement, indépendamment de toute chose. 'L'arabesque est de tous les dessins celui qui porte le plus d'esprit'. Hiéroglyphe d'une irrésistible séduction, l'arabesque comme synonyme de la ligne serpentine, signifie la volupté dont l'Orient est synonyme. Quand il parle de l'ondulation des collines, le poète constate que 'la ligne serpentine qui se déploie sur le torse d'une belle femme couchée, n'a pas une grâce plus voluptueuse et plus molle'.[32]

L'image du serpent, de la femme serpent (dont Clarimonde est un exemple) s'impose : 'Si la beauté vient de la ligne courbe, comme le prétend Hogarth, rien ne serait plus gracieux que le reptile, dont la démarche est une suite d'ondulations et de sinuosités harmonieuses, écrit Gautier.[33] L'arabesque a à voir avec l'Eros : elle a la même puissance, celle de 'faire éprouver un plaisir sans nom'. Et je terminerai sur ce point en évoquant l'arc-en-ciel des couleurs de la couleuvre qui se love au cœur de Venise pour Gautier ou dans le fouillis végétal d'une architecture de rêve chez Keats pour qui elle devient image du rêve lui-même, mis en abyme :

> a gordian shape of dazzling hue,
> Vermilion-spotted, golden, green, and blue;
> Striped like a zebra, feckled like a pard,
> Eyed like a peacock, and all crimson barr'd;
> And full of silver moons, that, as she breathed,
> Dissolv'd, or brighter shone, or interwreathed
> Their lustres with the gloomier tapestries –
> So rainbow-sided, touch's with miseries,
> She seem'd, at once, some penanced lady elf,
> Some demon's mistress, or the demon's self.[34]

Mise en abyme

Nous avons évoqué la rupture introduite par le rêve, le changement de registre qu'elle implique et induit dans son mouvement transgressif. Ainsi le rêve apparaît-il comme fortement encadré. Je ne parle pas ici de l'épanchement du songe dans la vie réelle comme chez un Nerval dans *Aurélia* ou dans les déambulations nocturnes d'un Florio chez Eichendorff, je voudrais mettre l'accent sur un phénomène d'encadrement qui désignant explicitement le rêve comme tel, participe de la construction d'une mise en abyme et dont le rôle est d'avertir que l'on change de code herméneutique, que l'on passe d'un récit prosaïque à une narration poétique par exemple, d'une mimesis à une allégorie.

L'utilisation anamorphotique des matériaux diurnes, comme par exemple dans le rêve d'Elis dans *Mines de Falun* d'Hoffmann, permet non seulement une transformation du regard, mais aussi une mise en abyme qui peut prendre un tour parodique comme dans le *Vase d'Or* ou la *Fée aux miettes* de par la surdétermination que favorise l'encadrement.

Les procédés d'inclusion participent également de l'ironie romantique comme chez Hoffmann qui aime jouer avec différents niveaux de narration. Je dis ironie parce que Hoffmann joue dans le *Vase d'or* de l'écart entre l'histoire qui se passe à Dresde et le mythe lui-même, livré par fragments, comme bribes d'une mémoire disparue et pourtant fondatrice. La mise en abyme est un procédé romantique d'infinitisation et de merveilleux fréquent.

Lucien Dällenbach souligne deux fonctions importantes du procédé: la mise en relation de similitude de la partie et du tout d'abord (et on pourra se demander quelle est la partie et quel est le tout). Ensuite il a pour fonction de mettre en évidence la construction mutuelle de l'écrivain et de l'écrit (l'activité de copiste d'Anselme est évidemment une mise en abyme de la création littéraire elle-même du conte).[35] L'ouverture d'une perspective avec similitude et changement de niveaux a fasciné les romantiques. L'auto-enchâssement narratif permet d'aborder une triple transgression: celle du principe de causalité (un produit se donne comme le produit de son produit), celle de la temporalité et celle de l'espace puisqu'il représente comme sa partie et se laisse enfermer parce qu'il contient. Ainsi la mise en abyme ouvre-t-elle au récit sa dimension poétique en y apportant non seulement un aspect ludique, la légèreté et la grâce de la fiction aux vivantes arabesques, mais elle suspend le mécanisme de l'enchaînement des causes et des effets (ce qui est bien entendu une exigence de l'idéalisme magique), elle suspend la temporalité en introduisant l'éternel retour du même et en brisant les chaînes du temps (ce qui projetera Anselme dans cet âge d'or paradisiaque, vert paradis d'amour idyllique où c'est l'éternité qui marque la mesure) et enfin elle bouscule les lois de l'espace. On peut être en plusieurs endroits à la fois. Bref, nous entrons dans le monde merveilleux où les personnages sont déclarés jeunes quand ils n'ont que 700 ans, où l'on passe l'après-midi en Orient pour prendre le thé à Dresde …

La mise en abyme se fait par l'introduction du Märchen qui, comme le rêve, est une forme de récit, comme l'a remarqué déjà Herder, qui échappe au temps de l'histoire. Novalis rompt avec le vieil adage du XVIIIe qui veut que songe n'est que mensonge et les fables ne sont que radotages. Le conte, comme le rêve, jouissent d'une liberté singulière. Le conte est pour lui prophétique de l'âge d'or: 'Le véritable auteur du Märchen est un voyant de l'avenir'.

Dans un Märchen authentique, tout doit être merveilleux – mystérieux, incohérent, – tout doit être animé. Spontané. Et chaque chose à sa façon. Toute la nature doit se mêler étrangement au monde des esprits – (ce doit être) l'époque de l'universelle anarchie, de l'irrégularité – de la liberté – l'état de nature de la Nature – l'époque d'avant le monde. Cette époque des origines présente les traits épars de l'époque d'après le monde, de même que l'état de nature est une étrange image du royaume éternel …
Tous les Märchen ne sont que rêves de cette patrie qui est partout et nulle part.[36]

'Alles Poetische muss märchenhaft sein'. Une caractéristique importante du Märchen est semblable au rêve: son animation au sens fort du terme. Dans un Märchen tout vit et toutes les choses sont douées d'une vie fantastique. Le rêve est véritablement 'une seconde vie'.

Un autre exemple me semble particulièrement riche, bien qu'il ne me soit pas possible de le développer longuement comme il le mériterait, le poème *Lamia* de Keats. L'adjonction d'une prodiégèse au récit poétique avec l'histoire d'Hermes amoureux d'une belle nymphe met en place tous les thèmes relatifs à l'objet d'amour impossible, qui ne peut se laisser regarder et appréhender du fait de l'opacité reptilienne et rétinienne.[37] Particulièrement intéressante dans ce poème est la série de reduplication, de répétition, de répliques (ainsi le labyrinthe végétal est-il redoublé par le palais inconnu) que le pré-récit embrayeur met en place sous le signe de la métamorphose et de l'anamorphose qui selon l'angle du regard fait de l'obscur objet du désir une femme ou un serpent. La vision de face d'Apollonius la présente comme l'être repoussant; ce n'est que dans la vision oblique, de côté, qu'elle apparaît comme suscitant l'élan érotique. On pourrait longtemps gloser sur ce regard de biais qui autorise une levée de l'interdit et qui permet au récit de se dérouler. De fait nous avons affaire exactement à la position topique du rêve qui lui aussi opère une focalisation[38] indirecte. Lamia n'est objet du désir du discours que parce qu'elle est elle-même rêvante et imaginante. La source du poème est le rêve de Lamia et Keats pose la source onirique comme fondement au récit poétique.

Pour conclure, je proclamerai bien haut le sortilège bu. Car il en va d'une profession de foi: 'Ce qui m'étonne, c'est que le poète éveillé ait si rarement profité dans ses œuvres des fantaisies du poète endormi, ou du moins qu'il ait si rarement avoué son emprunt, car la réalité de cet emprunt dans les conceptions les plus audacieuses du génie est une chose qu'on ne peut pas contester (…) J'avais besoin aussi pour moi de l'expression vive et cependant élégante et harmonieuse de ces caprices du rêve qui n'avaient jamais été écrits', écrit Nodier pour qui 'La vie du sommeil [est] plus solennelle que l'autre' dans sa préface de *Smarra*.

Il y a certes une dimension symbolique du rêve, longuement étudié par la critique, d'Albert Béguin à Werner Vortriedte par exemple, mais il en est une allégorique qui mérite toute notre attention. Dans l'autotélisme de l'œuvre/rêve, Moritz relevait déjà ceci dans sa *Götterlehre:*

La nature du beau consiste en ce que les parties et le tout deviennent parlantes et signifiantes, une partie toujours à travers une autre et le tout à travers lui-même; en ce que le beau s'explique lui-même – se décrit à travers lui-même – et donc n'ait besoin d'aucune explication ni description, en dehors du doigt qui ne fait qu'en indiquer le contenu. Aussitôt qu'une belle œuvre exigerait, en dehors de ce doigt index, une explication particulière, elle deviendrait par là même déjà imparfaite: puisque la première exigence du beau est cette clarté par laquelle il se déploie devant les yeux.[39]

Le rêve, paradigme de l'œuvre, lieu de cohérence et de surdétermination, n'a besoin que de cet index qui est justement la fonction allégorique pour désigner ce qui se signifie soi-même. L'art, le rêve, n'imite pas la nature, il est la nature. Cet autotélisme, ce tautégorisme (terme employé par Coleridge et Schelling) porte son attention moins sur le produit que sur la production, sur le dynamisme d'une imagination au travail que sur ses résidus. Ce qui ne signifie nullement que la dimension symbolique soit absente, mais c'est dans le jeu du symbolisme et de l'allégorique, entre une appréhension du langage comme expression de l'Etre[40] et une compré- hension de celle-ci comme ce qui désigne, s'auto-désigne comme allégorie, intro- duisant une distance de soi à soi que s'élabore le jeu de l'absence et de la présence qui est au fondement de toute poésie.

NOTES

1.   Cité par Beguin 1946, 209.

2.   La confusion délibérée de l'art et de la nature, du sujet et de l'objet, de la vie et du rêve, toutes ces oscillations et ambivalences propres au romantisme caractérisent l'autonomie du langage poétique qui est pour Novalis le signe même de son naturalisme.

3.   *L'Encyclopédie* définit le songe comme une 'fiction que l'on a employée dans tous les genres de poésie, épique, lyrique, élégiaque, dramatique'.

4.   *La nouvelle Héloïse.* Rousseau 1967.

5.   Chateaubriand 1964.

6.   Cf. Mercier: 'Ce sol dépouillé, cette vaste étendue de neige, ces arbres sans feuilles qui semblent plutôt défigurer la terre que l'embellir, ces ouragans qui achèvent de briser leurs branchages four- chus et languissans , ces longs gémissements de la nature qui errent au milieu de ces troncs noir- cis, ont encore quelque chose de frappant et de sublime, tant cette nature est belle, même au mi- lieu des horreurs qui environnent son tombeau (…)' (Mercier 1787, 110).

7.   Novalis 1960.

8.   Mercier 1789.

9.   Ibid.

10. *Heinrich von Ofterdingen.* Novalis 1960.

11. Voir Patterson 1951.

12. Sa description du paradis dans le 3e livre des Martyrs par exemple (Voir Clayton 1934).

13. 'Unser Leben ist ein Traum, heißt soviel als: unser Leben ist ein Gedanke' (Novalis).

14. Cité par Beguin 1946, 209.

15. Beguin 1946, 167.

16.   Jean Paul 1932.

17. Schubert 1968, 1.

18. Le modèle de ce langage est la langue éternelle que parle la nature, langue de la solitude, d'un monde primitif, langue du génie, de la simplicité et de la profondeur dont Senancour évoque les 'effets romantiques' dans *Oberman (De l'expression romantique et du ranz des vaches).* Les hiéroglyphes

de la nature, 'monuments de nos destinées inconnues' révèlent l'infinitisation et l'approfondissement du paysage dans la contemplation de ses métamorphoses. 'Je cherche dans le mouvement de
la forêt, dans le bruit des pins, quelques-uns des accents de la langue éternelle'. Or de tels accents
'que la foule ne sait point', signes du sentiment, sont appréhendés sous le signe de la reminiscen-
ce.

19. Pour Byron, la poésie 'is the lava of the imagination whose eruption prevents an earthquake'.

20. 'Ce monde de l'imagination est le monde de l'éternité; il est le cœur du divin, dans lequel nous
entrerons après la fin du corps vivant. Ce monde est infini et éternel, alors que le monde de la gé-
nération, ou de la vie organique, est fini et temporel. En ce monde éternel existe la realité perma-
nente de chaque chose que nous voyons réfléchie dans ce miroir organique de la nature. Toutes
choses sont comprises en leurs formes éternelles, dans le corps divin du Sauveur, la véritable
vigne de l'éternite. L'imagination humaine, elle n'est apparue venant au Jugement avec ses Saints,
et rejetant le temporel afin que l'éternité pût s'établir; autour d'elle se trouvaient les images des
existants suivant un ordre accordé à mon regard' (*The Last Judgment*).

21. Jean Paul 1932, 37.

22. Uhland 1807.

23. Mercier 1783-89, 71-72.

24. Mercier 1801.

25. Capharnäum, Les nuits d'octobre. Nerval 1960.

26. *Kreisleriana*. Hoffmann 1966.

27. *Auréalia*. Nerval 1960.

28. Baudelaire 1961, 1077-78.

29. 'Ce qui serait vraiment surprenant, c'est que le son ne pût pas suggérer la couleur, que les couleurs ne pussent pas donner l'idée d'une mélodie, et que le son et la couleur fussent impropres à
traduire des idées; les choses s'étant toujours exprimées par une analogie réciproque, depuis le
jour où Dieu a proféré le monde comme une complexe et indivisible totalité'. *L'Art romantique*,
article sur Richard Wagner et *Tannhäuser*. Voir mon article: Montandon 1995.

30. 'Toute entière', *Fleurs du Mal*. Baudelaire 1961.

31. L'arabesque est indice *d'artificialité* chez un Huysmans et dans l'art nouveau.

32. Gautier 1990, 337.

33. Gautier 1991, 69.

34. *Lamia*. Keats 1973.

35. On peut songer aux *Flegeljahre* de Jean Paul où Walt et Vult, deux jumeaux antithétiques, écrivent
un roman. Jean Paul est le maître de ces mises en abymes (avec la référence à l'auberge de l'auberge) qu'il appelle dans sa théorie de l'humour (*Propédeutique à l'esthétique*, § 46) le trait circulaire.

36. 'Ein Märchen ist wie ein Traumbild, ohne Zusammenhang. Ein Ensemble wunderbarer Dinge und Begebenheiten (…) In einem echten Märchen muß alles wunderbar, geheimnisvoll und unzusammenhängend sein; alles belebt. Jedes auf anderer Art. Die Ganze Natur muß auf wunderliche Art mit der ganzen Geisterwelt vermischt sein (…)' (Novalis, Fragment 415 et 416).

37. Christian Lacassagnère a analysé avec acuité la topique constitué par le sujet divisé et la triangulation du désir où Apollonius et Jove, sujet à éclipse mais toujours déjà là assume le rôle de la parole du Père symbolique.

38. Pour ce qui regarde la focalisation, il faudrait aussi rappeler l'importance toute nouvelle accordée au détail. L'art romantique par ailleurs veut en finir avec les hiérarchies, en promouvant les arts mineurs. Novalis parlant de *Wilhelm Meister:* 'cette merveilleuse ordonnance romantique − qui ignore rang et valeur, premier et dernier − grand et petit'. (Fragment 445). Ceci légitime l'attention donnée au minuscule, au détail, au grain de sable qui comme on le sait renferme un monde infini.

39. Moritz 1948, 95.

40. Le poète parle alors le langage du monde, dit 'le premier chant des êtres dans toute sa fraîcheur' (Guérin, *Le cahier vert*). Pour Hugo, 'tout parle'. 'Tout dit dans l'infini quelque chose à quelqu'un' (Hugo, *Ce que dit la bouche d'ombre*) et le poète n'est que l'interprète du 'langage des fleurs et des choses muettes' (Baudelaire, 'Elévation').

BIBLIOGRAPHIE

Abrams, M.H. 1953. *The Mirror and the Lamp: Romantic Theory and the Critical Tradition*. Oxford.

Baudelaire, Charles 1961. *Œuvres complètes*. Paris.

Béguin, Albert 1946. *L'Âme romantique et le rêve*. Paris.

Blake, William 1976. *Complete Writings*. Oxford.

Bousquet, Jacques 1964. *Les thèmes du rêve dans la littérature romantique*. Paris.

Byron, George Gordon, Lord 1975. *Poetical Works*. Oxford.

Chateaubriand, François René de 1863. *Les Martyrs*. Paris.

Chateaubriand, François René de 1964. *René*. Paris.

Clayton, Vista 1934. 'A Contemporary Source for the Description of Heaven', in *Les Martyrs. Romanic Review,* XXV.

Coleridge, S.T. 1978. *Poetical Works*. Oxford.

Constant, Benjamin 1973. *Adolphe*. Paris.

Dällenbach, Lucien 1977. *Le récit spéculaire*. Paris.

de Man, Paul 1984. 'Intentional Structure of the Romantic Image'. *The Rhetoric of Romanticism*. New York.

De Quincey, Thomas 1990. *Les Confessions d'un mangeur d'opium anglais.* Traduction de Pierre Leyris. Paris.

Diderot, Denis 1970. *Œuvres complètes.* Le Club francais du Livre. Paris.

Gautier, Théophile 1990. *Constantinople et autres textes sur la Turquie.* La Boîte à documents.

Gautier, Théophile 1991. *Voyage en Egypte.* La Boîte à documents.

Guérin, Maurice de 1998. *Le Cahier Vert.* Edition des Amis de Guérin par C. Gély.

Herder, Johann Gottfried 1967. *Sämtliche Werke.* Hildesheim.

Hoffmann, E.T.A. 1966. *Werke.* München.

Hugo, Victor 1969. *Œuvres complètes.* Le Club francais du Livre. Paris.

Jean Paul 1932. *Choix de rêves.* Paris.

Jean Paul 1971. *Werke.* München.

Keats, John 1973. *Poetical Works.* Oxford.

Lichtenberg, G. C. 1967. *Sämtliche Schriften.* München.

Mercier, L.-S. 1770 *Songes d'un hermite.* Paris.

Mercier, L.-S. 1787. *Mon Bonnet de Nuit.* Lausanne.

Mercier, L.-S. 1788. *Voyages imaginaires, Songes, Visions.* Amsterdam.

Mercier, L.-S. 1783-89. *Tableau de Paris.* Amsterdam.

Mercier, L.-S. 1789. *Songes philosophiques.* Paris.

Mercier, L.-S. 1801. *Néologie.* Paris.

Montandon, Alain 1995. 'Castel en Allemagne. Synesthésies et correspondances dans le romantisme allemand'. *Etudes sur le XVIIIe siècle.*

Moritz, Karl Philipp 1948. *Götterlehre.* Lahr.

Nerval, Gérard de 1960. *Œuvres.* Paris.

Novalis 1960. *Schriften.* Stuttgart.

Patterson, Helen Temple 1951. 'Petites clefs de grands mystères'. *RLC,* janvier.

Ricœur, Paul 1960. *Finitude et culpabilité.* Montaigne.

Rousseau, J.-J. 1967. *La nouvelle Héloïse.* Paris, GF.

Schubert, G.H. von 1968. *Die Symbolik des Traumes.* Faksimiledruck nach der Ausgabe von 1814. Heidelberg.

Senancour, Etienne Pivert de 1965. *Oberman.* UGE. Paris.

Todorov, Tzvetan 1977. *Théories du symbole.* Paris.

Uhland, L. 1865-73. *Schriften zur Geschichte der Dichtung und Sage.*

About the Contributors

DIANA BEHLER is Professor of Germanics and Comparative Literature at the University of Washington, Seattle, USA. Her publications include *The Theory of the Novel in Early German Romanticism* (1978), translations for *The German Library,* Vols. 23 and 24, and book chapters and articles on Lessing, Wieland, Henry Crabb Robinson, Novalis, the Schlegel Brothers, and Friedrich Nietzsche.

ERNST BEHLER (1928-1997) was Professor and Chairman in the Department of Comparative Literature at the University of Washington, Seattle, USA, and a leading authority on German Romanticism. Ernst Behler has edited the *Kritische Friedrich Schlegel Ausgabe* and authored several books on German Romanticism and literary theory, including *Klassische Ironie, Romantische Ironie, Tragische Ironie* (1972), *Die Zeitschriften der Brüder Schlegel: Ein Beitrag zur Geschichte der deutschen Romantik* (1983), *Derrida − Nietzsche, Nietzsche − Derrida* (1988), *Unendliche Perfektibilität: Europäische Romantik und französische Revolution* (1989), *Irony and the Discourse of Modernity* (1990), *Frühromantik* (1992), *German Romantic Literary Theory* (1993), and *Ironie und literarische Moderne* (1997).

ANDREAS BÖHN has taught modern German Literature and Media Studies at the Universities of Mannheim, Karlsruhe, Waterloo (Ontario), and Sarajevo, and is currently holder of a Heisenberg fellowship of Deutsche Forschungs-Gemeinschaft (DFG). His publications include *Vollendende Mimesis. Wirklichkeitsdarstellung und Selbstbezüglichkeit in Theorie und literarische Praxis* (1992), *Das zeitgenössische deutsch-sprachige Sonett (1999),* and *Das Formzitat. Bestimmung einer Textstrategie im Spannungs-feld zwischen Inter-textualitätsforschung und Gattungstheorie* (forthcoming). In addition, he has edited *Formzitate, Gattungsparodien, ironische Formwendung* (1999).

ANGELA ESTERHAMMER is Professor of English and Comparative Literature at the University of Western Ontario, Canada. Her publications include *Creating*

States: Studies on the Performative Languages of John Milton and William Blake (1994), *Two Stories of Prague, by R.M: Rilke* (1994), *The Romantic Performative: Language and Action in British and German Romanticism* (2000), and articles on Blake, Coleridge, Wordsworth, Milton, German Romanticism, philosophy of language, and the Bible.

MARIE-THERES FEDERHOFER holds an M.A. from the University of Berlin and a doctorate from the University of Tromsø, Norway, where she teaches German Literature. She has published *'Moi simple amateur'. Johann Heinrich Merck und der naturwissenschaftliche Dilettantismus im 18. Jahrhundert* (forthcoming), and several articles on the history of natural sciences in the 18th century (mineralogy, paleontology, meteorology) and its cultural context.

OTTO FISCHER is researcher and lecturer at the Department of Literature, Uppsala University, and at the Department of Thematic Studies, Linköping University, Sweden. His publications include *Tecknets tragedi. Symbol och allegori i Atterboms sagospel Lycksalighetens ø* [The Tragedy of the Sign. Symbol and Allegory in Atterbom's saga, Island of Happiness] (1998). He is currently directing a media history research project on Swedish Romanticism.

ISAK WINKEL HOLM is Assistant Professor at the Department of Comparative Literature, University of Copenhagen, Denmark. He is author of *Tanken i Billedet. Søren Kierkegaards Poetik* [Thought in Image. Søren Kierkegaard's Poetics] (1998).

IB JOHANSEN is Associate Professor of English at the University of Aarhus, Denmark. He was Guest Lecturer at SUNY Binghamton in 1981. His publications include articles on Blake, Poe, and fantastic literature. He is author of *Sfinksens forvandlinger* [Metamorphoses of the Sfinx] (1986) – a study of fantastic literature in Denmark from ca. 1820 to the mid-1980s.

ALICE A. KUZNIAR is Professor of German and Comparative Literature at the University of North Carolina, Chapel Hill, USA. She has published several articles on German Romantic literature and painting in such journals as *German Quarterly, Germanic Review, PMLA,* and *Studies in Romanticism*. In addition, she has written *Delayed Endings: Nonclosure in Novalis and Hölderlin* (1987) and *The Queer German Cinema* (2000). She has also edited *Outing Goethe and His Age* (1996).

IDE HEJLSKOV LARSEN, has a Ph.D. in Comparative Literature from the University of Copenhagen, Denmark. She is currently employed in the publishing business, writes on literature for newspapers, journals and websites, translates literary theory and writes fiction. Her last published work was a co-production on science fiction, *Kloner og Stjernekrig: Science fiction fra H. G. Wells til Svend Åge Madsen* [Clones and Starwar: Science Fiction from H.G. Wells to Svend Åge Madsen] (2000).

ALAIN MONTANDON is Professor of Comparative Literature at Université Blaise Pascal, Director of the Centre de Recherches sur les Littératures Modernes et Contemporaines (CRLMC), and member of the Institut Universitaire de France (chaire de Littérature comparée et de sociopoétique). His publications include *La réception de Laurence Sterne en Allemagne* (1985), *Jean Paul romancier* (1987), *Dictionnaire raisonné de la politesse et du savoir-vivre* (1995), *Le roman en Europe au XVIIIe siècle* (1999), and *Sociopoétique de la promenade* (2000).

KLAUS P. MORTENSEN is Professor of Danish Literature at the Danish Educational University. His publications include *Himmelstormerne. En linje i dansk naturdigtning* [The Titans. A Line in the Danish Poetry of Nature] (1993), *The Time of Unrememberable Being. Wordsworth and the Sublime* (1998), *Johan Thomas Lundbyes kærlighed* [Johan Thomas Lundbye's Love] (2000), and *Spejlinger. Litteratur og refleksion* [Mirrorings. Literature and Reflection] (2000).

CECILIA SJÖHOLM has a Ph.D. in Comparative Literature from the University of Stockholm and is currently teaching at the South Stockholm University College, Sweden. Her published work includes *Alone and Perverted* (with Sara Arrhenius; 1995) and *Representations of the Unconscious: Stagnelius, Ekelöf, and Norén* (1996). She is currently working on a project called 'The Antigone Complex. Modernity and the Invention of Feminine Desire'.

BENGT ALGOT SØRENSEN is Professor of German Literature at the University of Odense, Denmark. His publications include *Symbol und Symbolismus* (1963), *Herrschaft und Zärtlichkeit* (1984), *Jens Peter Jacobsen* (1994), and *Funde und Forschungen* (1997).

CHENXI TANG is Assistant Professor of Germanic Studies at the University of Chicago, USA. He is the author of *Writing World History: The Emergence of Modern Global Consciousness in Late Eighteenth-Century Europe* (forthcoming). He is currently working on a study of Søren Kierkegaard and the advent of Modern Media, and is one of the translators of Søren Kierkegaard's collected works from Danish into Chinese. His translation of *Om Begrebet Ironi* is forthcoming.

Index